AF572166

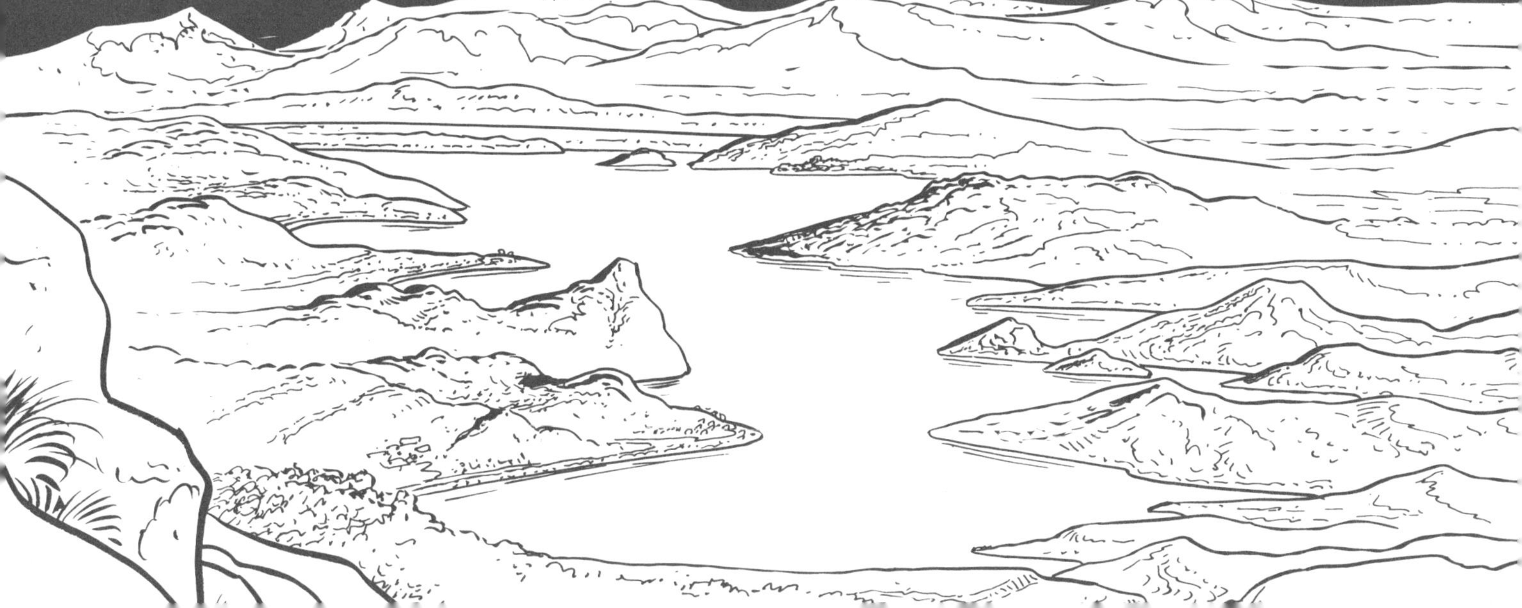

M. WEYLAND

ARIA

ARIA TAKES OFF

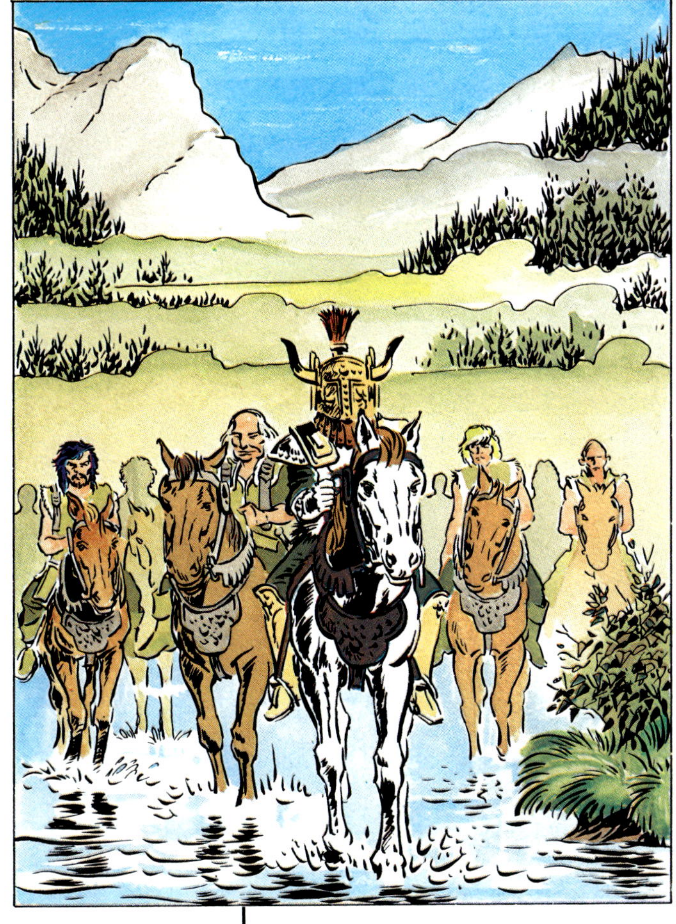

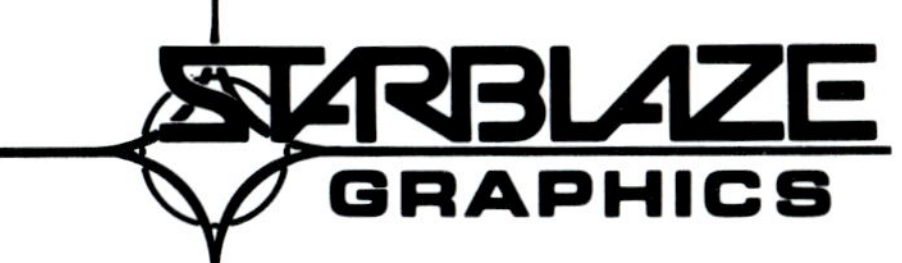

Starblaze Graphics—The Donning Company/Publishers
Norfolk/Virginia Beach • 1986

The Donning Company/Publishers
5659 Virginia Beach Boulevard
Norfolk, Virginia 23502

Library of Congress Cataloging-in-Publication Data:

TO COME

ISBN 0-89865-468-8

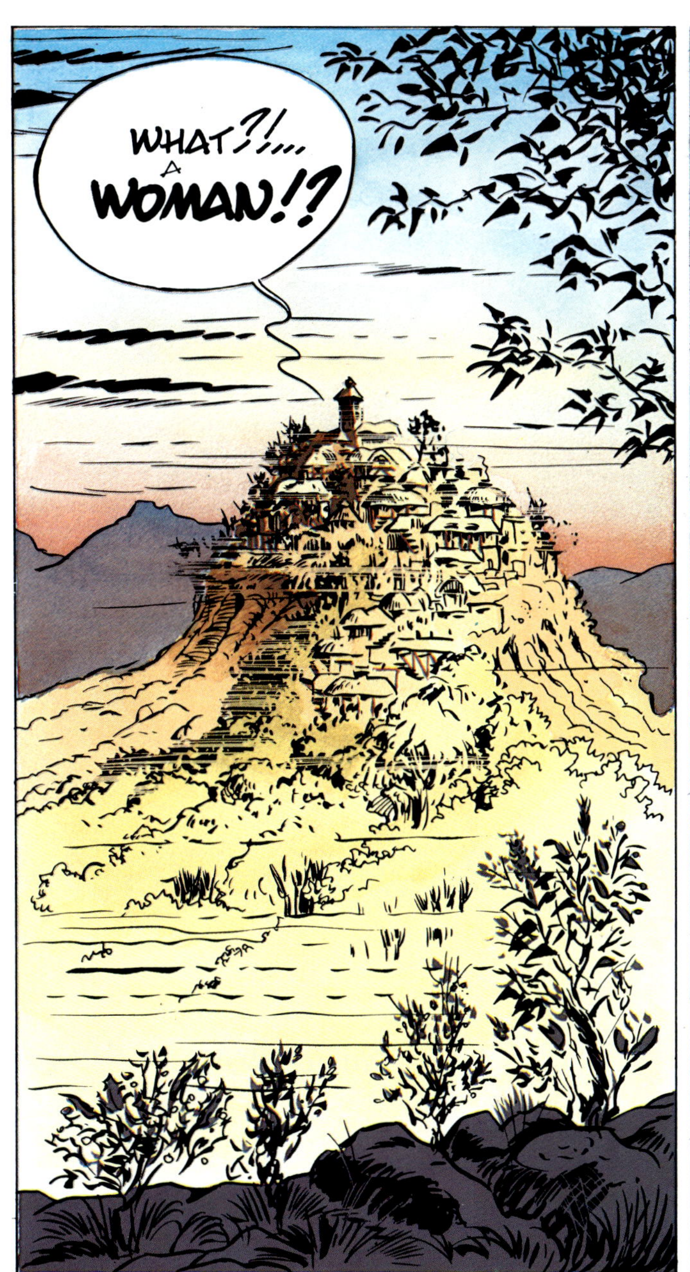
WHAT?!... A WOMAN!?

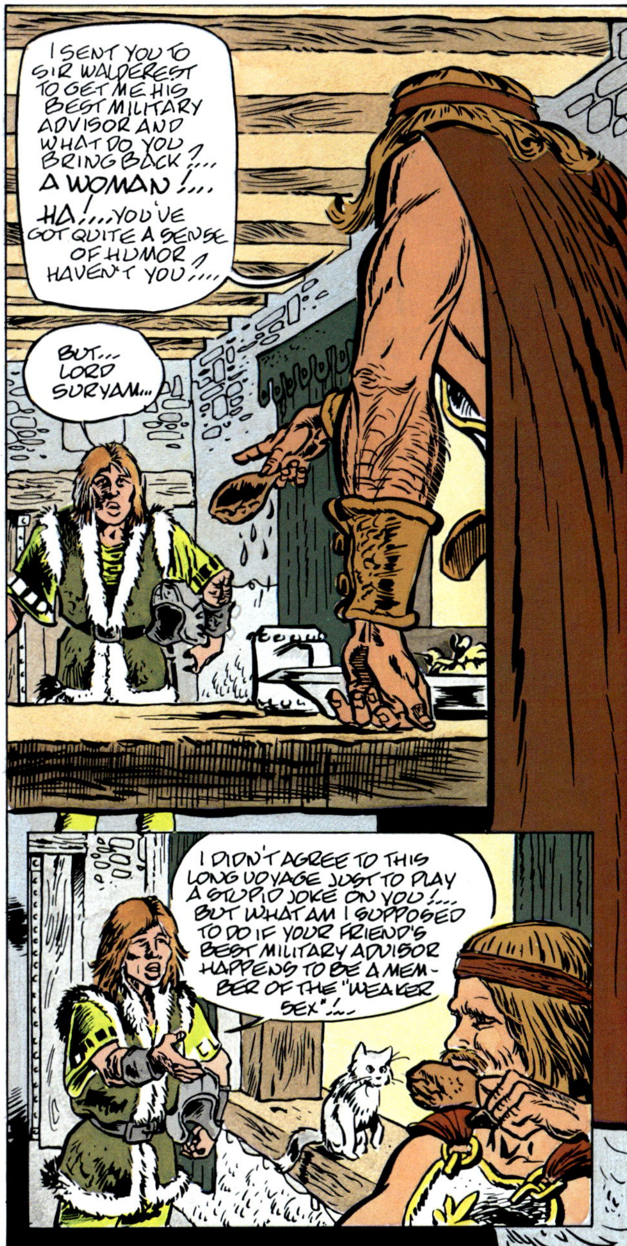
I SENT YOU TO SIR WALDEREST TO GET ME HIS BEST MILITARY ADVISOR AND WHAT DO YOU BRING BACK?... A WOMAN!... HA!... YOU'VE GOT QUITE A SENSE OF HUMOR HAVEN'T YOU?!...
BUT... LORD SURYAM...
I DIDN'T AGREE TO THIS LONG VOYAGE JUST TO PLAY A STUPID JOKE ON YOU!... BUT WHAT AM I SUPPOSED TO DO IF YOUR FRIEND'S BEST MILITARY ADVISOR HAPPENS TO BE A MEMBER OF THE "WEAKER SEX"!...

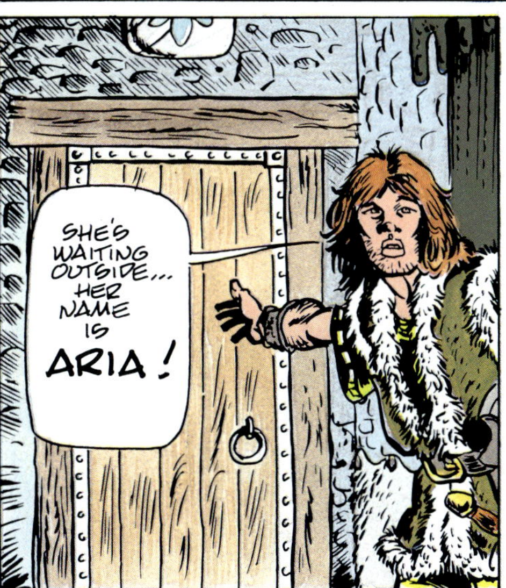
SHE'S WAITING OUTSIDE... HER NAME IS ARIA!

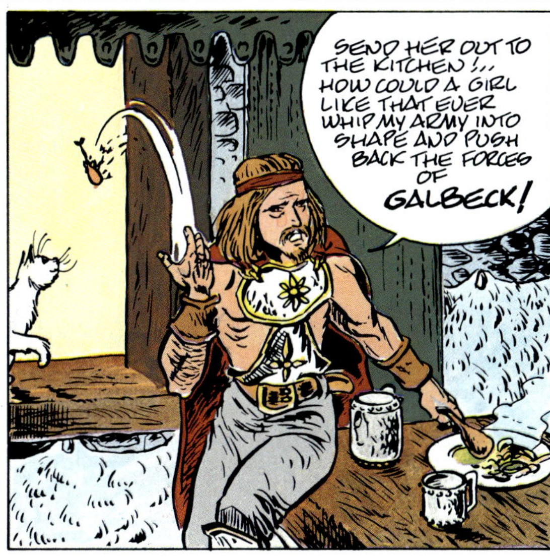
SEND HER OUT TO THE KITCHEN!... HOW COULD A GIRL LIKE THAT EVER WHIP MY ARMY INTO SHAPE AND PUSH BACK THE FORCES OF GALBECK!

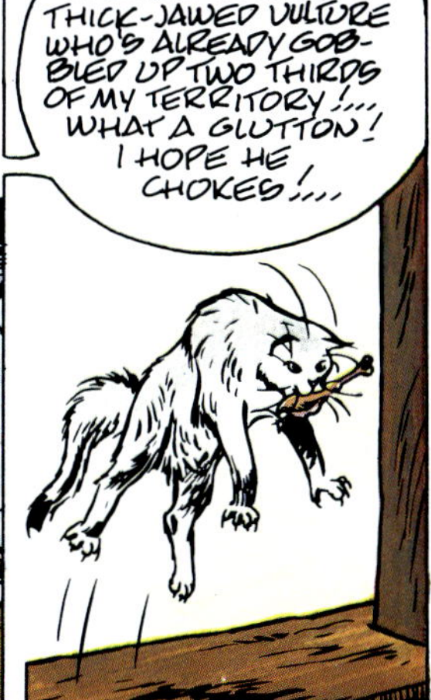
OH! THAT BLASTED GALBECK... THAT THICK-JAWED VULTURE WHO'S ALREADY GOBBLED UP TWO THIRDS OF MY TERRITORY!... WHAT A GLUTTON! I HOPE HE CHOKES!...

1.

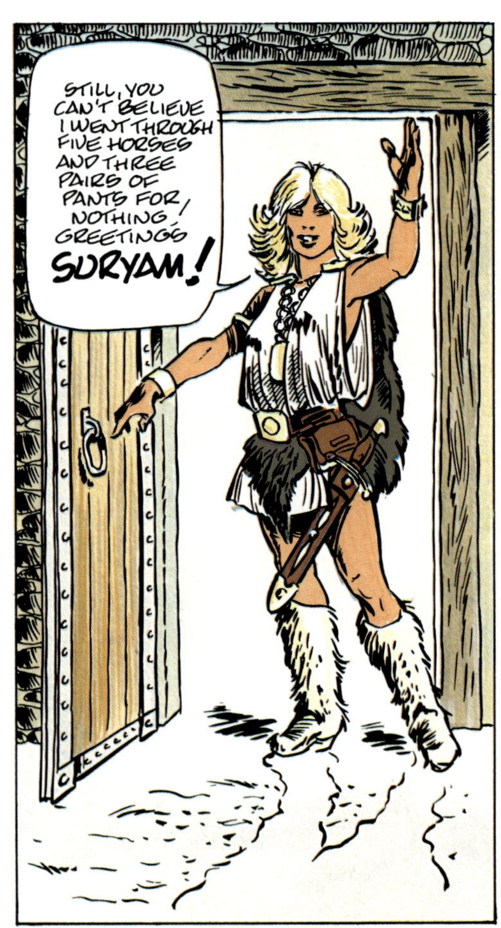
STILL, YOU CAN'T BELIEVE I WENT THROUGH FIVE HORSES AND THREE PAIRS OF PANTS FOR NOTHING! GREETINGS SURYAM!

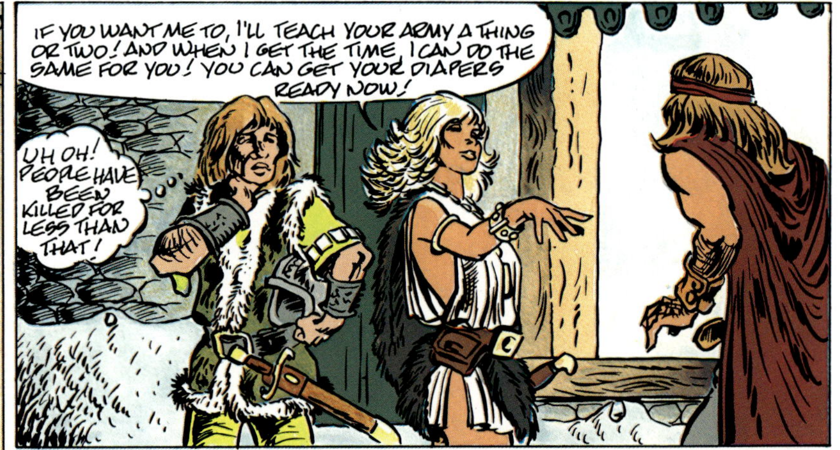
IF YOU WANT ME TO, I'LL TEACH YOUR ARMY A THING OR TWO! AND WHEN I GET THE TIME, I CAN DO THE SAME FOR YOU! YOU CAN GET YOUR DIAPERS READY NOW!
UH OH! PEOPLE HAVE BEEN KILLED FOR LESS THAN THAT!

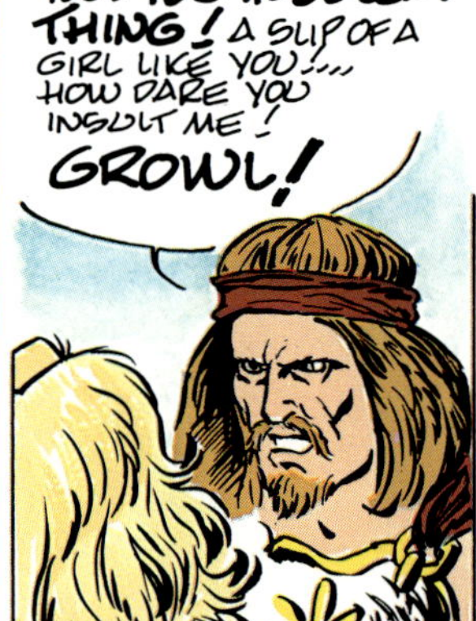
YOU! YOU INSOLENT THING! A SLIP OF A GIRL LIKE YOU... HOW DARE YOU INSULT ME! GROWL!

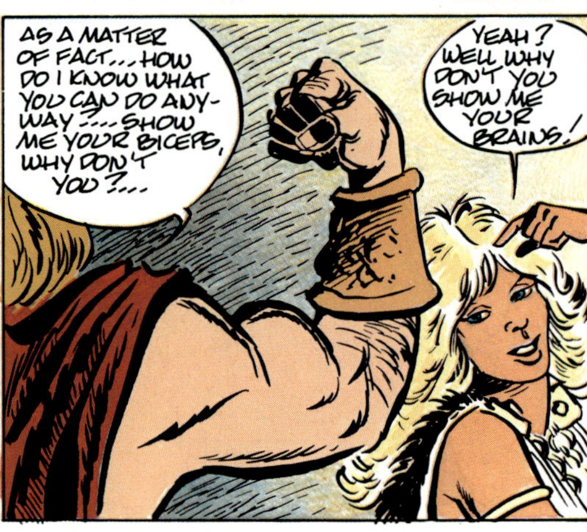
AS A MATTER OF FACT... HOW DO I KNOW WHAT YOU CAN DO ANYWAY?... SHOW ME YOUR BICEPS, WHY DON'T YOU?...
YEAH? WELL WHY DON'T YOU SHOW ME YOUR BRAINS!

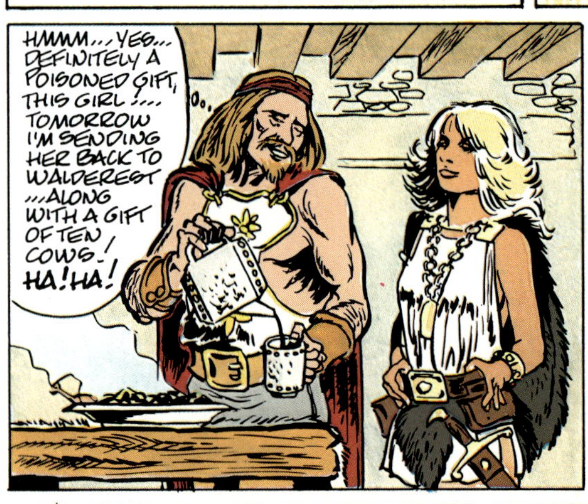
HMMM... YES... DEFINITELY A POISONED GIFT, THIS GIRL... TOMORROW I'M SENDING HER BACK TO WALDEREST ...ALONG WITH A GIFT OF TEN COWS! HA! HA!

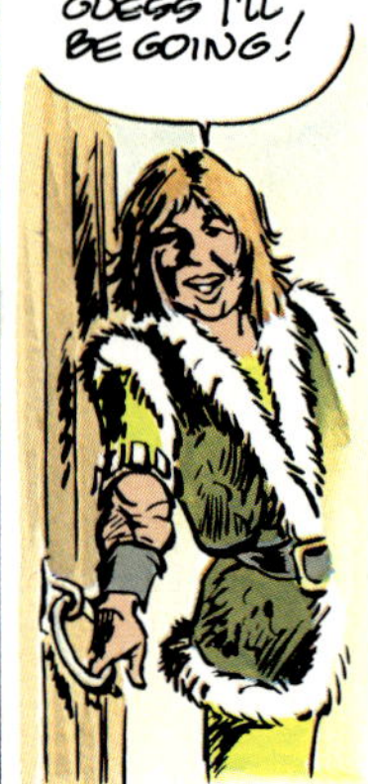
WELL... I GUESS I'LL BE GOING!

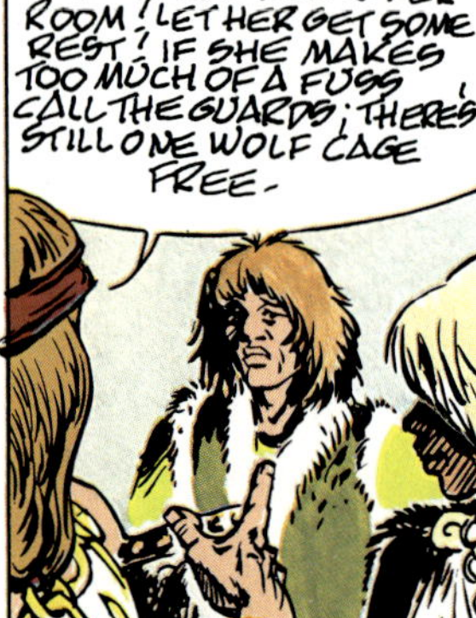
WAIT... SHOW HER TO HER ROOM! LET HER GET SOME REST! IF SHE MAKES TOO MUCH OF A FUSS CALL THE GUARDS; THERE'S STILL ONE WOLF CAGE FREE.

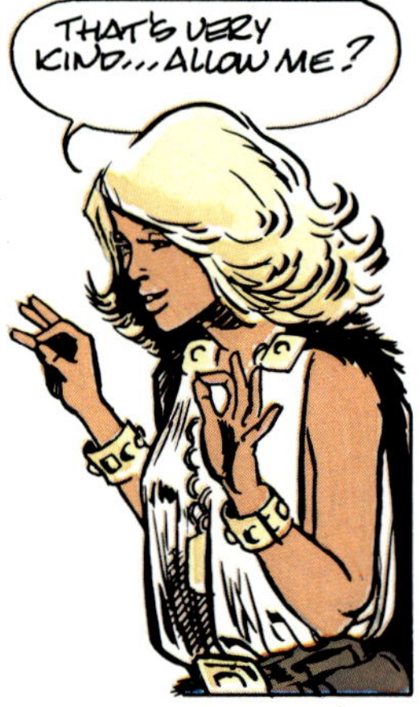
THAT'S VERY KIND... ALLOW ME?

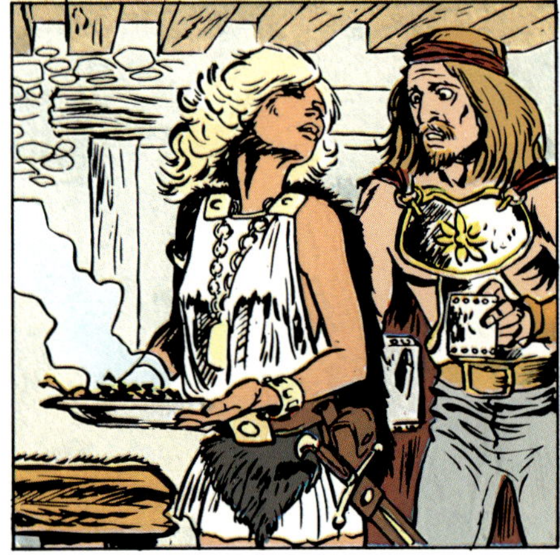

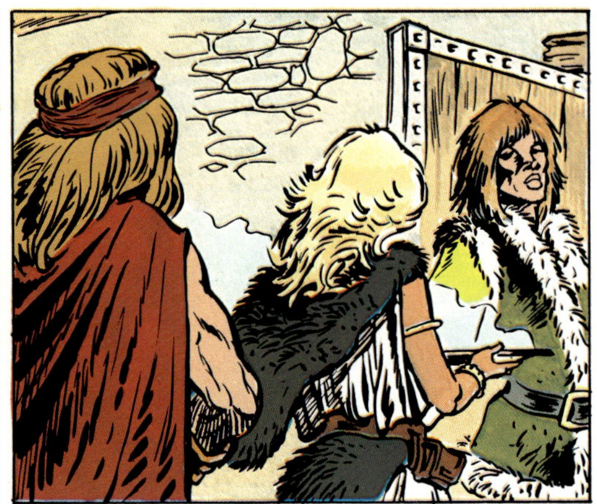

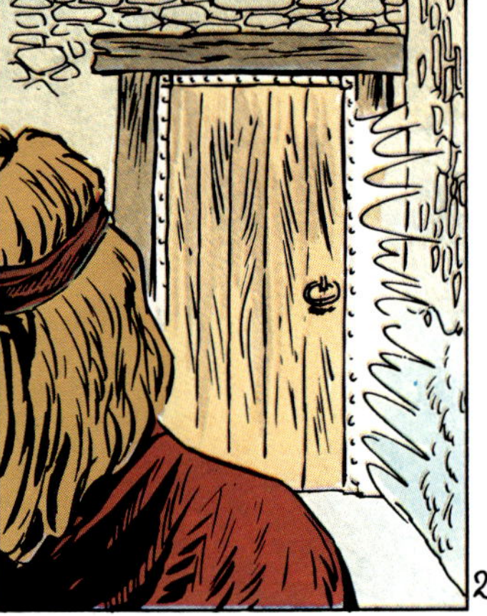

2

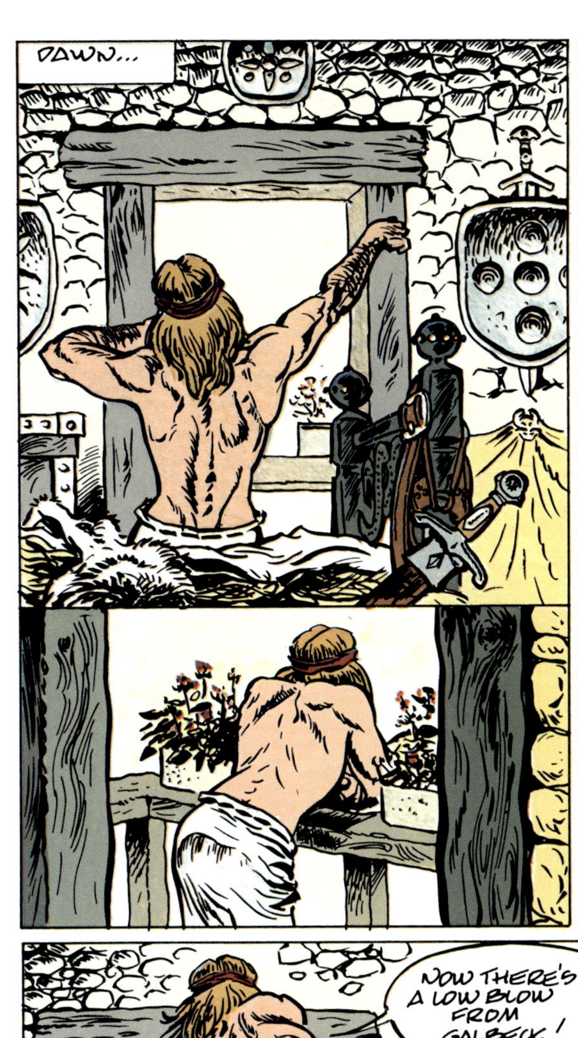
DAWN...
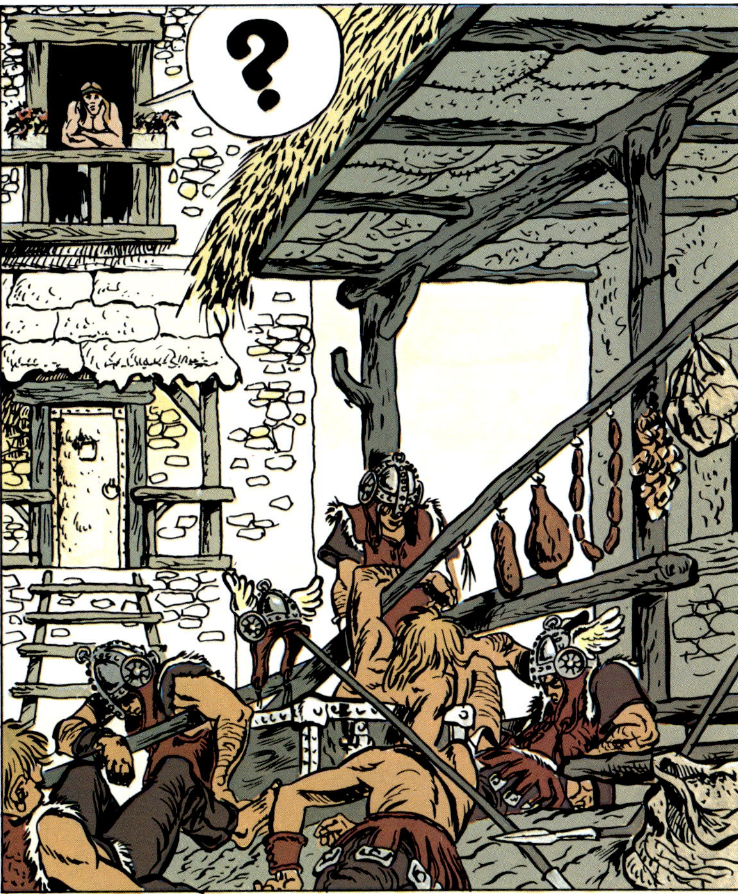
?
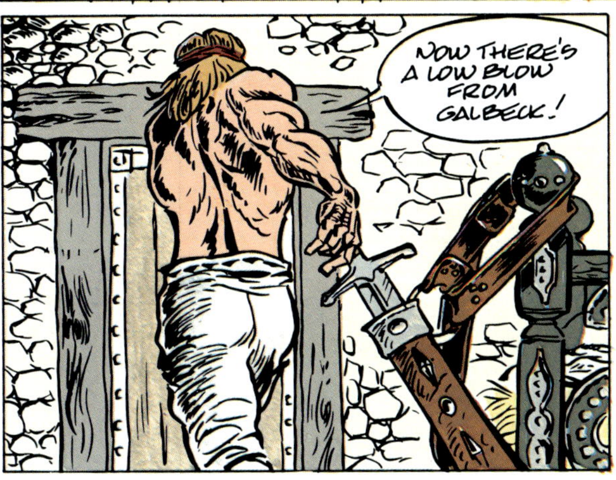
NOW THERE'S A LOW BLOW FROM GALBECK!
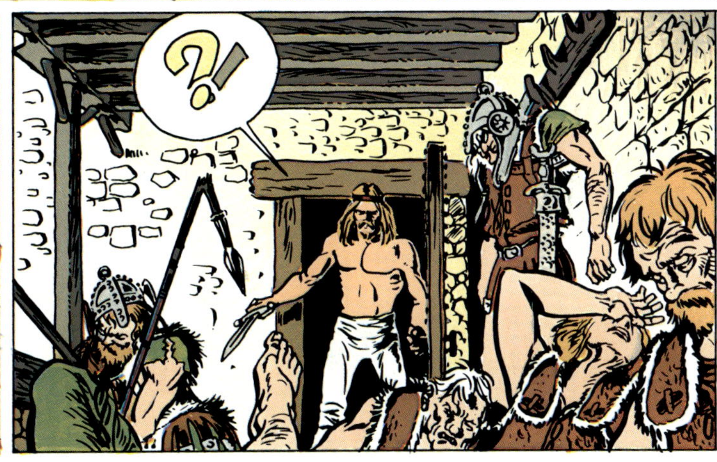
?!
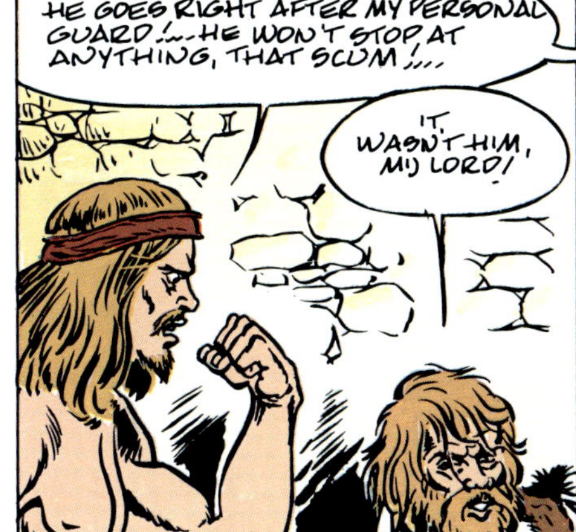
HE GOES RIGHT AFTER MY PERSONAL GUARD!... HE WON'T STOP AT ANYTHING, THAT SCUM!...
IT WASN'T HIM, MY LORD!
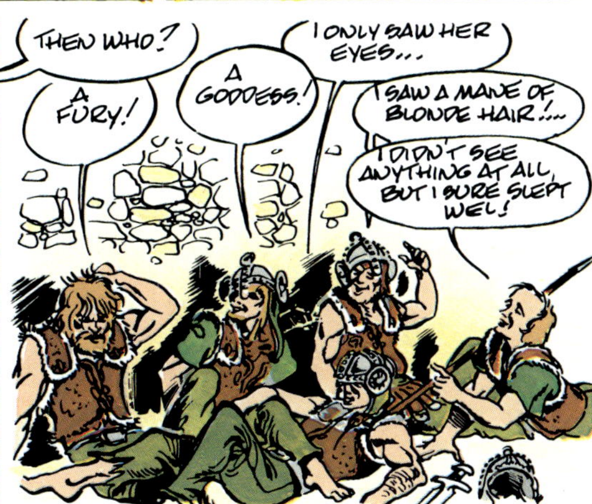
THEN WHO?
A FURY!
A GODDESS!
I ONLY SAW HER EYES...
I SAW A MANE OF BLONDE HAIR!...
I DIDN'T SEE ANYTHING AT ALL, BUT I SURE SLEPT WEL!
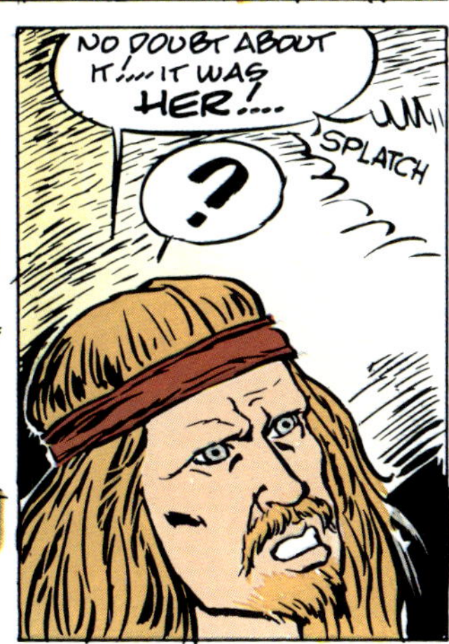
NO DOUBT ABOUT IT!... IT WAS HER!...
SPLATCH
?
3

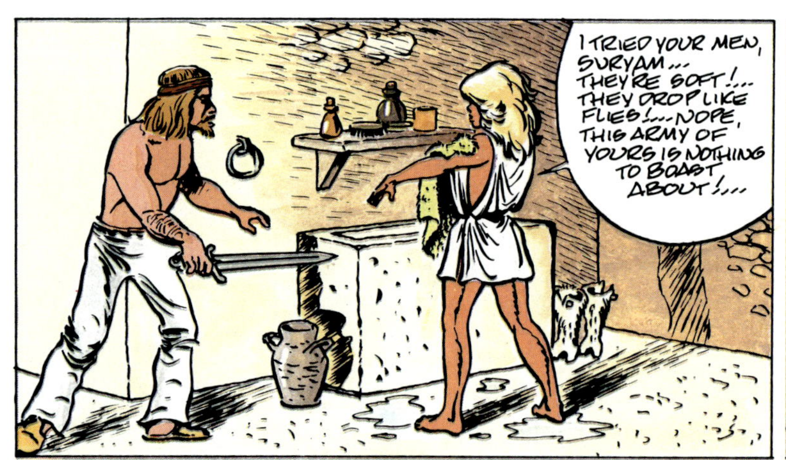

I TRIED YOUR MEN, SURYAM... THEY'RE SOFT!... THEY DROP LIKE FLIES!... NOPE, THIS ARMY OF YOURS IS NOTHING TO BOAST ABOUT!...

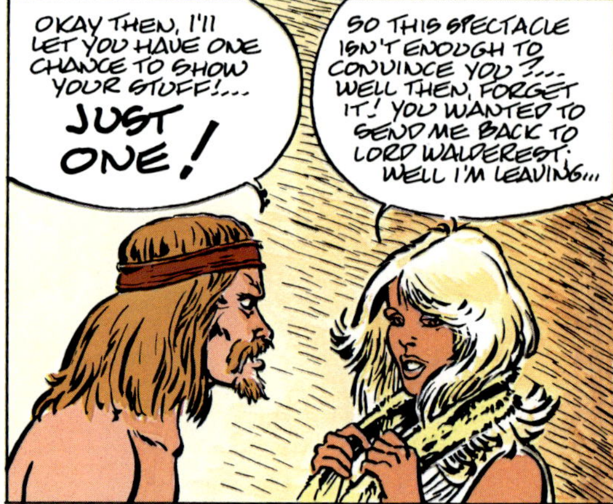

OKAY THEN, I'LL LET YOU HAVE ONE CHANCE TO SHOW YOUR STUFF!... JUST ONE!
SO THIS SPECTACLE ISN'T ENOUGH TO CONVINCE YOU?... WELL THEN, FORGET IT! YOU WANTED TO SEND ME BACK TO LORD WALDEREST. WELL I'M LEAVING...

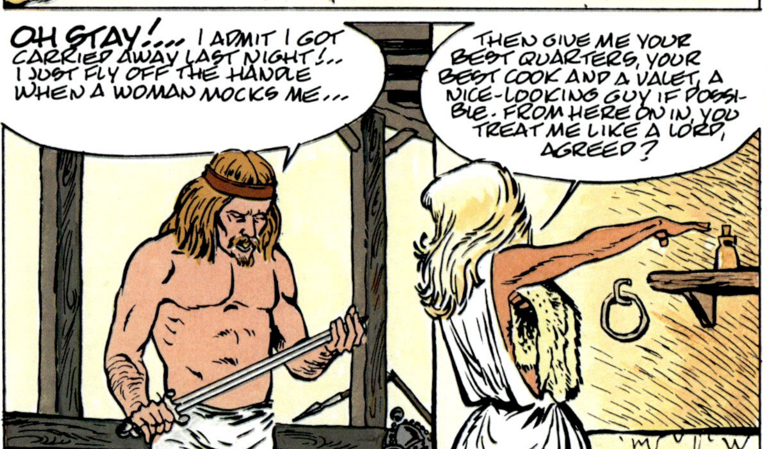

OH STAY!... I ADMIT I GOT CARRIED AWAY LAST NIGHT!... I JUST FLY OFF THE HANDLE WHEN A WOMAN MOCKS ME...
THEN GIVE ME YOUR BEST QUARTERS, YOUR BEST COOK AND A VALET, A NICE-LOOKING GUY IF POSSIBLE. FROM HERE ON IN, YOU TREAT ME LIKE A LORD, AGREED?

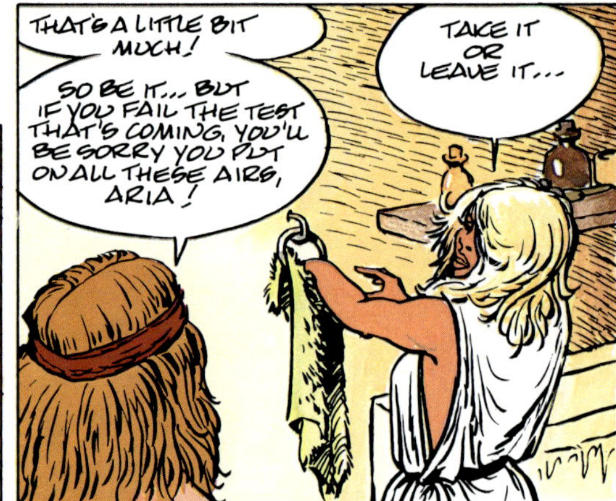

THAT'S A LITTLE BIT MUCH!
SO BE IT... BUT IF YOU FAIL THE TEST THAT'S COMING, YOU'LL BE SORRY YOU PUT ON ALL THESE AIRS, ARIA!
TAKE IT OR LEAVE IT...

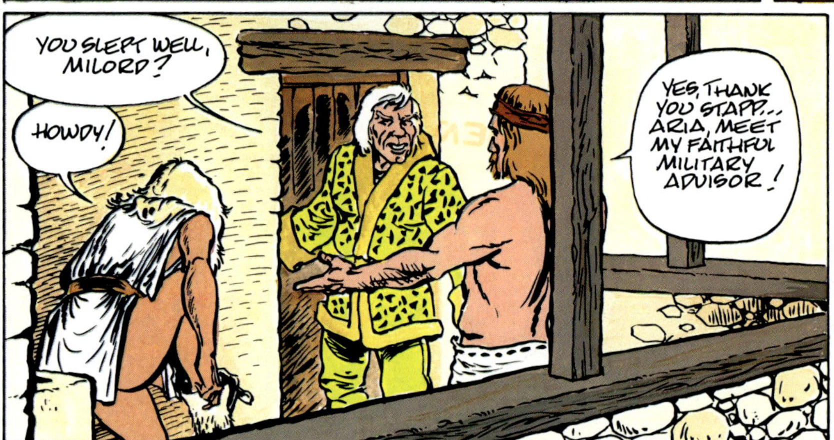

YOU SLEPT WELL, MILORD?
HOWDY!
YES, THANK YOU STAPP... ARIA, MEET MY FAITHFUL MILITARY ADVISOR!

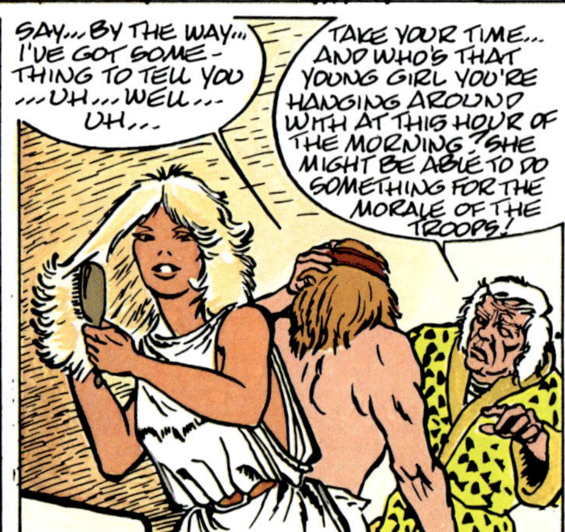

SAY... BY THE WAY... I'VE GOT SOMETHING TO TELL YOU ...UH... WELL... UH...
TAKE YOUR TIME... AND WHO'S THAT YOUNG GIRL YOU'RE HANGING AROUND WITH AT THIS HOUR OF THE MORNING? SHE MIGHT BE ABLE TO DO SOMETHING FOR THE MORALE OF THE TROOPS!

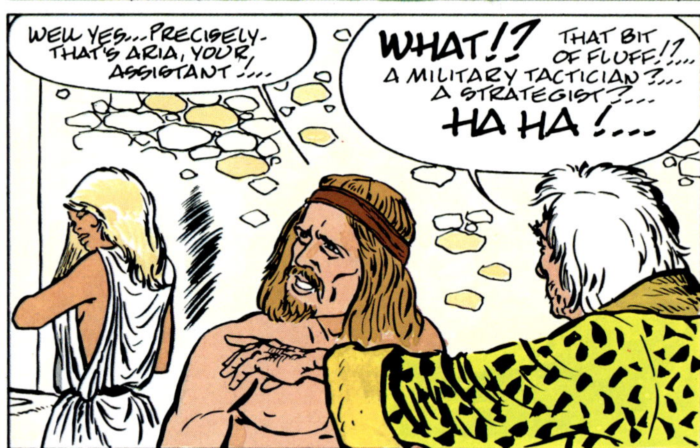

WELL YES... PRECISELY. THAT'S ARIA, YOUR ASSISTANT!...
WHAT!? THAT BIT OF FLUFF!?... A MILITARY TACTICIAN?... A STRATEGIST?... HA HA!...

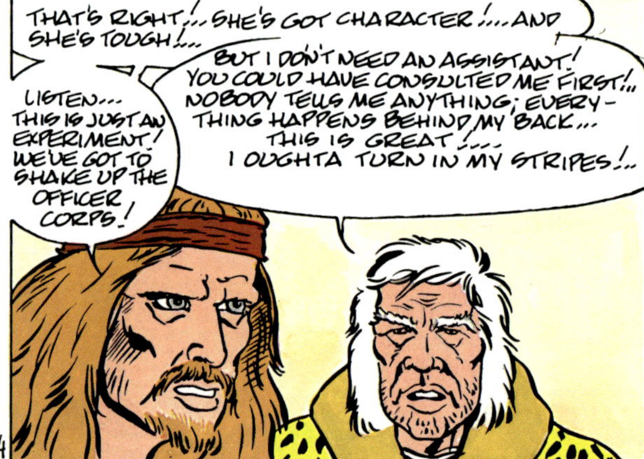

THAT'S RIGHT!... SHE'S GOT CHARACTER!... AND SHE'S TOUGH!...
BUT I DON'T NEED AN ASSISTANT! YOU COULD HAVE CONSULTED ME FIRST!... NOBODY TELLS ME ANYTHING; EVERYTHING HAPPENS BEHIND MY BACK... THIS IS GREAT!... I OUGHTA TURN IN MY STRIPES!...
LISTEN... THIS IS JUST AN EXPERIMENT! WE'VE GOT TO SHAKE UP THE OFFICER CORPS!

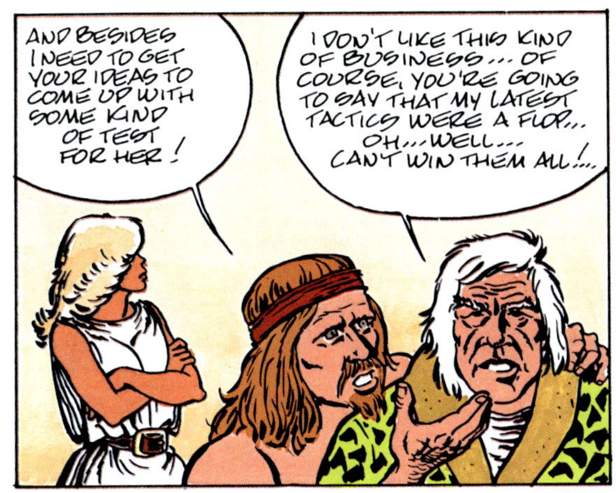
AND BESIDES I NEED TO GET YOUR IDEAS TO COME UP WITH SOME KIND OF TEST FOR HER!
I DON'T LIKE THIS KIND OF BUSINESS... OF COURSE, YOU'RE GOING TO SAY THAT MY LATEST TACTICS WERE A FLOP... OH... WELL... CAN'T WIN THEM ALL!...

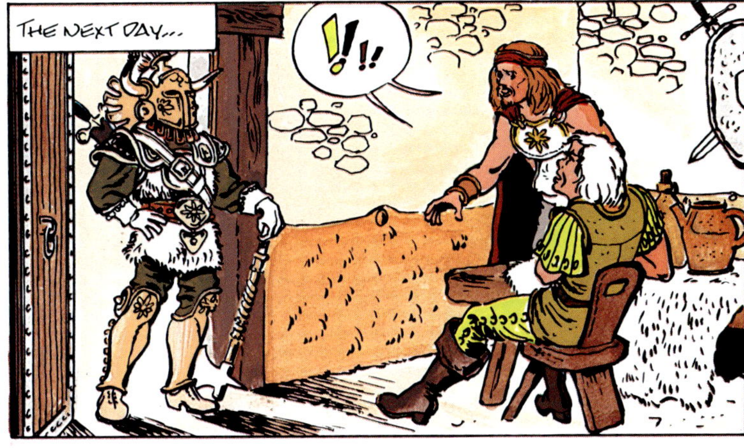
THE NEXT DAY...
!!!!

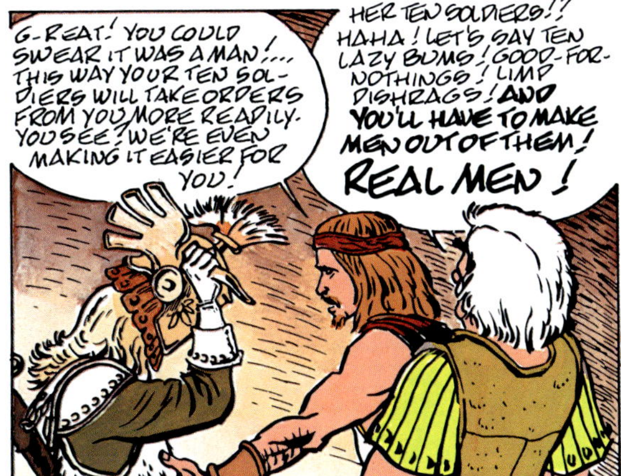
G-REAT! YOU COULD SWEAR IT WAS A MAN!... THIS WAY YOUR TEN SOLDIERS WILL TAKE ORDERS FROM YOU MORE READILY. YOU SEE! WE'RE EVEN MAKING IT EASIER FOR YOU!
HER TEN SOLDIERS!? HAHA! LET'S SAY TEN LAZY BUMS! GOOD-FOR-NOTHINGS! LIMP DISHRAGS! AND YOU'LL HAVE TO MAKE MEN OUT OF THEM! REAL MEN!

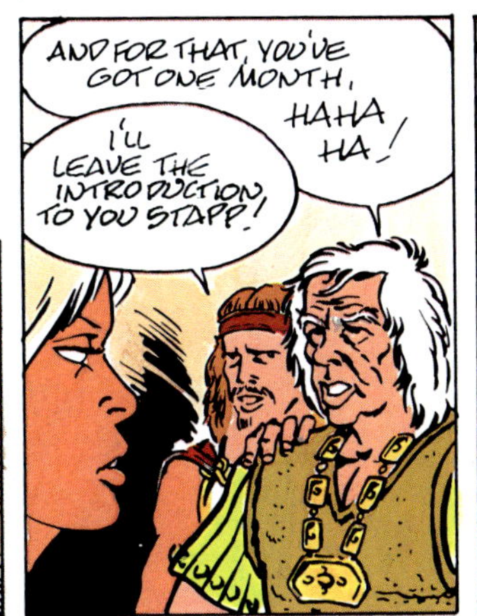
AND FOR THAT, YOU'VE GOT ONE MONTH.
HAHA HA!
I'LL LEAVE THE INTRODUCTION TO YOU STAPP!

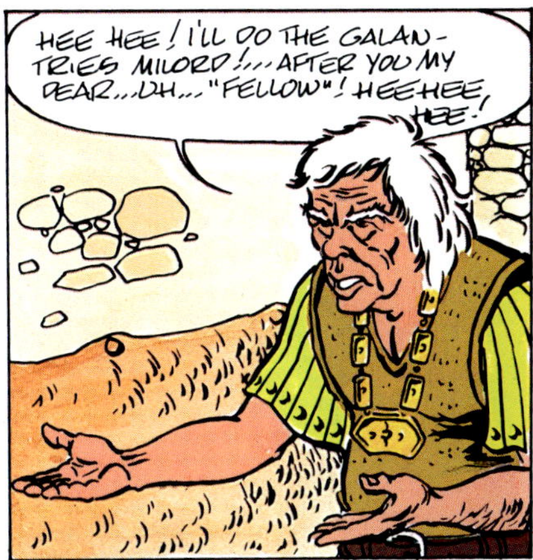
HEE HEE! I'LL DO THE GALANTRIES MILORD!... AFTER YOU MY DEAR... UH... "FELLOW"! HEE HEE HEE!

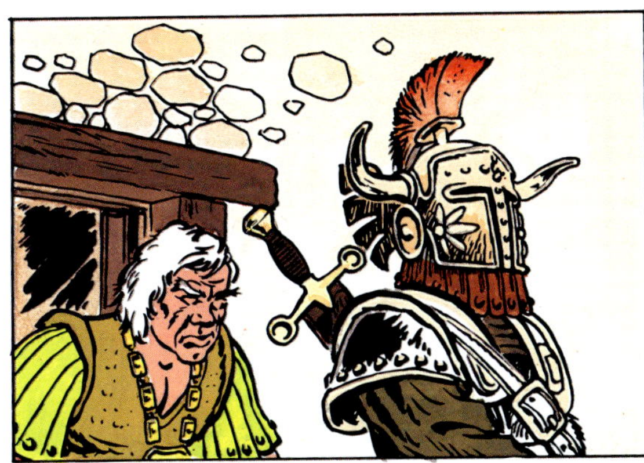

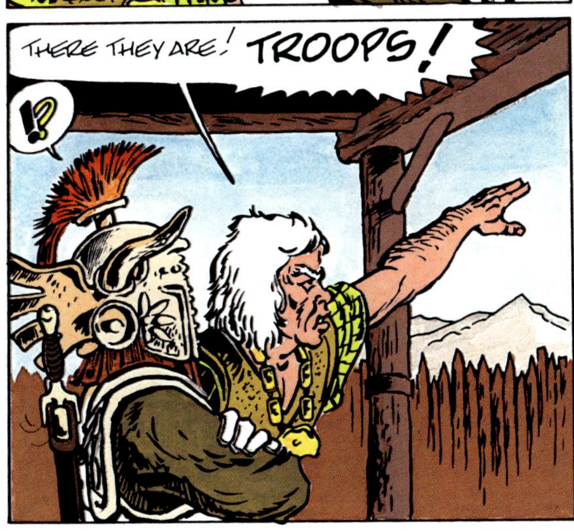
THERE THEY ARE! TROOPS!
!?

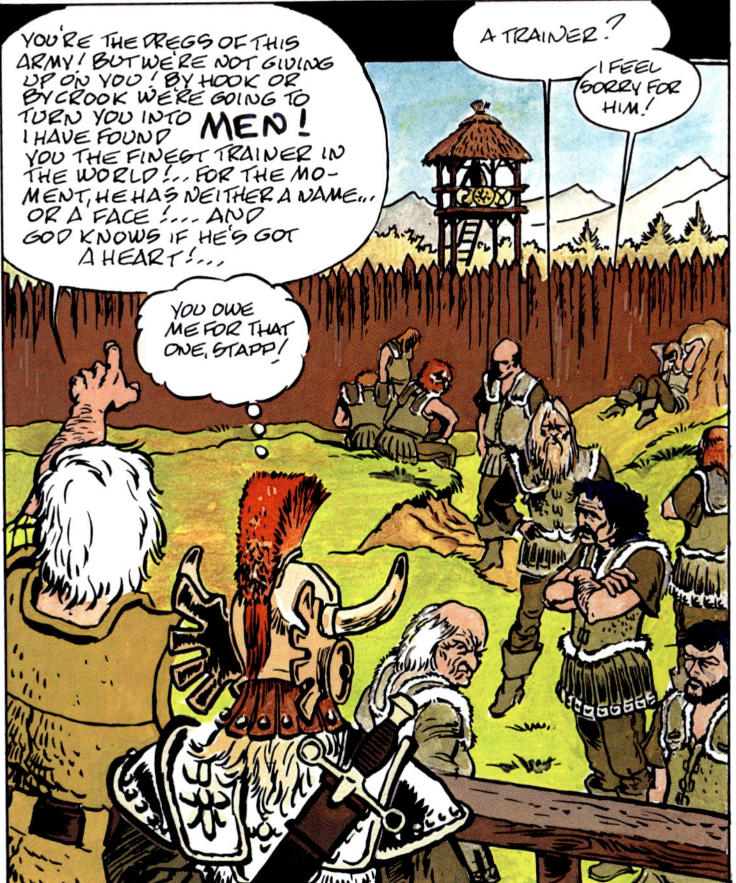
YOU'RE THE DREGS OF THIS ARMY! BUT WE'RE NOT GIVING UP ON YOU! BY HOOK OR BY CROOK WE'RE GOING TO TURN YOU INTO MEN! I HAVE FOUND YOU THE FINEST TRAINER IN THE WORLD!... FOR THE MOMENT, HE HAS NEITHER A NAME... OR A FACE!... AND GOD KNOWS IF HE'S GOT A HEART!...
A TRAINER?
I FEEL SORRY FOR HIM!
YOU OWE ME FOR THAT ONE, STAPP!

5

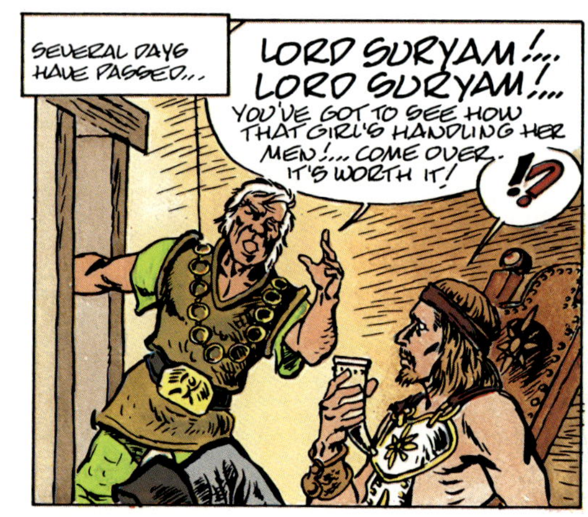
SEVERAL DAYS HAVE PASSED...
LORD SURYAM!... LORD SURYAM!...
YOU'VE GOT TO SEE HOW THAT GIRL'S HANDLING HER MEN!... COME OVER. IT'S WORTH IT!
!?

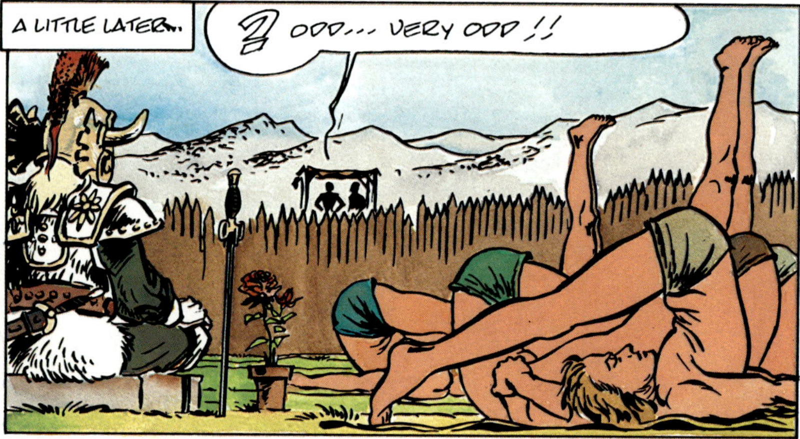
A LITTLE LATER...
?
ODD... VERY ODD!!

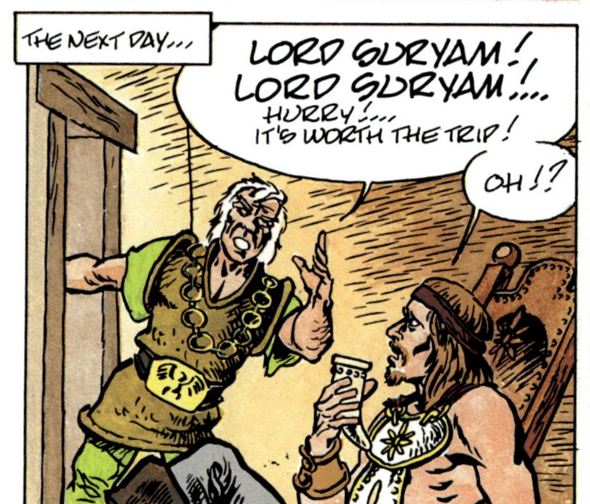
THE NEXT DAY...
LORD SURYAM! LORD SURYAM!...
HURRY!... IT'S WORTH THE TRIP!
OH!?

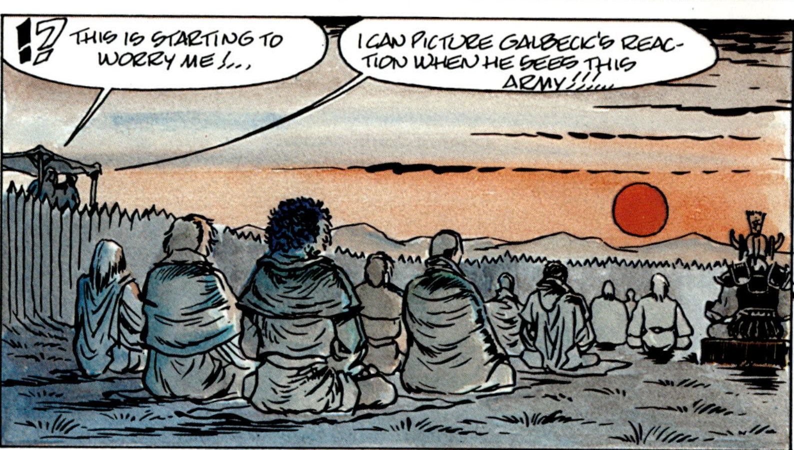
!?
THIS IS STARTING TO WORRY ME!...
I CAN PICTURE GALBECK'S REACTION WHEN HE SEES THIS ARMY!!!...

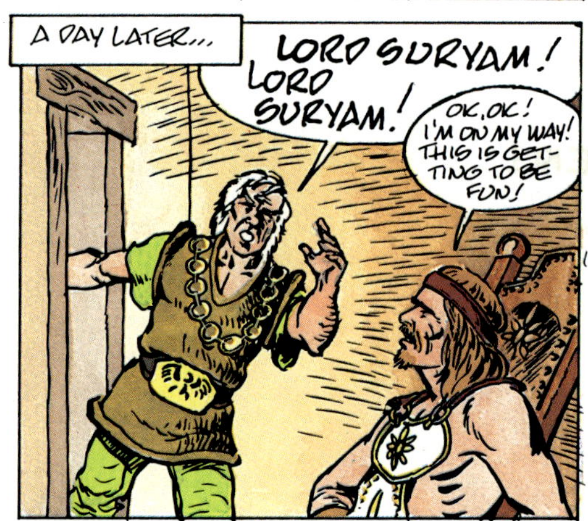
A DAY LATER...
LORD SURYAM! LORD SURYAM!
OK, OK! I'M ON MY WAY! THIS IS GETTING TO BE FUN!

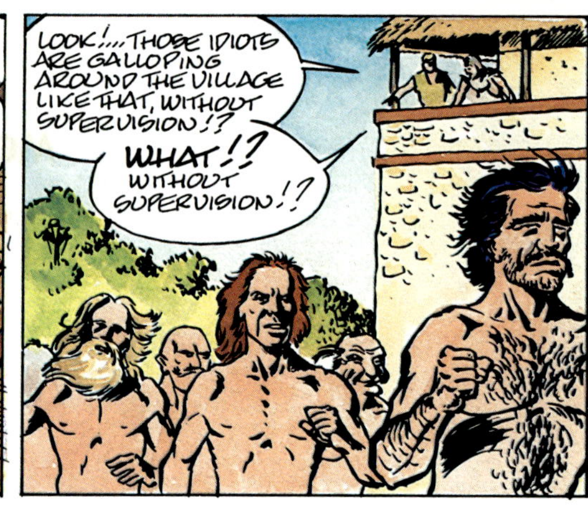
LOOK!... THOSE IDIOTS ARE GALLOPING AROUND THE VILLAGE LIKE THAT, WITHOUT SUPERVISION!?
WHAT!? WITHOUT SUPERVISION!?

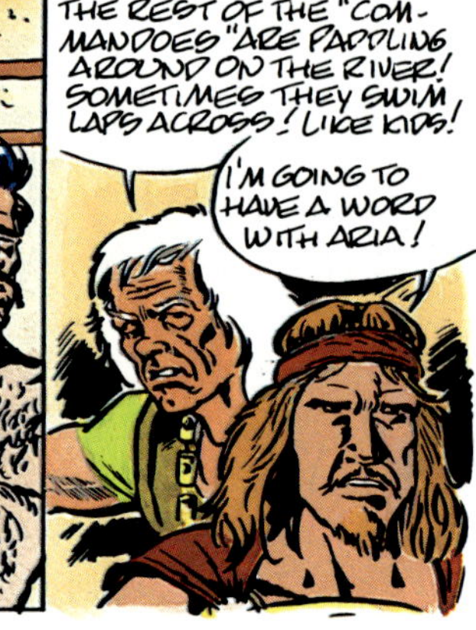
AND IT GETS BETTER YET! THE REST OF THE "COMMANDOES" ARE PADDLING AROUND ON THE RIVER! SOMETIMES THEY SWIM LAPS ACROSS! LIKE KIDS!
I'M GOING TO HAVE A WORD WITH ARIA!

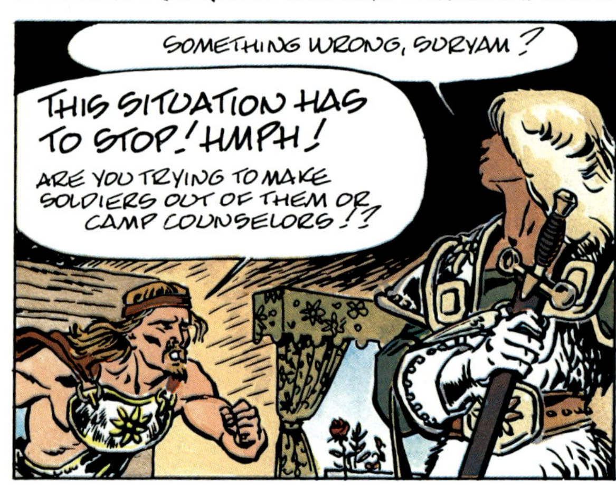
SOMETHING WRONG, SURYAM?
THIS SITUATION HAS TO STOP! HMPH!
ARE YOU TRYING TO MAKE SOLDIERS OUT OF THEM OR CAMP COUNSELORS!?

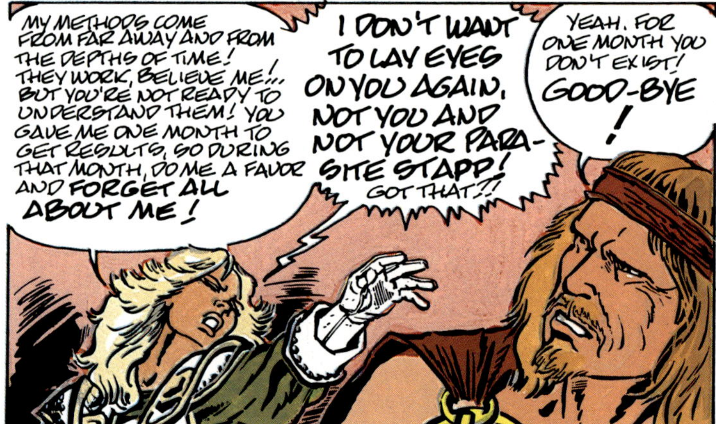
MY METHODS COME FROM FAR AWAY AND FROM THE DEPTHS OF TIME! THEY WORK, BELIEVE ME!... BUT YOU'RE NOT READY TO UNDERSTAND THEM! YOU GAVE ME ONE MONTH TO GET RESULTS, SO DURING THAT MONTH, DO ME A FAVOR AND FORGET ALL ABOUT ME!
I DON'T WANT TO LAY EYES ON YOU AGAIN, NOT YOU AND NOT YOUR PARASITE STAPP! GOT THAT!?
YEAH. FOR ONE MONTH YOU DON'T EXIST! GOOD-BYE!
6

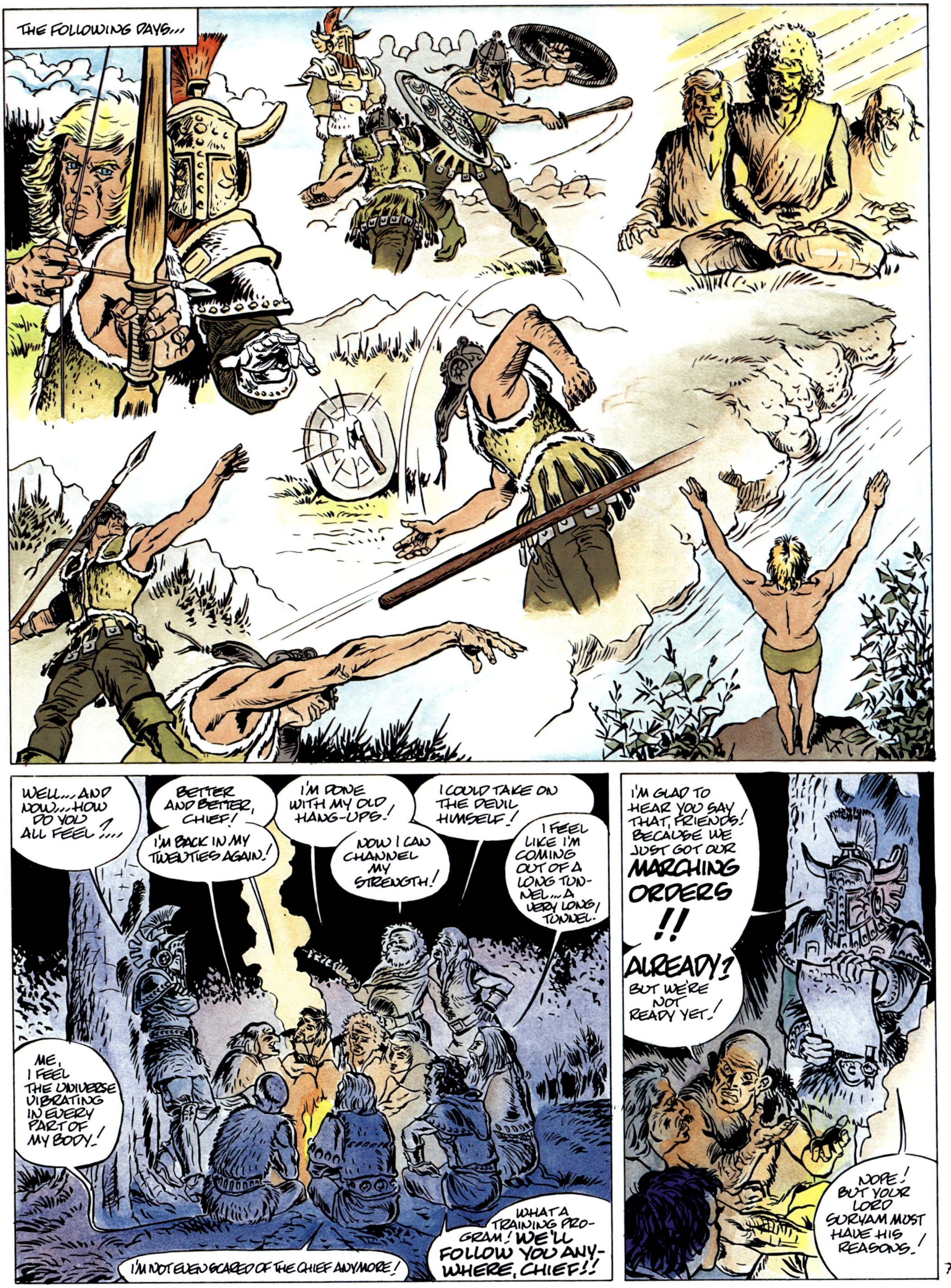

THE FOLLOWING DAYS...

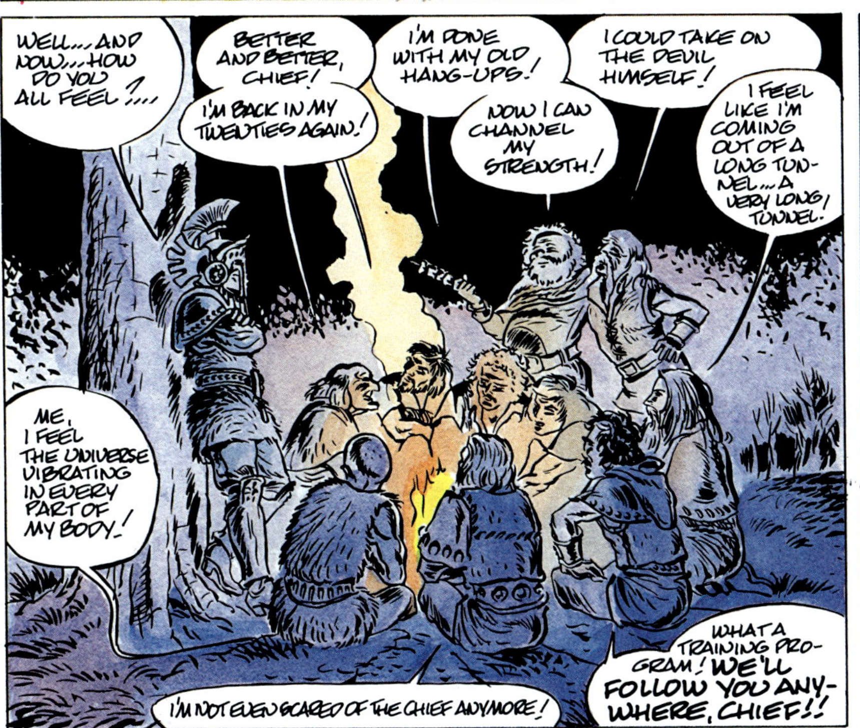

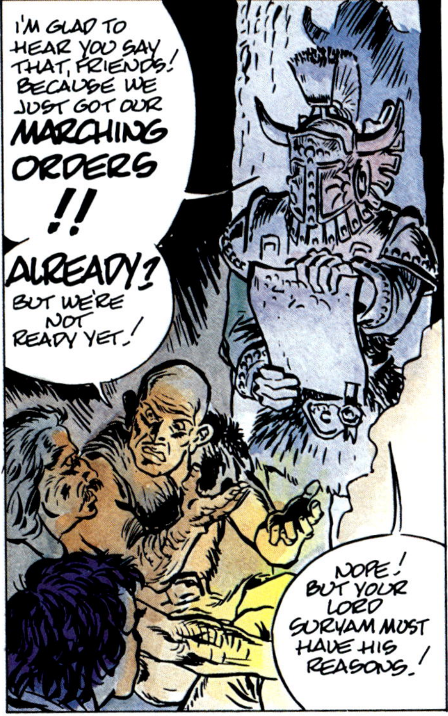

7

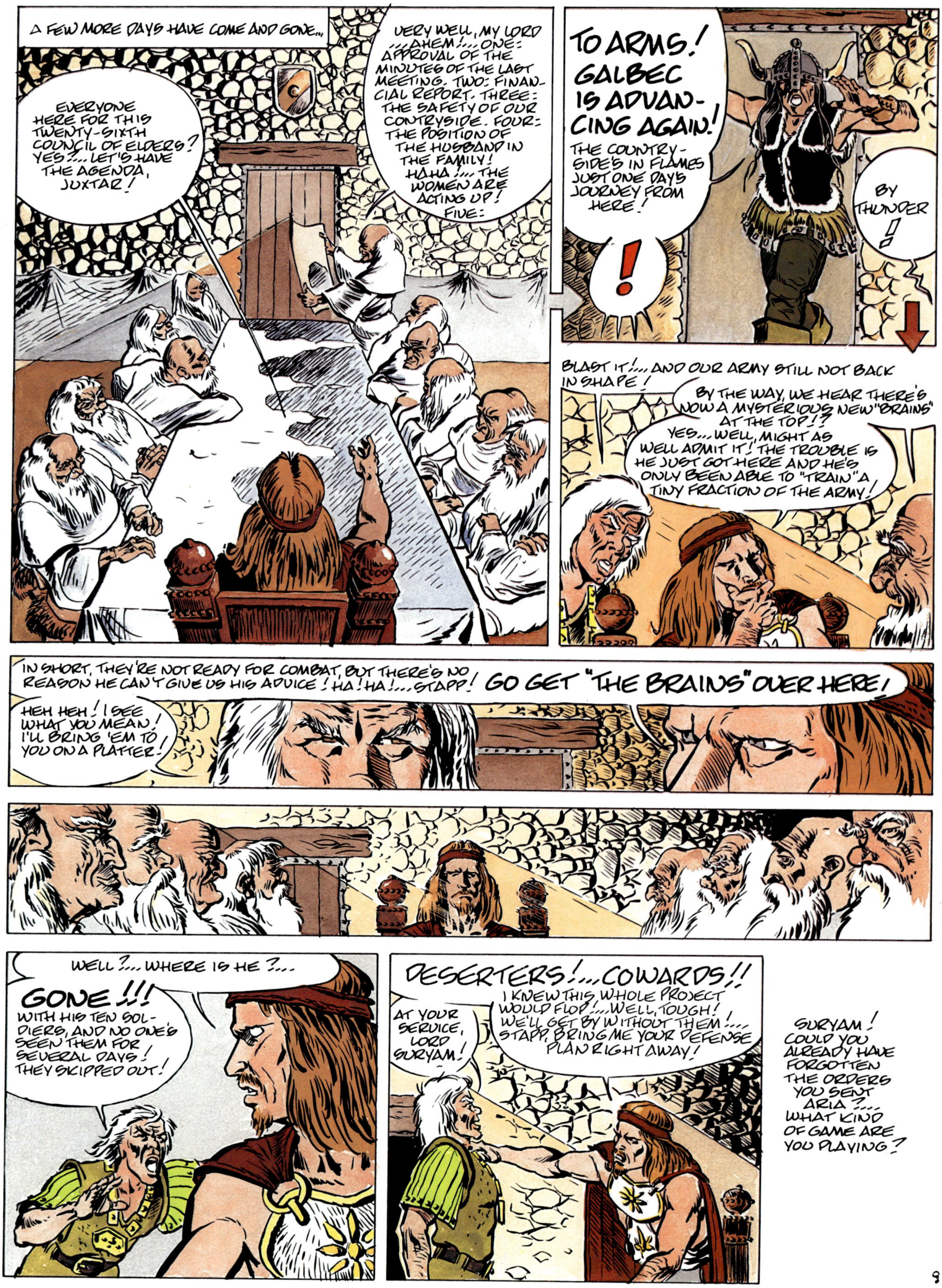

A FEW MORE DAYS HAVE COME AND GONE...

EVERYONE HERE FOR THIS TWENTY-SIXTH COUNCIL OF ELDERS? YES?... LET'S HAVE THE AGENDA, JUXTAR!

VERY WELL, MY LORD ...AHEM!... ONE: APPROVAL OF THE MINUTES OF THE LAST MEETING. TWO: FINANCIAL REPORT. THREE: THE SAFETY OF OUR CONTRYSIDE. FOUR: THE POSITION OF THE HUSBAND IN THE FAMILY! HAHA!... THE WOMEN ARE ACTING UP! FIVE:

TO ARMS! GALBEC IS ADVANCING AGAIN! THE COUNTRYSIDE'S IN FLAMES JUST ONE DAY'S JOURNEY FROM HERE!

!

BY THUNDER!

BLAST IT!... AND OUR ARMY STILL NOT BACK IN SHAPE!

BY THE WAY, WE HEAR THERE'S NOW A MYSTERIOUS NEW "BRAINS" AT THE TOP!?

YES... WELL, MIGHT AS WELL ADMIT IT! THE TROUBLE IS HE JUST GOT HERE AND HE'S ONLY BEEN ABLE TO "TRAIN" A TINY FRACTION OF THE ARMY!

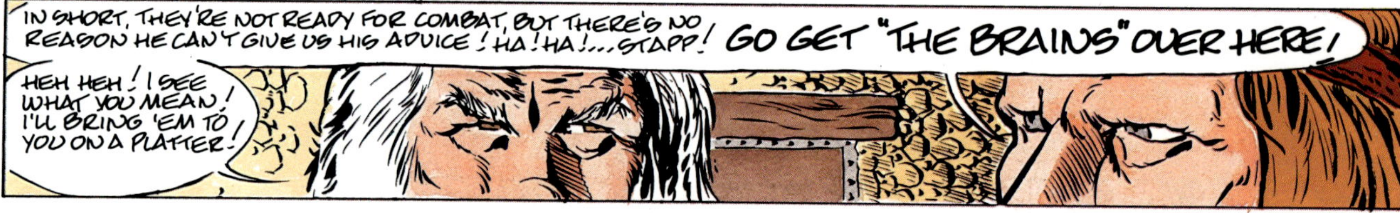

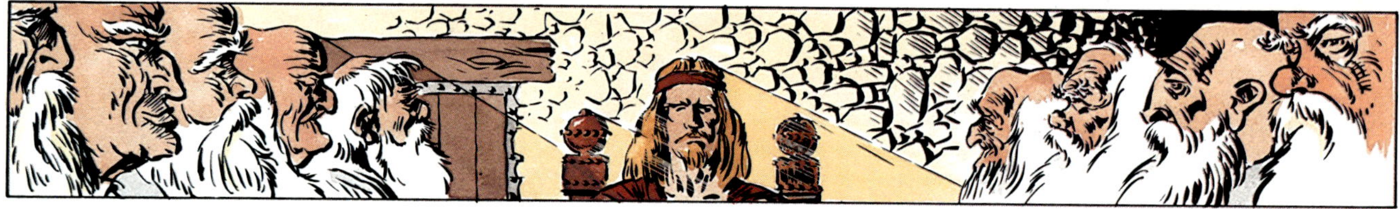

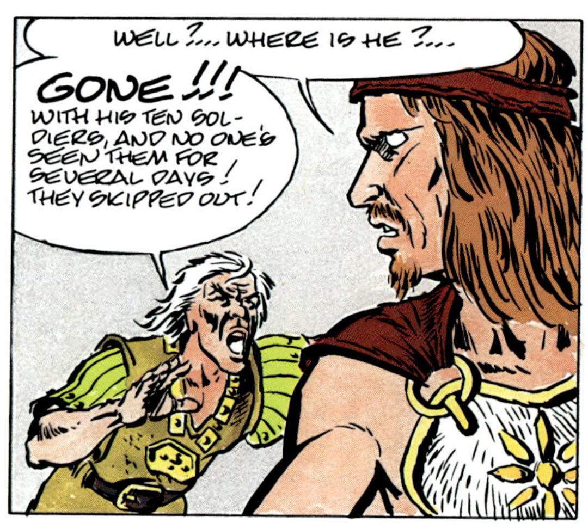

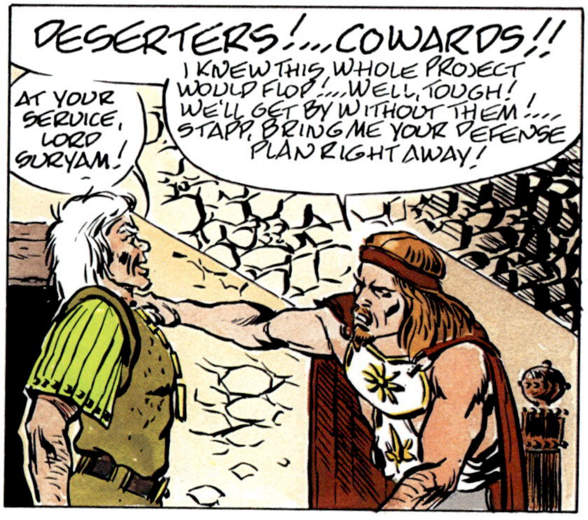

SURYAM! COULD YOU ALREADY HAVE FORGOTTEN THE ORDERS YOU SENT ARIA?... WHAT KIND OF GAME ARE YOU PLAYING?

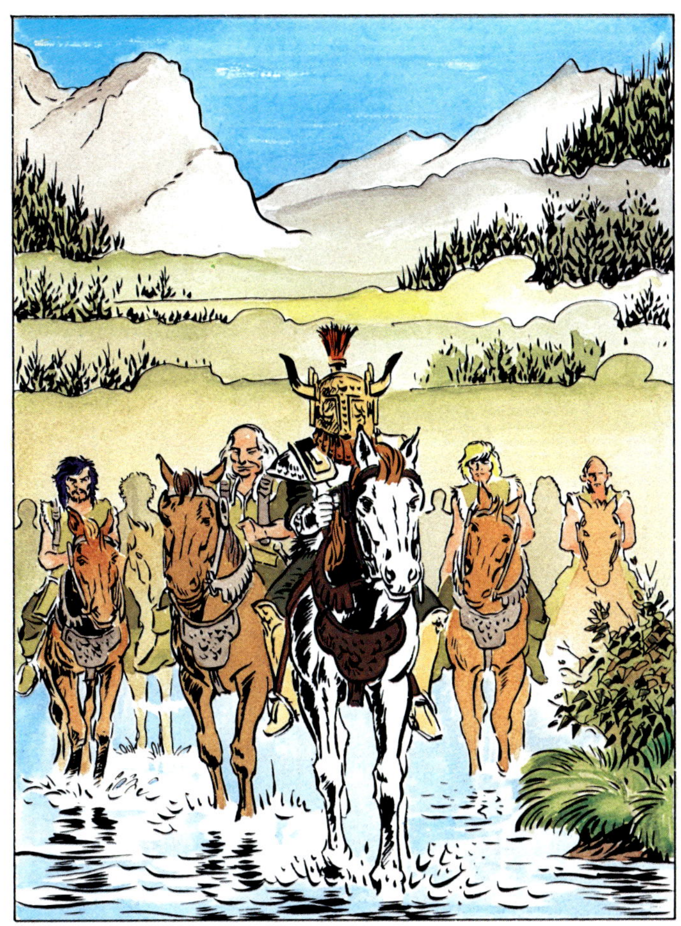

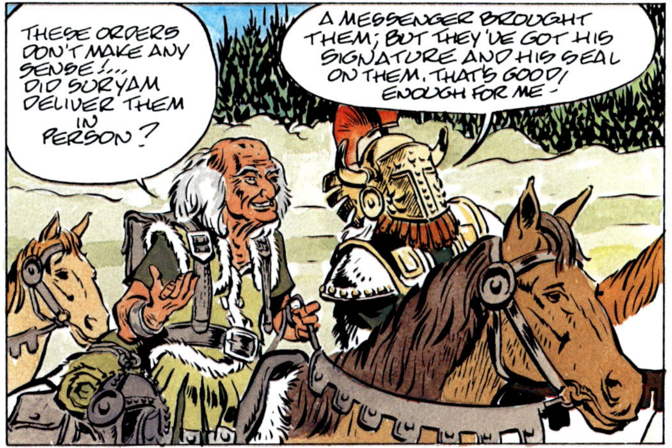
THESE ORDERS DON'T MAKE ANY SENSE!... DID SURYAM DELIVER THEM IN PERSON?
A MESSENGER BROUGHT THEM; BUT THEY'VE GOT HIS SIGNATURE AND HIS SEAL ON THEM. THAT'S GOOD ENOUGH FOR ME.

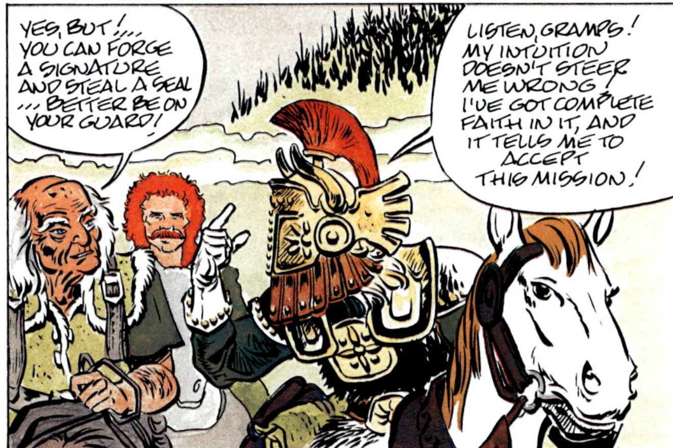
YES, BUT!... YOU CAN FORGE A SIGNATURE AND STEAL A SEAL... BETTER BE ON YOUR GUARD!
LISTEN, GRAMPS! MY INTUITION DOESN'T STEER ME WRONG. I'VE GOT COMPLETE FAITH IN IT, AND IT TELLS ME TO ACCEPT THIS MISSION!

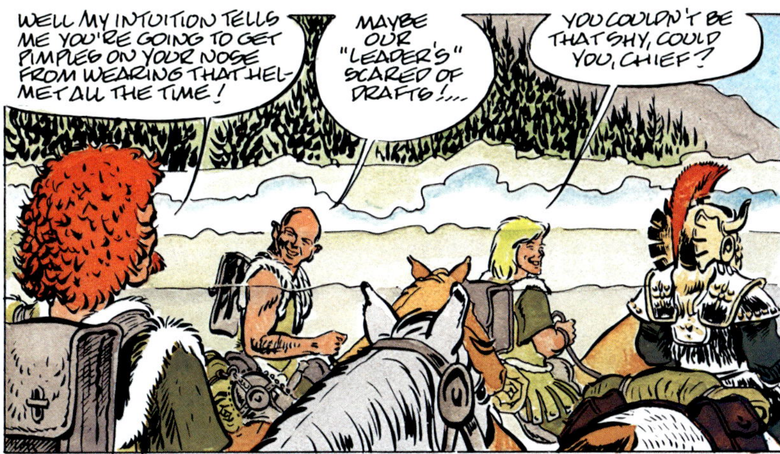
WELL MY INTUITION TELLS ME YOU'RE GOING TO GET PIMPLES ON YOUR NOSE FROM WEARING THAT HELMET ALL THE TIME!
MAYBE OUR "LEADER'S" SCARED OF DRAFTS!...
YOU COULDN'T BE THAT SHY, COULD YOU, CHIEF?

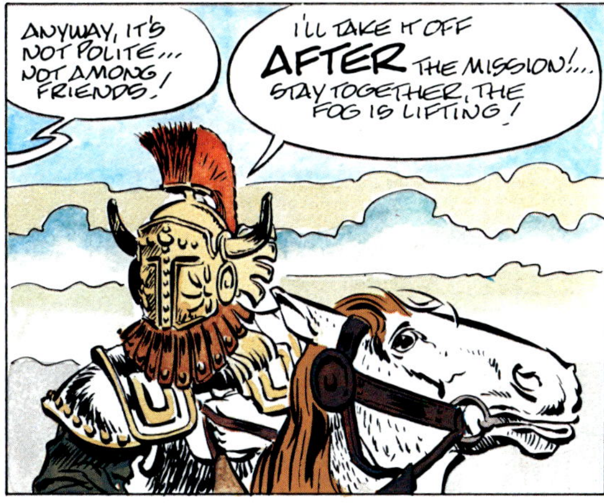
ANYWAY, IT'S NOT POLITE... NOT AMONG FRIENDS!
I'LL TAKE IT OFF AFTER THE MISSION!... STAY TOGETHER, THE FOG IS LIFTING!

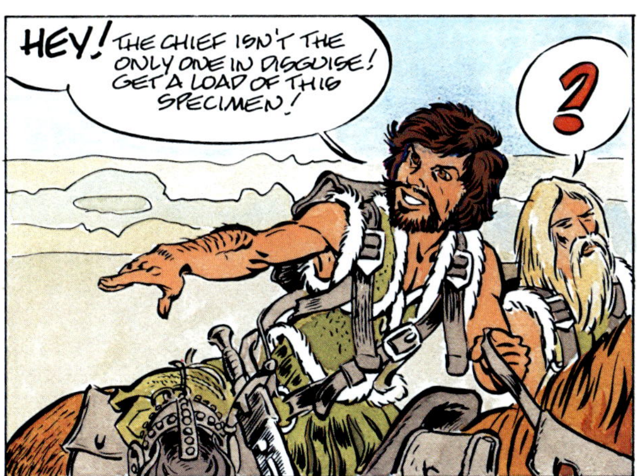
HEY! THE CHIEF ISN'T THE ONLY ONE IN DISGUISE! GET A LOAD OF THIS SPECIMEN!
?

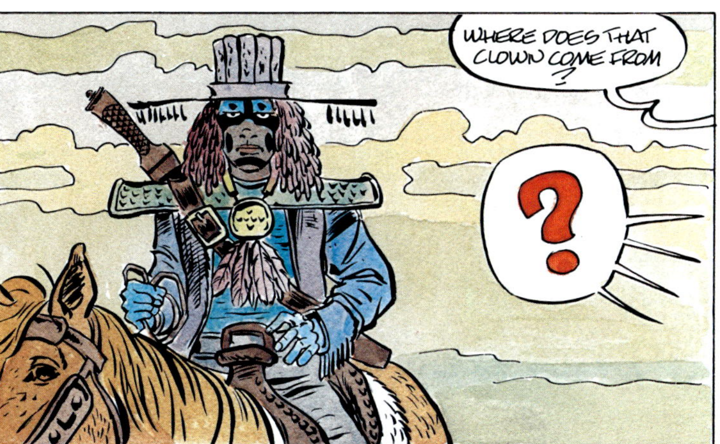
WHERE DOES THAT CLOWN COME FROM?
?

9

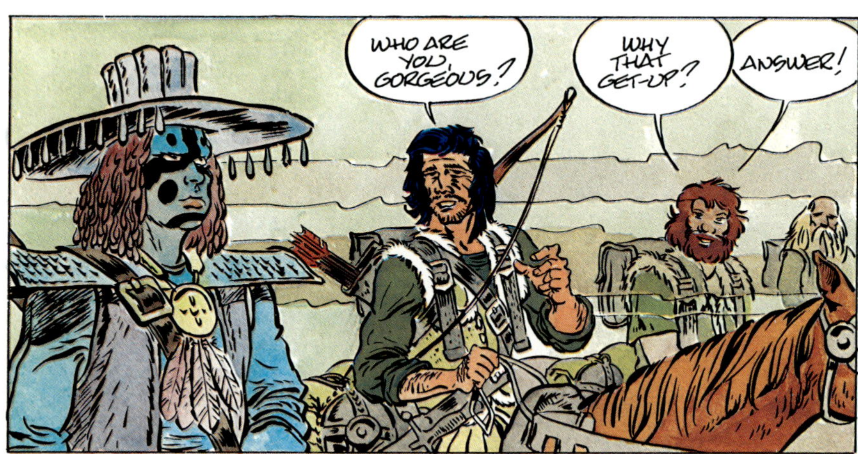
WHO ARE YOU, GORGEOUS?
WHY THAT GET-UP?
ANSWER!

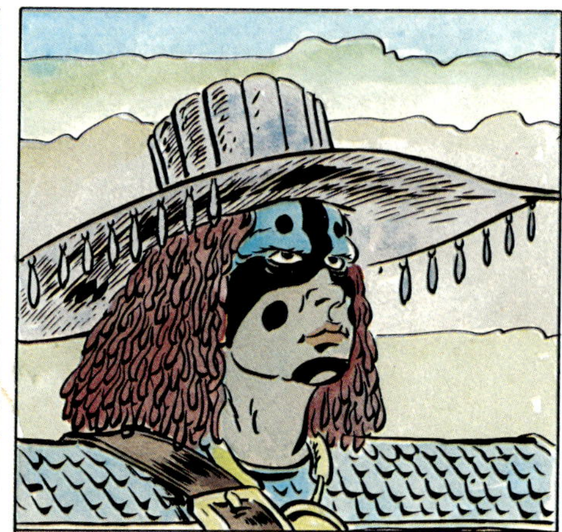

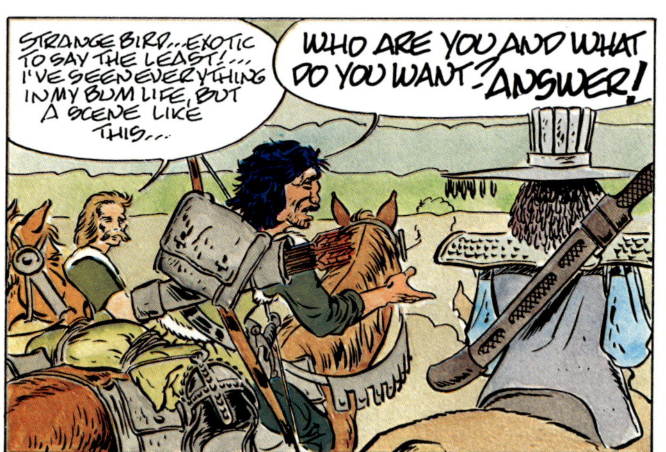
STRANGE BIRD... EXOTIC TO SAY THE LEAST!... I'VE SEEN EVERYTHING IN MY BUM LIFE, BUT A SCENE LIKE THIS...
WHO ARE YOU AND WHAT DO YOU WANT? ANSWER!

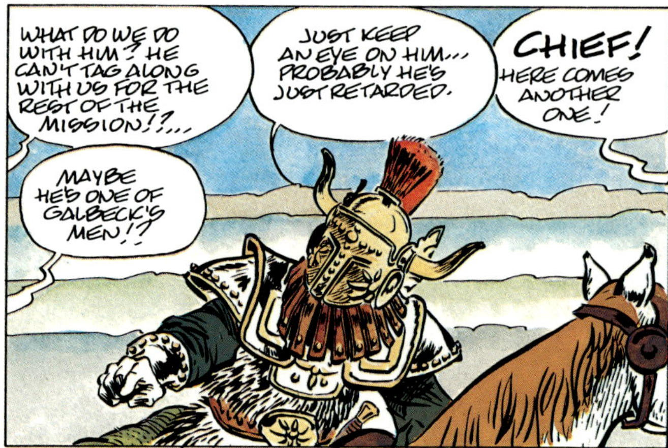
WHAT DO WE DO WITH HIM? HE CAN'T TAG ALONG WITH US FOR THE REST OF THE MISSION!?...
MAYBE HE'S ONE OF GALBECK'S MEN!?
JUST KEEP AN EYE ON HIM... PROBABLY HE'S JUST RETARDED.
CHIEF! HERE COMES ANOTHER ONE!

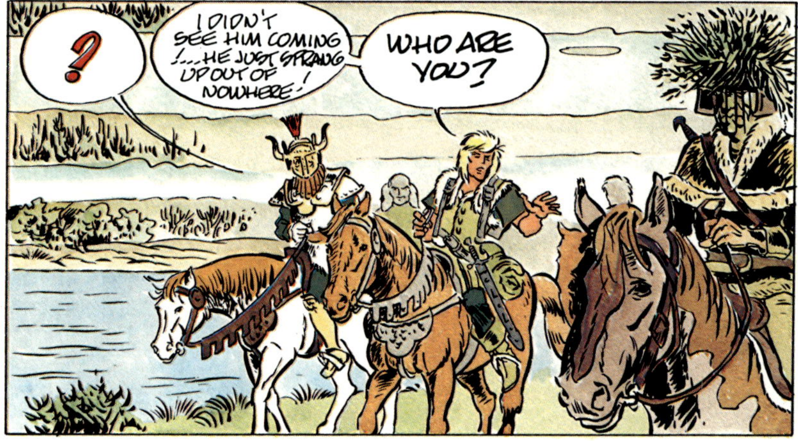
?
I DIDN'T SEE HIM COMING!... HE JUST SPRANG UP OUT OF NOWHERE!
WHO ARE YOU?

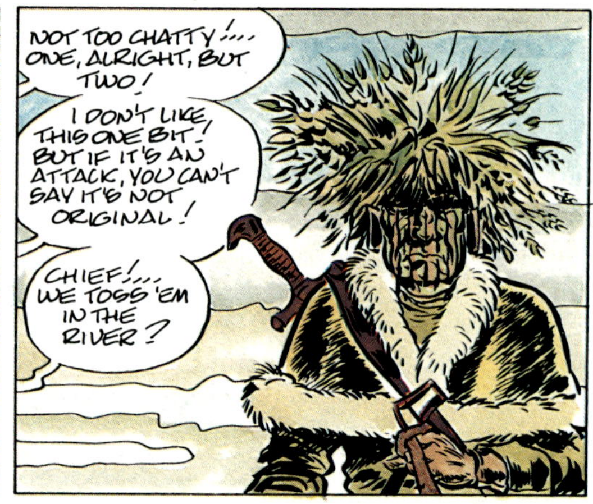
NOT TOO CHATTY!... ONE, ALRIGHT, BUT TWO!
I DON'T LIKE THIS ONE BIT! BUT IF IT'S AN ATTACK, YOU CAN'T SAY IT'S NOT ORIGINAL!
CHIEF!... WE TOSS 'EM IN THE RIVER?

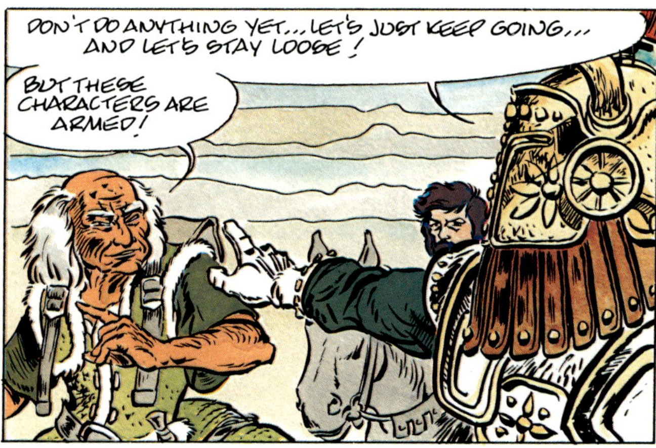
DON'T DO ANYTHING YET... LET'S JUST KEEP GOING... AND LET'S STAY LOOSE!
BUT THESE CHARACTERS ARE ARMED!

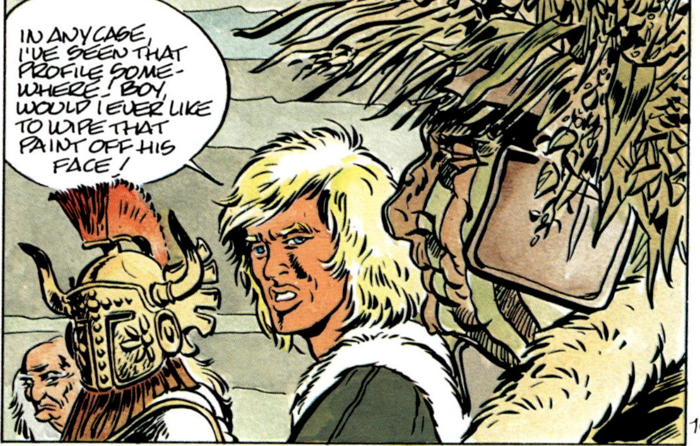
IN ANY CASE, I'VE SEEN THAT PROFILE SOMEWHERE! BOY, WOULD I EVER LIKE TO WIPE THAT PAINT OFF HIS FACE!
10.

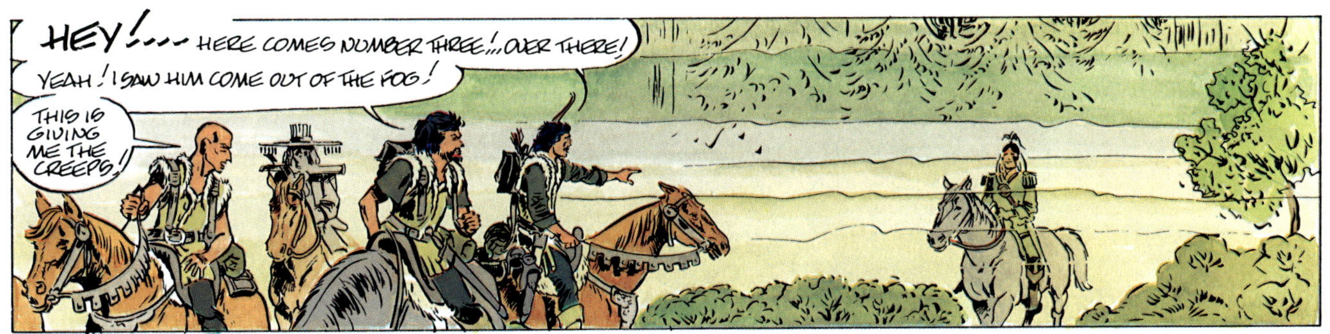
HEY!... HERE COMES NUMBER THREE!... OVER THERE!
YEAH! I SAW HIM COME OUT OF THE FOG!
THIS IS GIVING ME THE CREEPS!

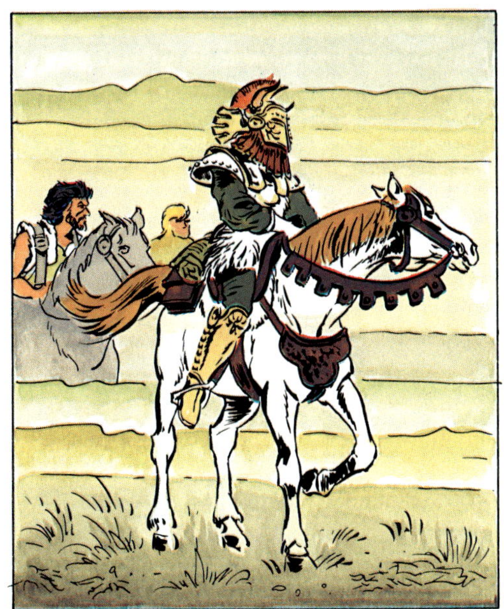

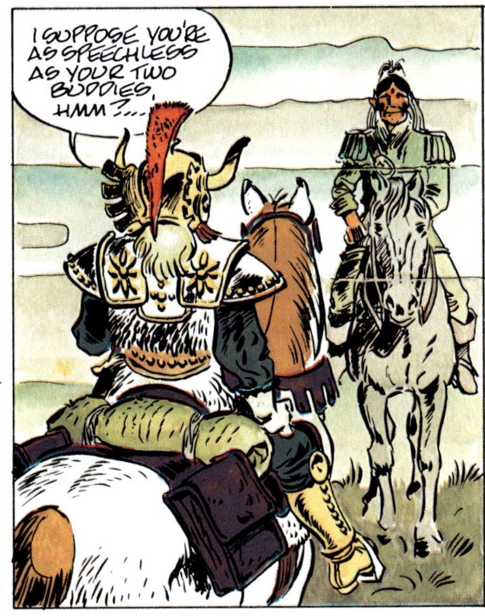
I SUPPOSE YOU'RE AS SPEECHLESS AS YOUR TWO BUDDIES, HMM?...

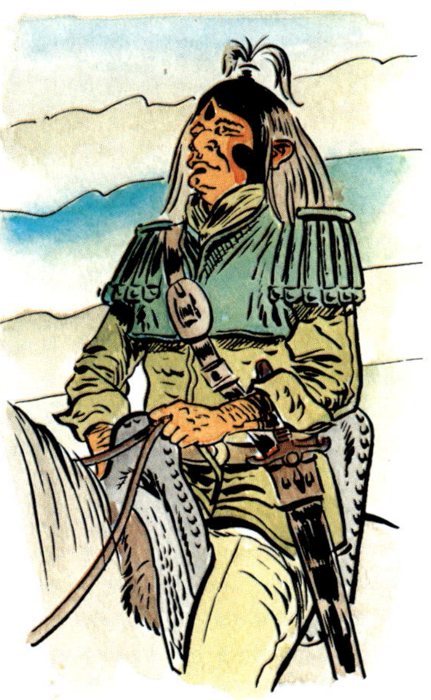

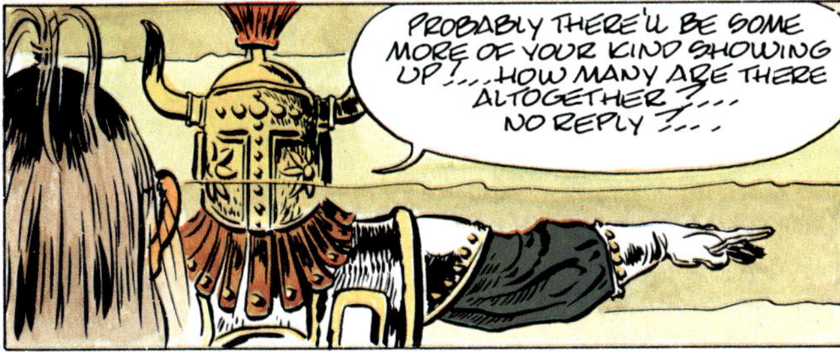
PROBABLY THERE'LL BE SOME MORE OF YOUR KIND SHOWING UP!... HOW MANY ARE THERE ALTOGETHER?... NO REPLY?...

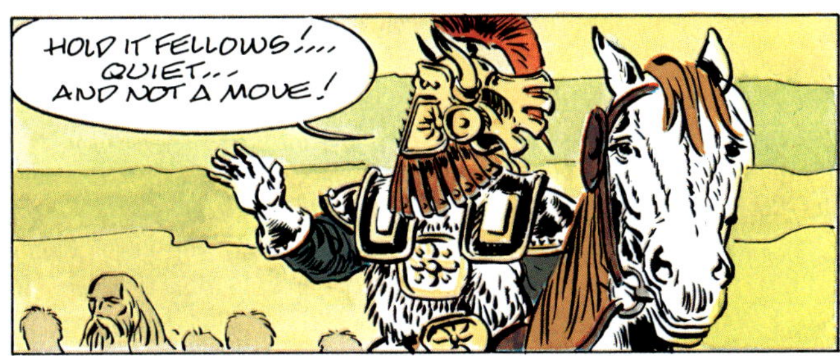
HOLD IT FELLOWS!... QUIET... AND NOT A MOVE!

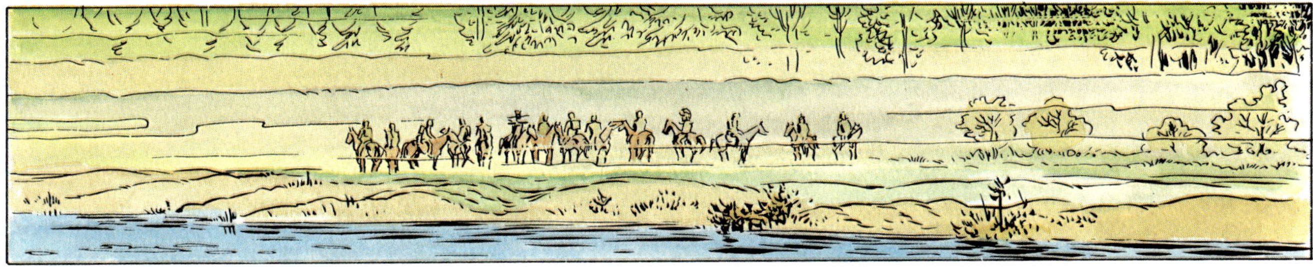

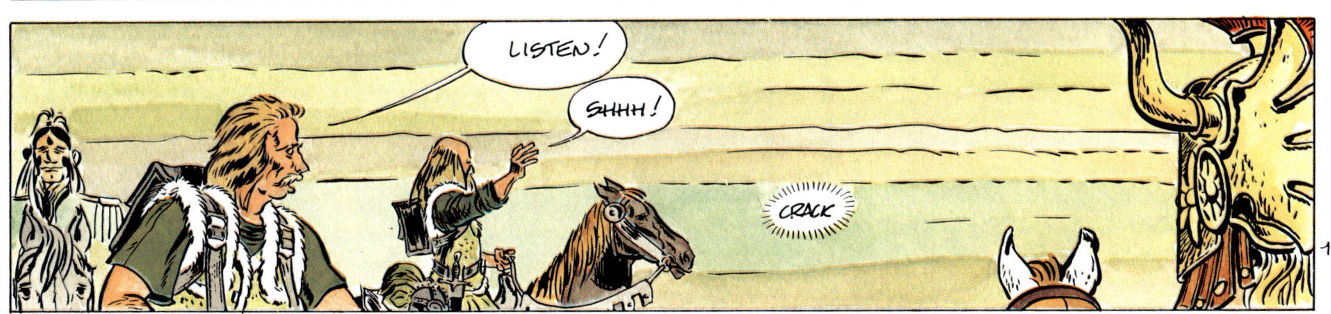
LISTEN!
SHHH!
CRACK
11.

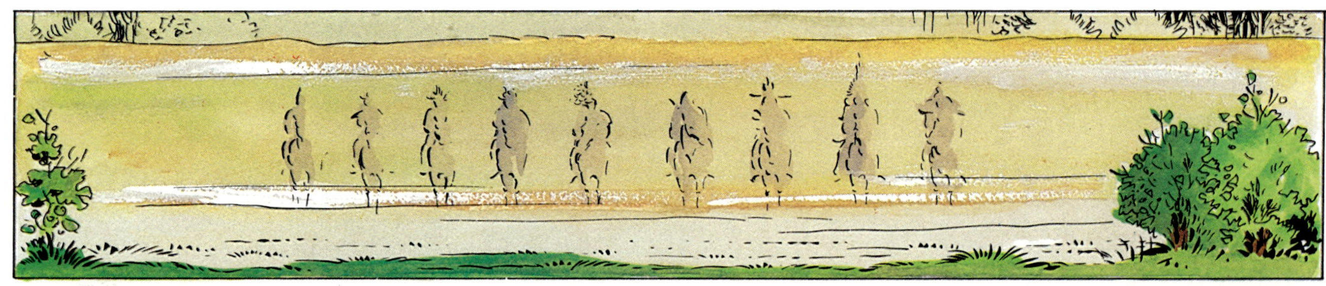

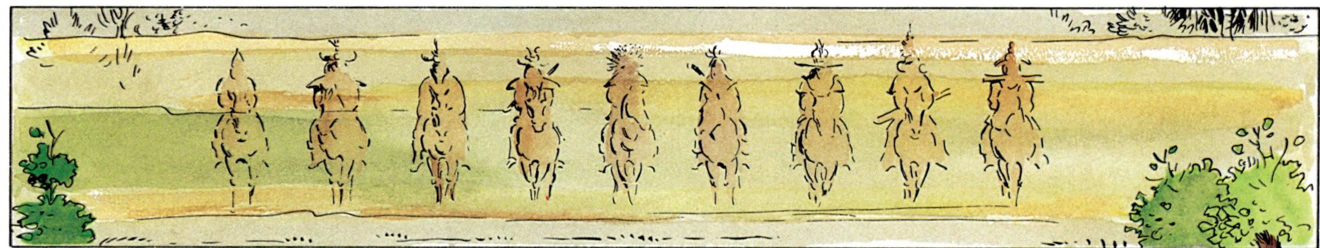

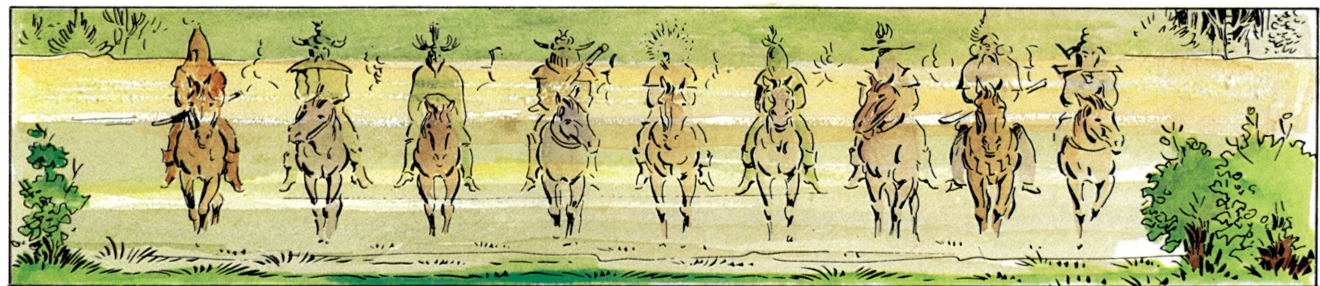

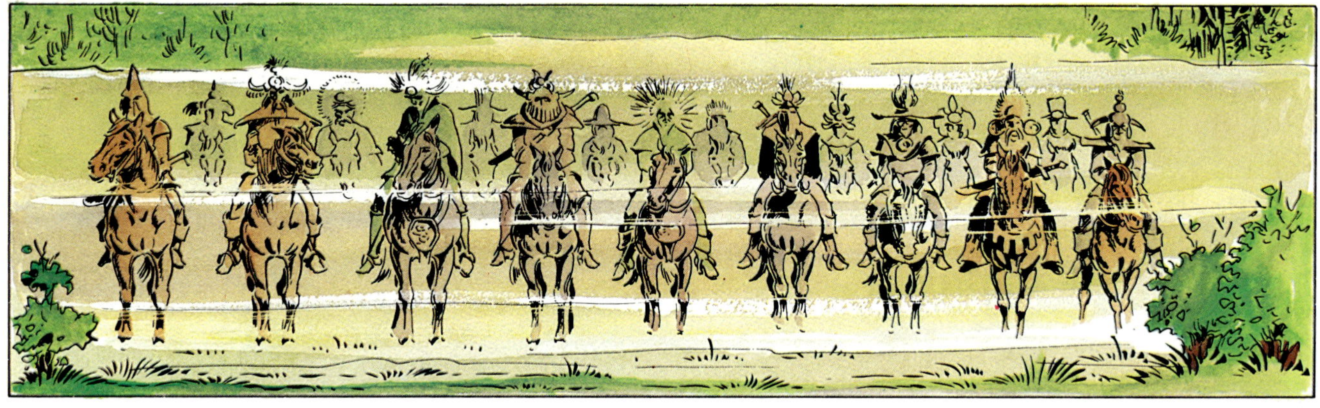

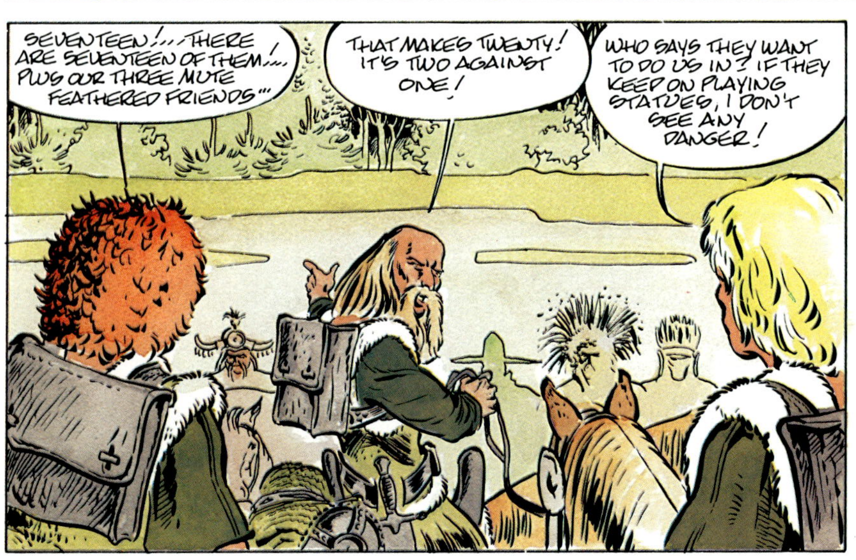

SEVENTEEN!... THERE ARE SEVENTEEN OF THEM!... PLUS OUR THREE MUTE FEATHERED FRIENDS!!!
THAT MAKES TWENTY! IT'S TWO AGAINST ONE!
WHO SAYS THEY WANT TO DO US IN? IF THEY KEEP ON PLAYING STATUES, I DON'T SEE ANY DANGER!

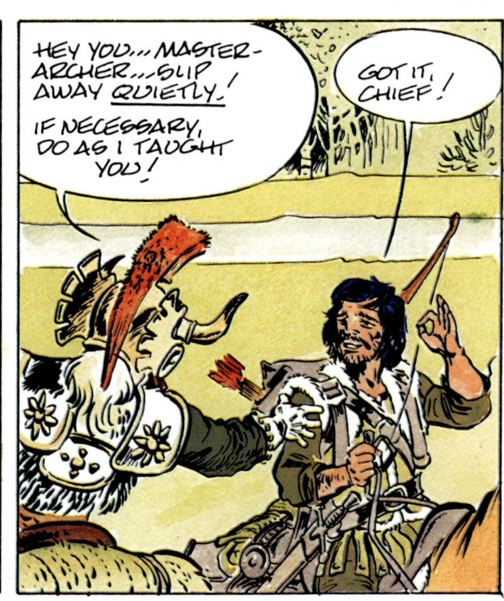

HEY YOU... MASTER-ARCHER... SLIP AWAY QUIETLY!
IF NECESSARY, DO AS I TAUGHT YOU!
GOT IT, CHIEF!
12.

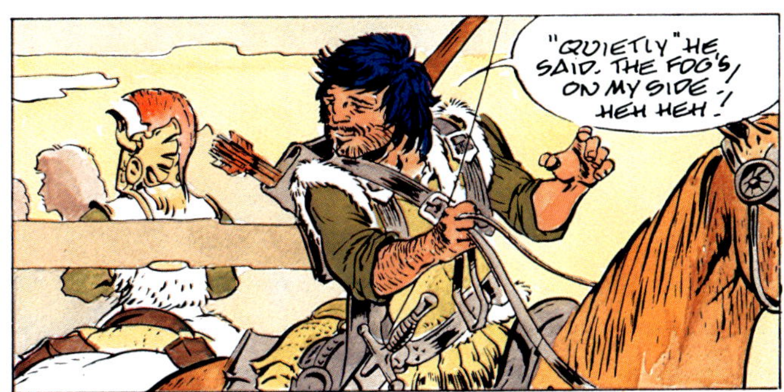
"QUIETLY" HE SAID. THE FOG'S ON MY SIDE! HEH HEH!
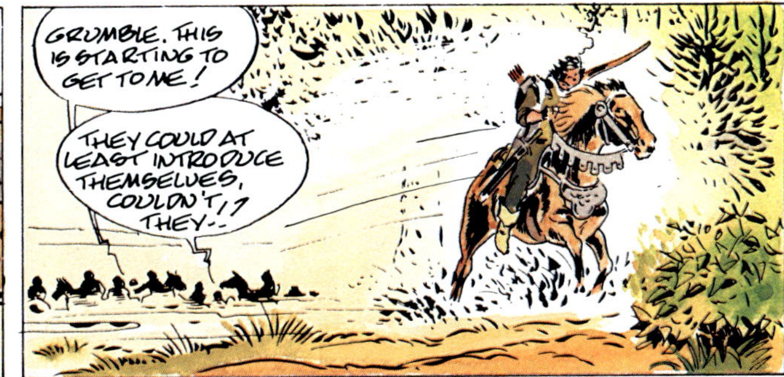
GRUMBLE. THIS IS STARTING TO GET TO ME!
THEY COULD AT LEAST INTRODUCE THEMSELVES, COULDN'T!? THEY--
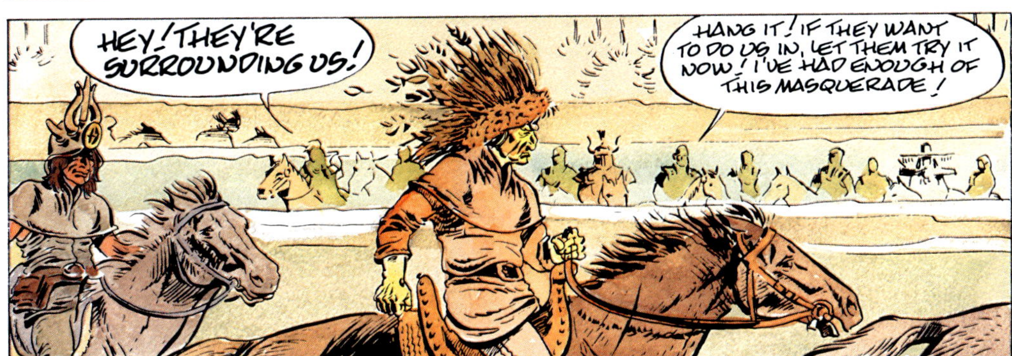
HEY! THEY'RE SURROUNDING US!
HANG IT! IF THEY WANT TO DO US IN, LET THEM TRY IT NOW! I'VE HAD ENOUGH OF THIS MASQUERADE!
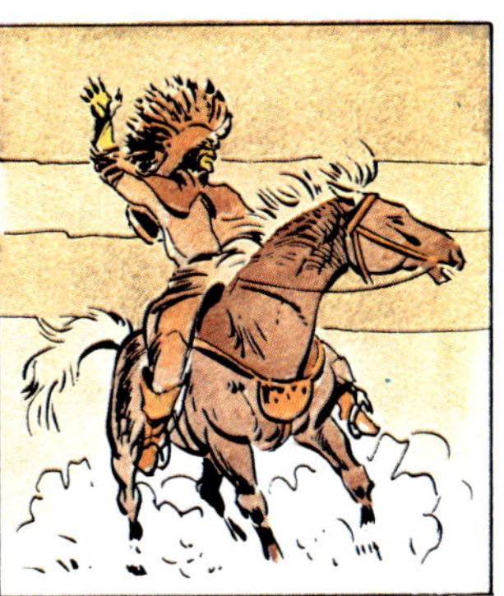
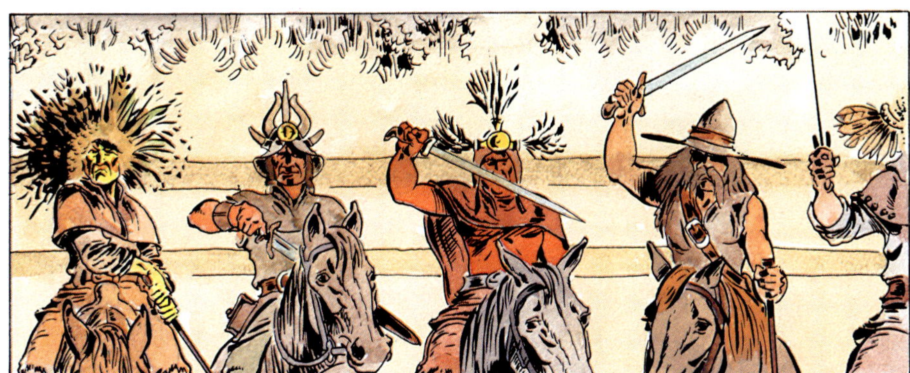
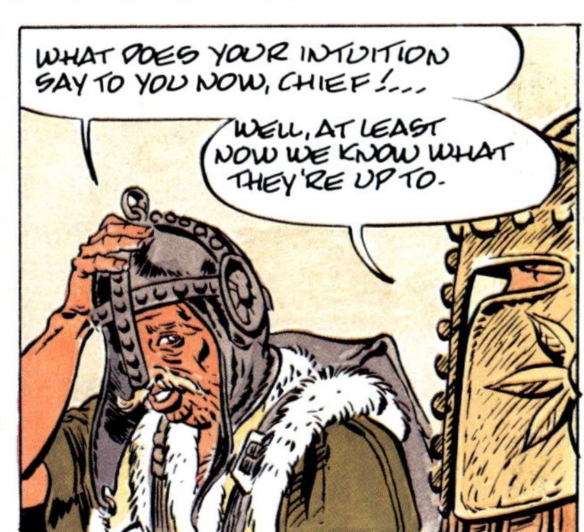
WHAT DOES YOUR INTUITION SAY TO YOU NOW, CHIEF!...
WELL, AT LEAST NOW WE KNOW WHAT THEY'RE UP TO.
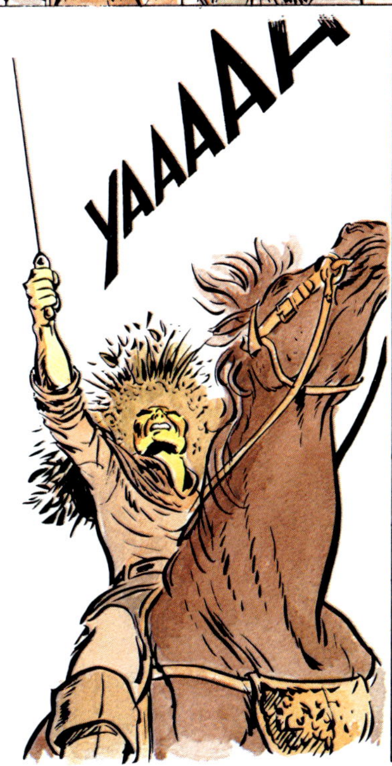
YAAAAA
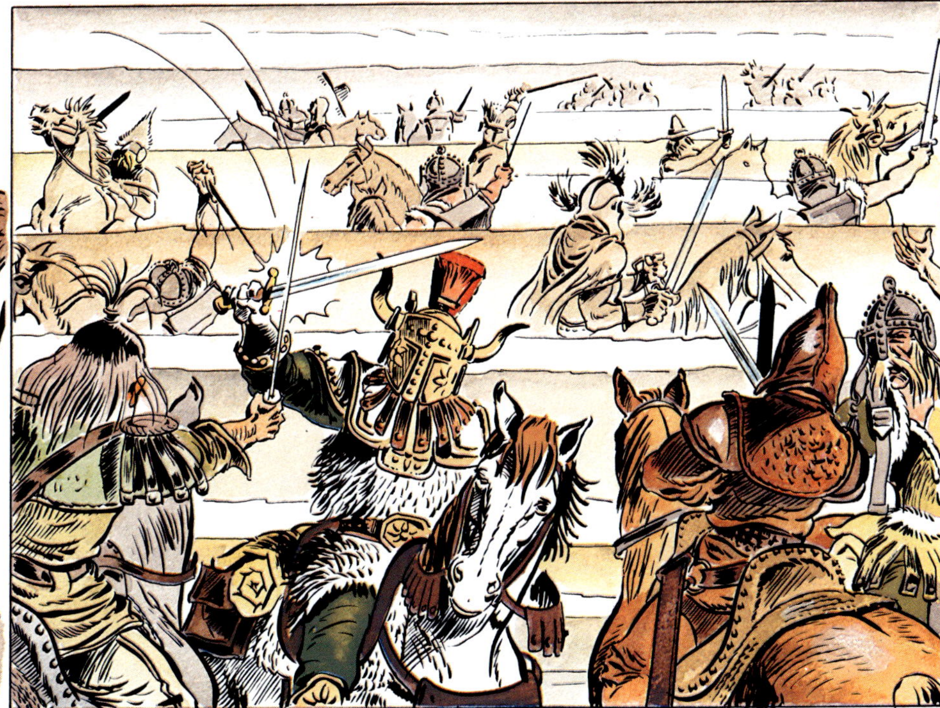

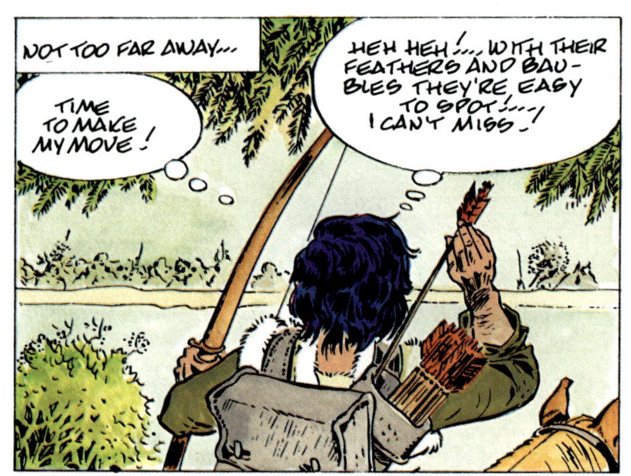
NOT TOO FAR AWAY...
TIME TO MAKE MY MOVE!
HEH HEH!... WITH THEIR FEATHERS AND BAUBLES THEY'RE EASY TO SPOT!...! I CAN'T MISS...!

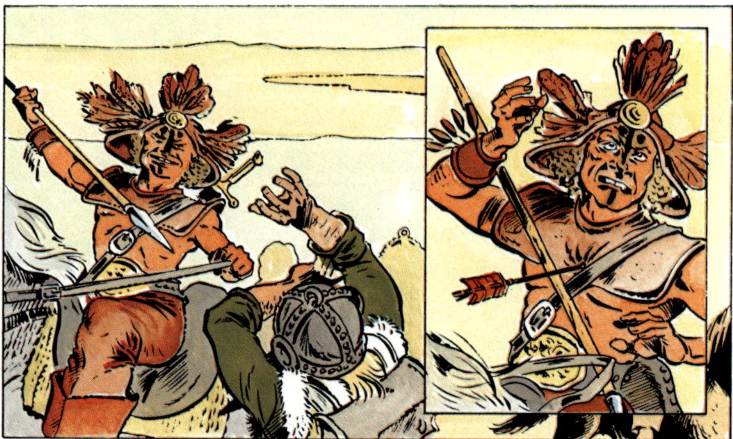

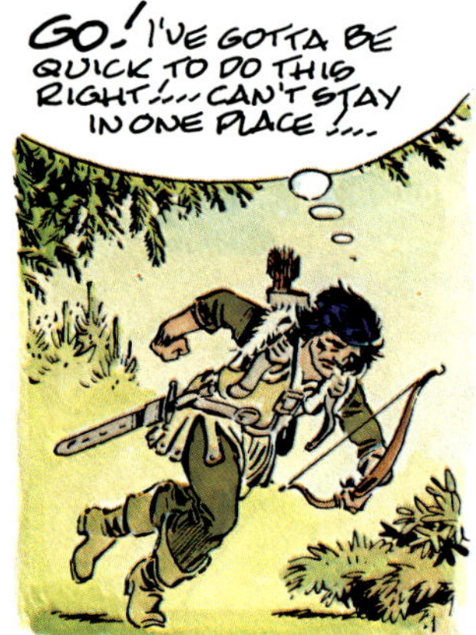
GO! I'VE GOTTA BE QUICK TO DO THIS RIGHT!... CAN'T STAY IN ONE PLACE...

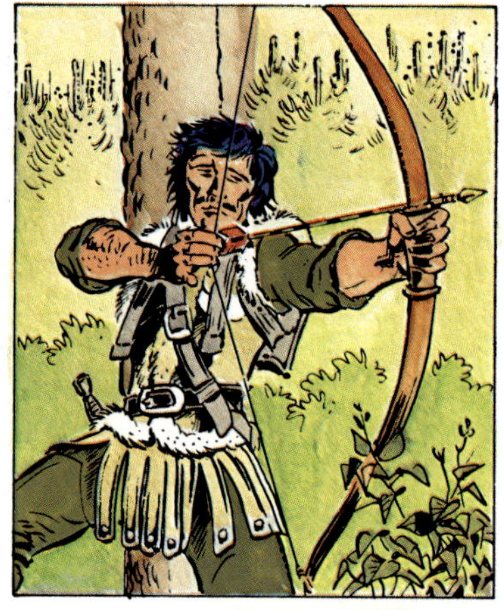

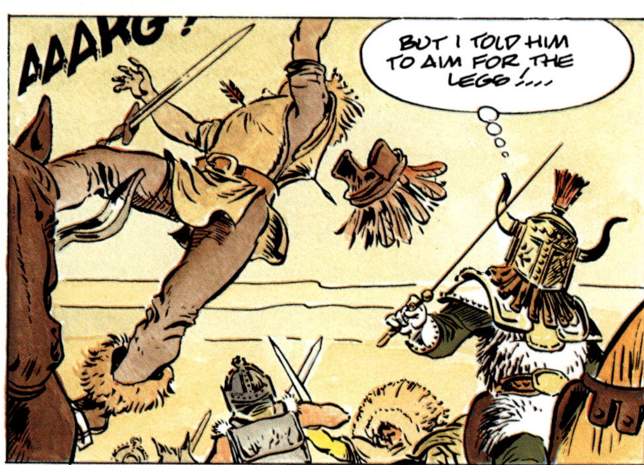
AAARG!
BUT I TOLD HIM TO AIM FOR THE LEGS!...

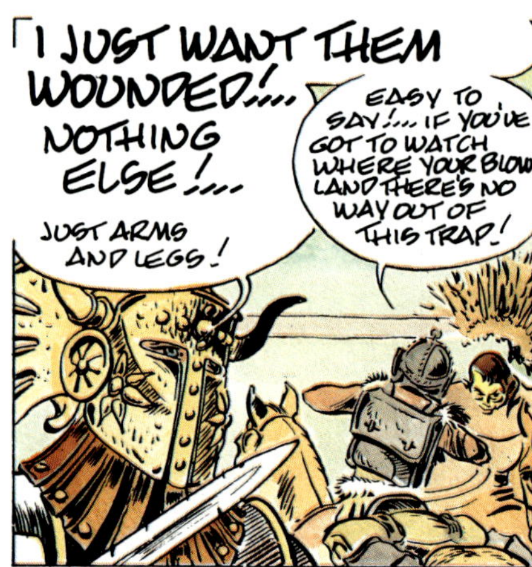
I JUST WANT THEM WOUNDED!... NOTHING ELSE!... JUST ARMS AND LEGS!
EASY TO SAY!... IF YOU'VE GOT TO WATCH WHERE YOUR BLOWS LAND THERE'S NO WAY OUT OF THIS TRAP!

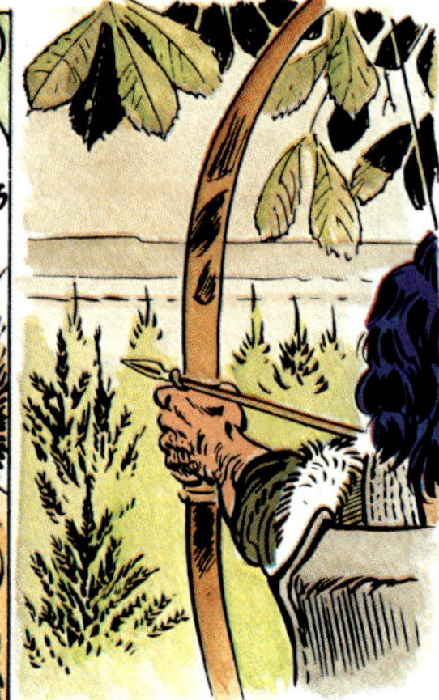

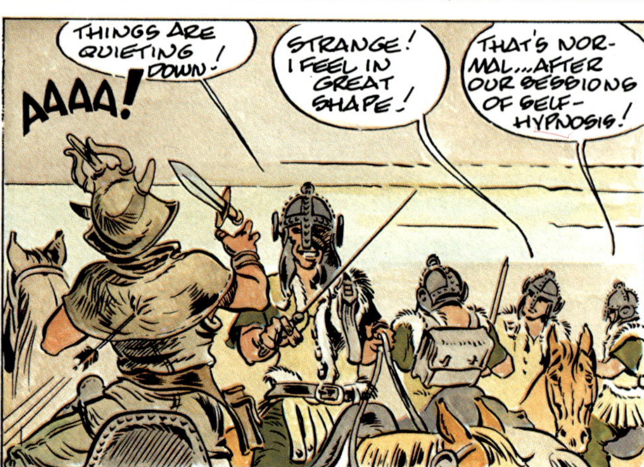
AAAA!
THINGS ARE QUIETING DOWN!
STRANGE! I FEEL IN GREAT SHAPE!
THAT'S NORMAL... AFTER OUR SESSIONS OF SELF-HYPNOSIS!

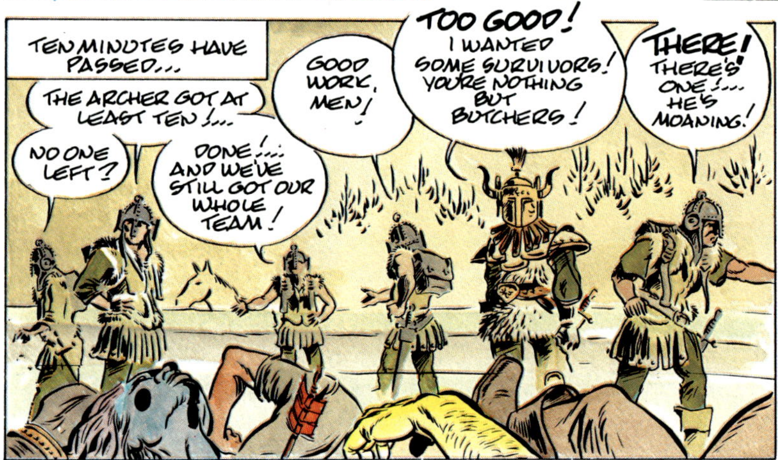
TEN MINUTES HAVE PASSED...
THE ARCHER GOT AT LEAST TEN!...
NO ONE LEFT?
DONE!... AND WE'VE STILL GOT OUR WHOLE TEAM!
GOOD WORK, MEN!
TOO GOOD! I WANTED SOME SURVIVORS! YOU'RE NOTHING BUT BUTCHERS!
THERE! THERE'S ONE!... HE'S MOANING!

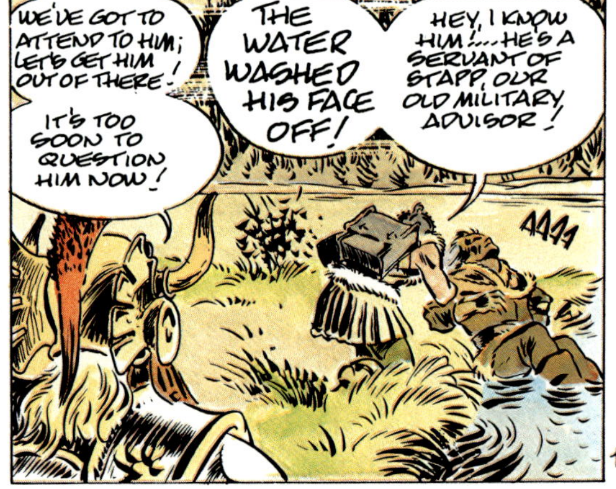
WE'VE GOT TO ATTEND TO HIM; LET'S GET HIM OUT OF THERE!
IT'S TOO SOON TO QUESTION HIM NOW!
THE WATER WASHED HIS FACE OFF!
HEY, I KNOW HIM!... HE'S A SERVANT OF STAPP, OUR OLD MILITARY ADVISOR!
AAAA
14

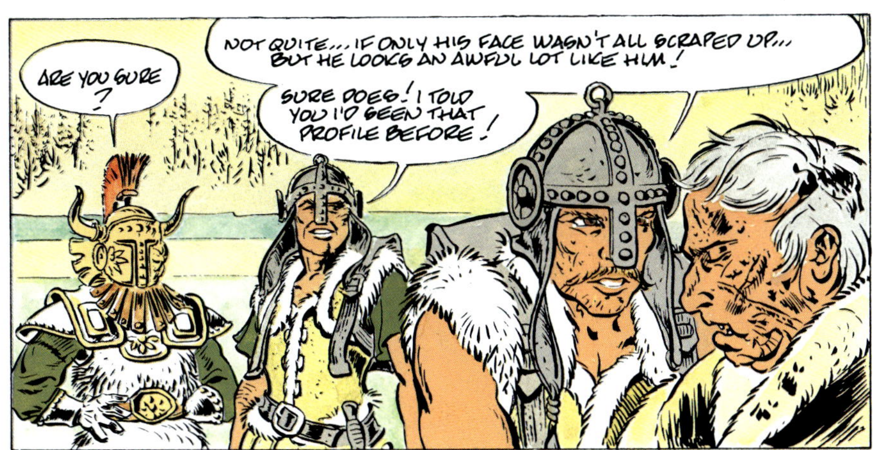
ARE YOU SURE ?
NOT QUITE... IF ONLY HIS FACE WASN'T ALL SCRAPED UP... BUT HE LOOKS AN AWFUL LOT LIKE HIM!
SURE DOES! I TOLD YOU I'D SEEN THAT PROFILE BEFORE!

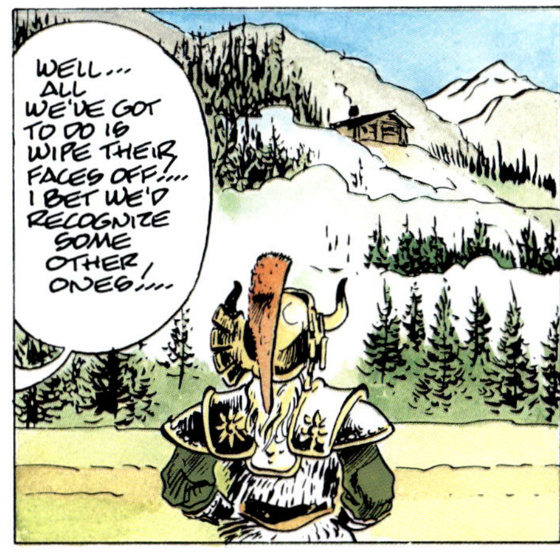
WELL... ALL WE'VE GOT TO DO IS WIPE THEIR FACES OFF!... I BET WE'D RECOGNIZE SOME OTHER ONES!...

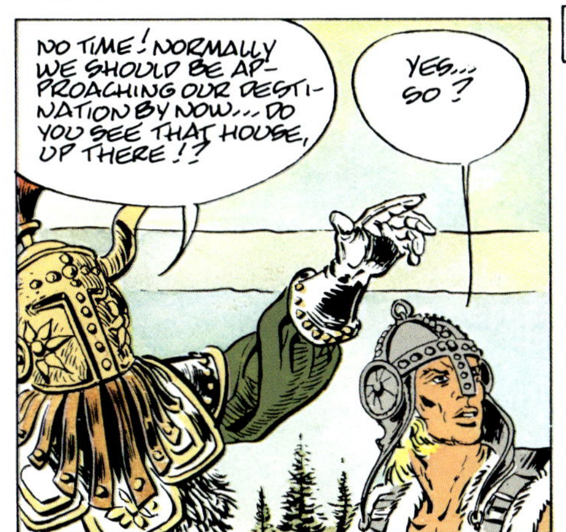
NO TIME! NORMALLY WE SHOULD BE APPROACHING OUR DESTINATION BY NOW... DO YOU SEE THAT HOUSE, UP THERE!?
YES... SO?

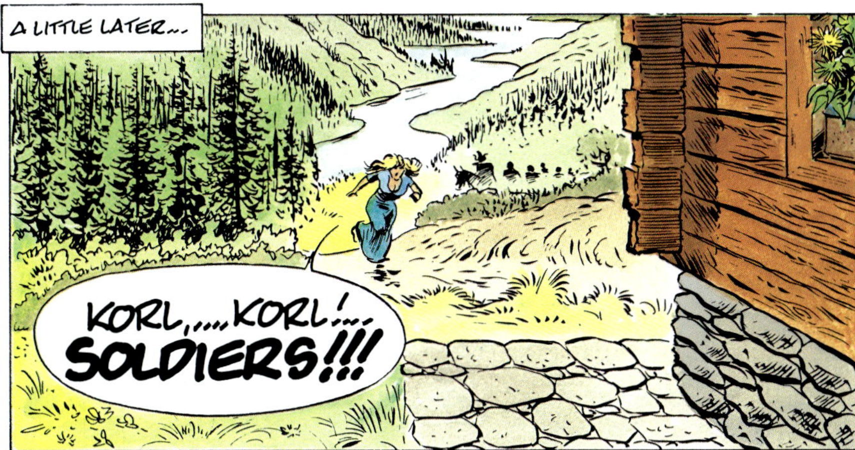
A LITTLE LATER...
KORL,... KORL!... SOLDIERS!!!

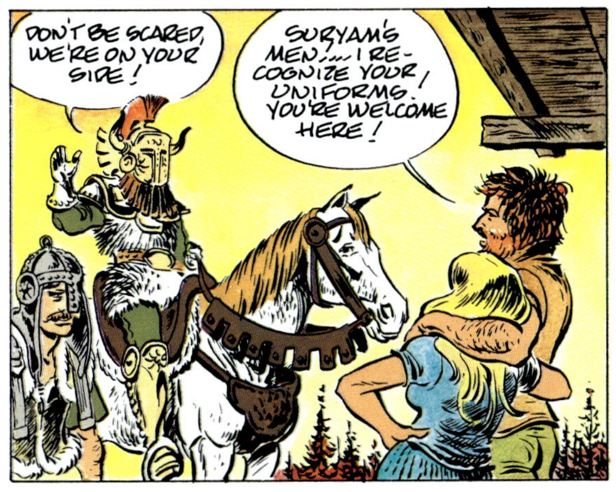
DON'T BE SCARED, WE'RE ON YOUR SIDE!
SURYAM'S MEN!... I RECOGNIZE YOUR UNIFORMS! YOU'RE WELCOME HERE!

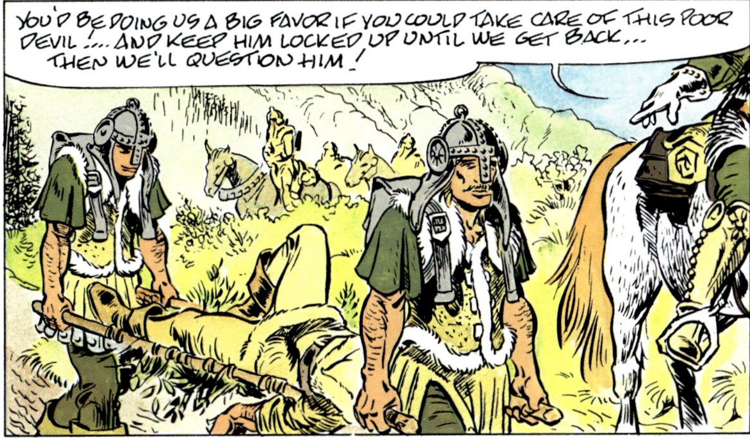
YOU'D BE DOING US A BIG FAVOR IF YOU COULD TAKE CARE OF THIS POOR DEVIL!... AND KEEP HIM LOCKED UP UNTIL WE GET BACK... THEN WE'LL QUESTION HIM!

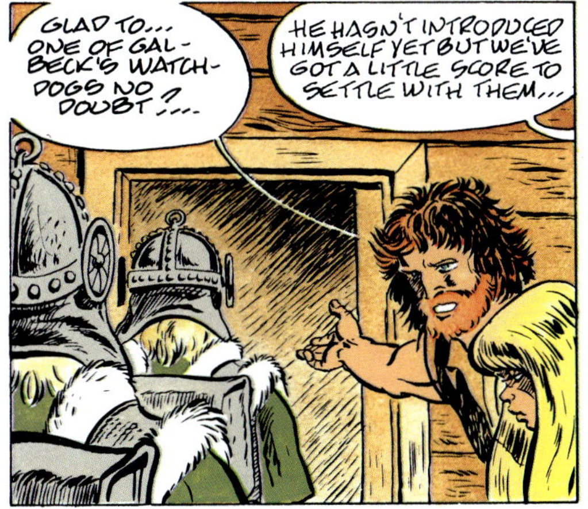
GLAD TO... ONE OF GALBECK'S WATCHDOGS NO DOUBT?...
HE HASN'T INTRODUCED HIMSELF YET BUT WE'VE GOT A LITTLE SCORE TO SETTLE WITH THEM...

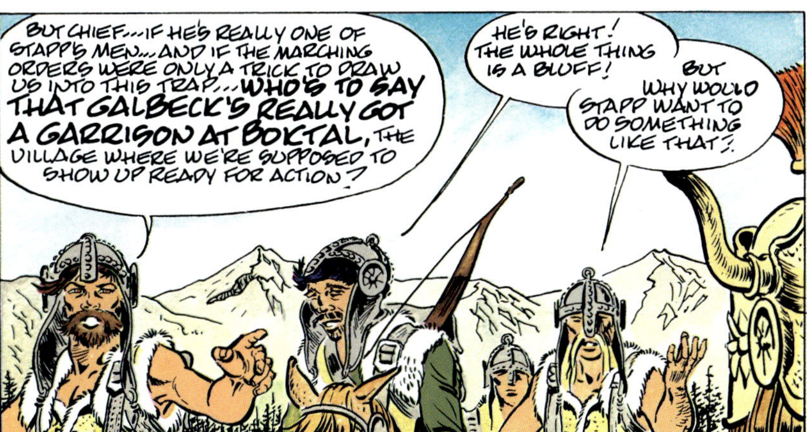
BUT CHIEF... IF HE'S REALLY ONE OF STAPP'S MEN... AND IF THE MARCHING ORDERS WERE ONLY A TRICK TO DRAW US INTO THIS TRAP... WHO'S TO SAY THAT GALBECK'S REALLY GOT A GARRISON AT BOKTAL, THE VILLAGE WHERE WE'RE SUPPOSED TO SHOW UP READY FOR ACTION?
HE'S RIGHT! THE WHOLE THING IS A BLUFF!
BUT WHY WOULD STAPP WANT TO DO SOMETHING LIKE THAT?

15.

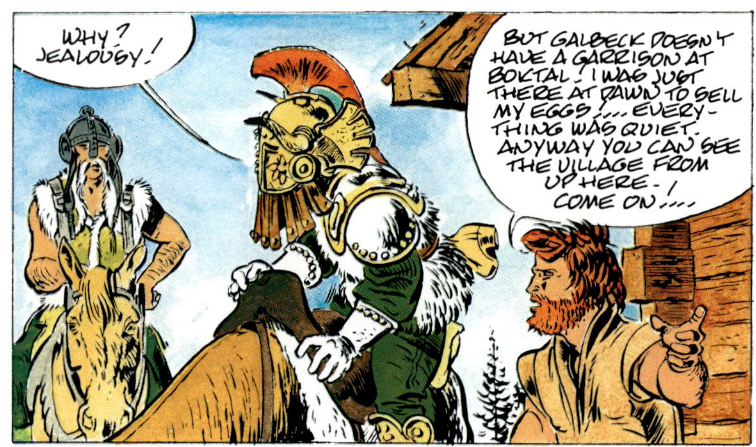
WHY? JEALOUSY!
BUT GALBECK DOESN'T HAVE A GARRISON AT BOKTAL! I WAS JUST THERE AT DAWN TO SELL MY EGGS!... EVERYTHING WAS QUIET. ANYWAY YOU CAN SEE THE VILLAGE FROM UP HERE.! COME ON!...

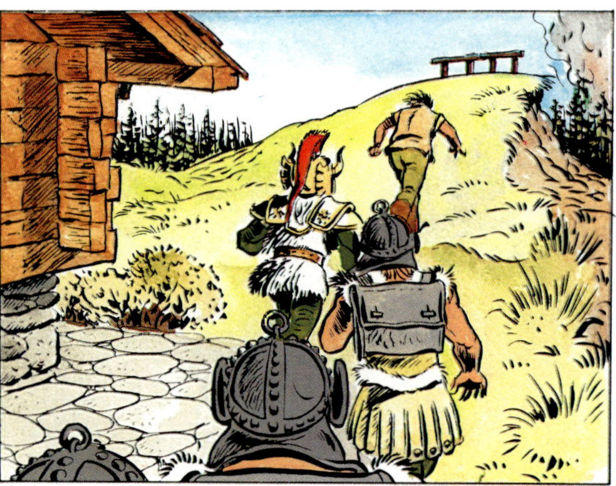

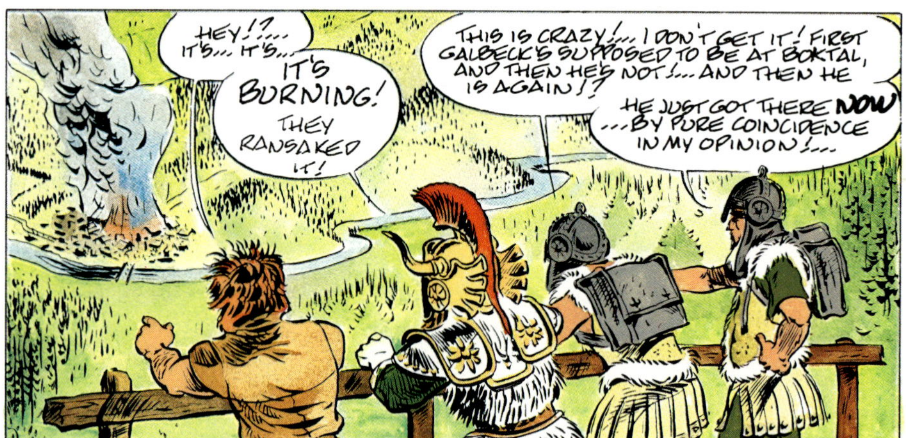
HEY!?... IT'S... IT'S...
IT'S BURNING!
THEY RANSAKED IT!
THIS IS CRAZY!... I DON'T GET IT! FIRST GALBECK'S SUPPOSED TO BE AT BOKTAL, AND THEN HE'S NOT!... AND THEN HE IS AGAIN!?
HE JUST GOT THERE NOW ...BY PURE COINCIDENCE IN MY OPINION!...

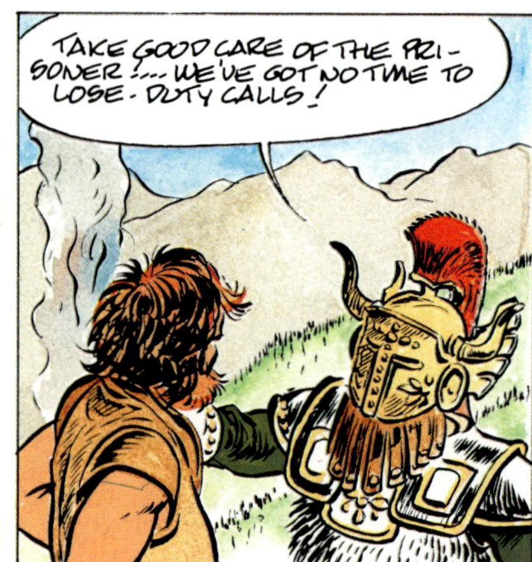
TAKE GOOD CARE OF THE PRISONER!... WE'VE GOT NO TIME TO LOSE. DUTY CALLS!

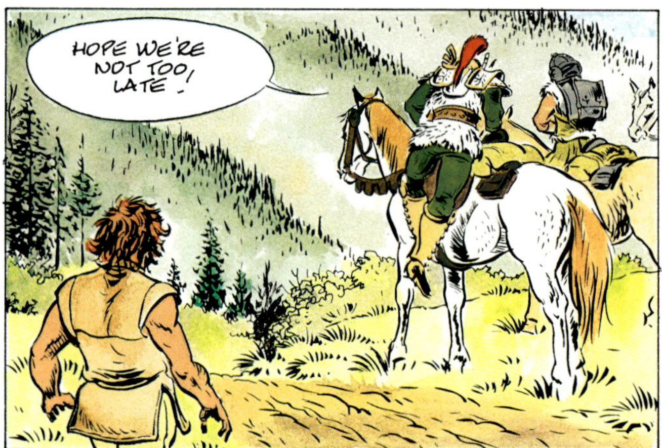
HOPE WE'RE NOT TOO LATE!

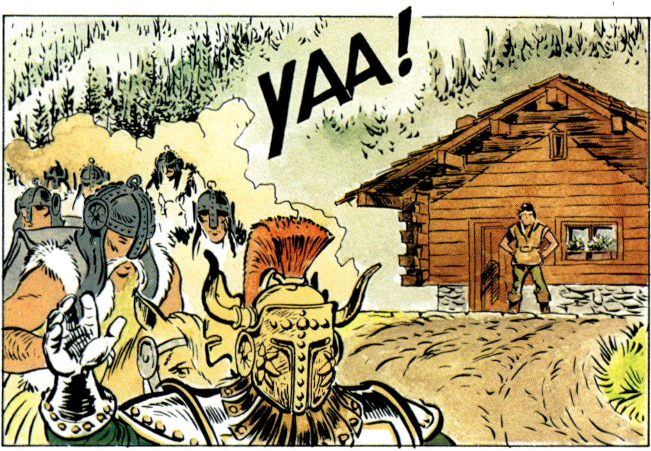
YAA!

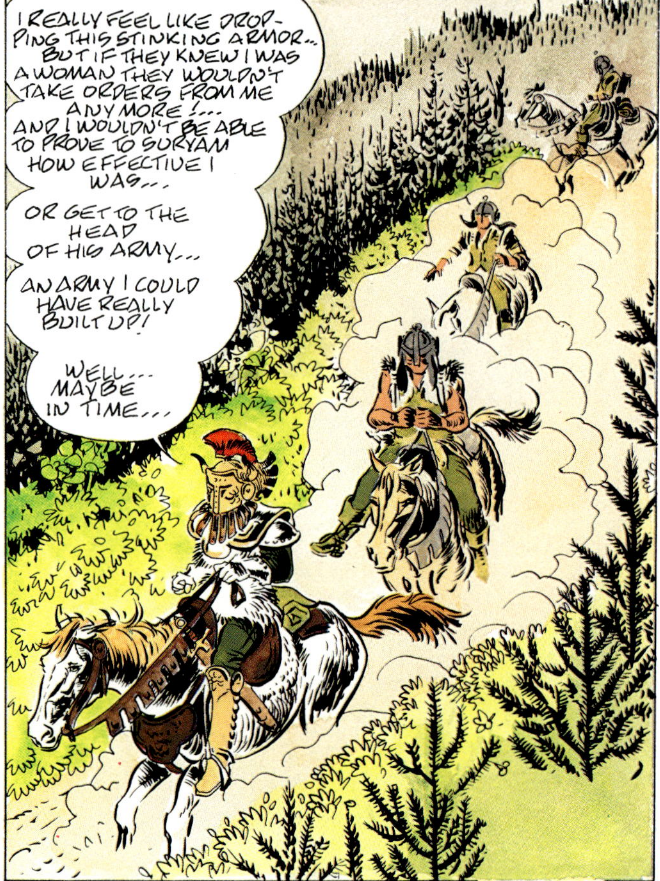
I REALLY FEEL LIKE DROPPING THIS STINKING ARMOR... BUT IF THEY KNEW I WAS A WOMAN THEY WOULDN'T TAKE ORDERS FROM ME ANYMORE!... AND I WOULDN'T BE ABLE TO PROVE TO SURYAM HOW EFFECTIVE I WAS...
OR GET TO THE HEAD OF HIS ARMY...
AN ARMY I COULD HAVE REALLY BUILT UP!
WELL... MAYBE IN TIME...

16

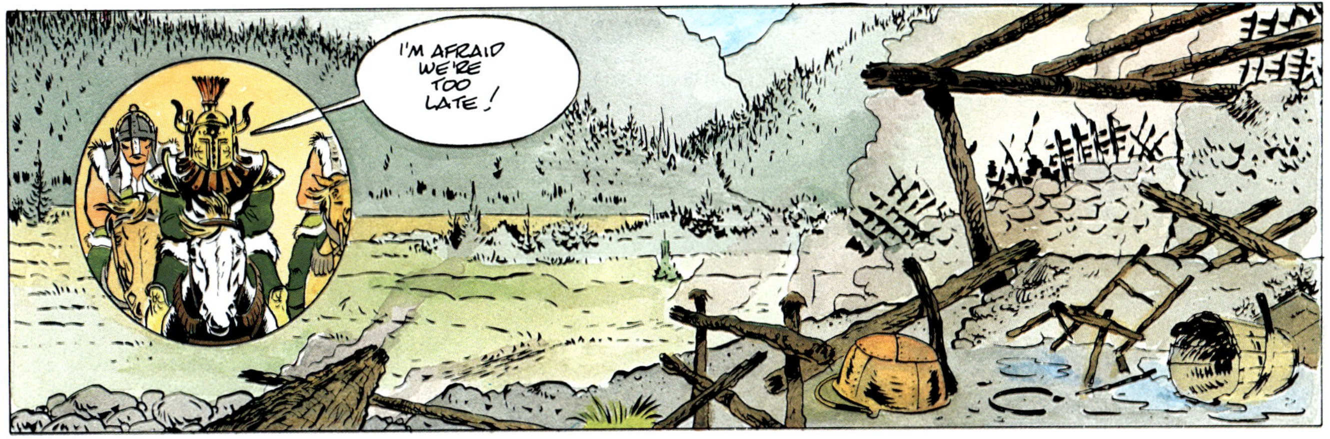
I'M AFRAID WE'RE TOO LATE!

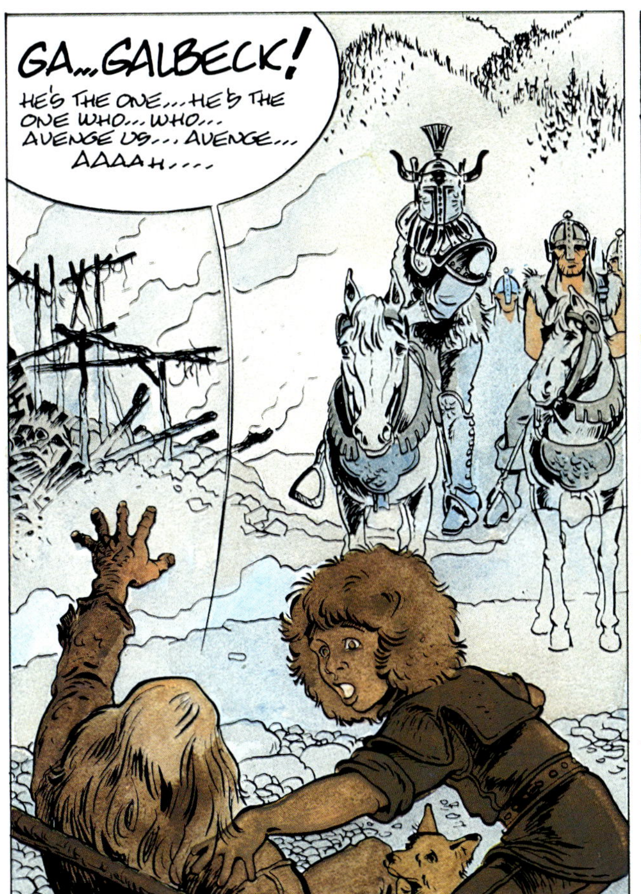
GA...GALBECK! HE'S THE ONE... HE'S THE ONE WHO... WHO... AVENGE US... AVENGE... AAAAH....

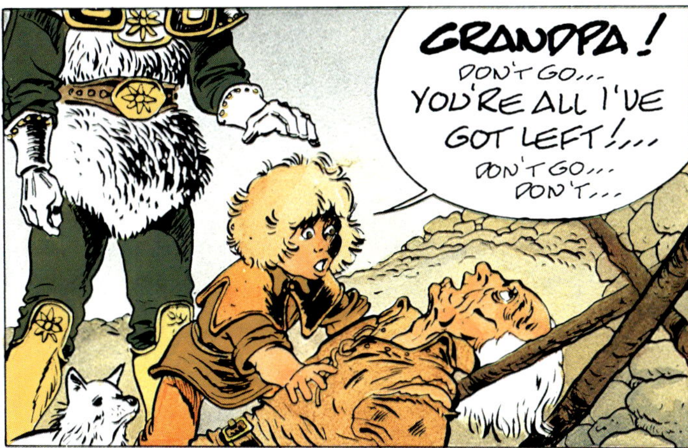
GRANDPA! DON'T GO... YOU'RE ALL I'VE GOT LEFT!... DON'T GO... DON'T...

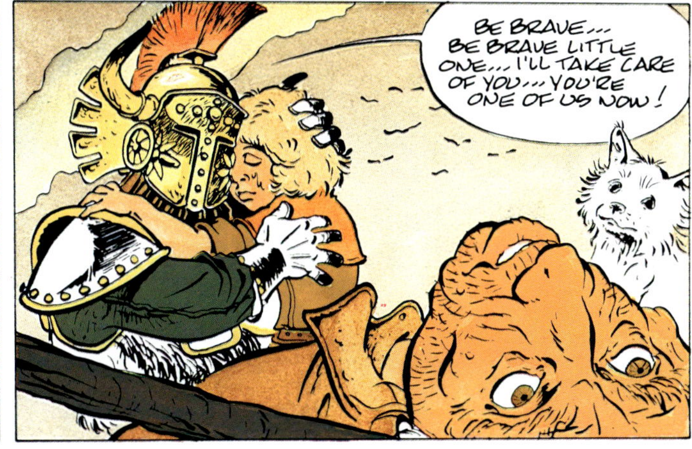
BE BRAVE... BE BRAVE LITTLE ONE... I'LL TAKE CARE OF YOU... YOU'RE ONE OF US NOW!

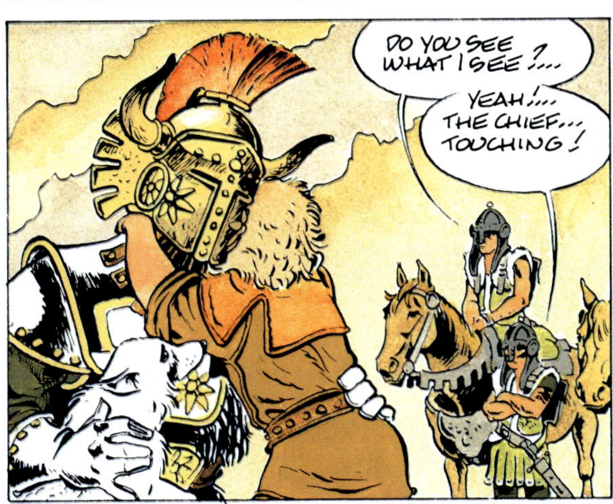
DO YOU SEE WHAT I SEE?...
YEAH!... THE CHIEF... TOUCHING!

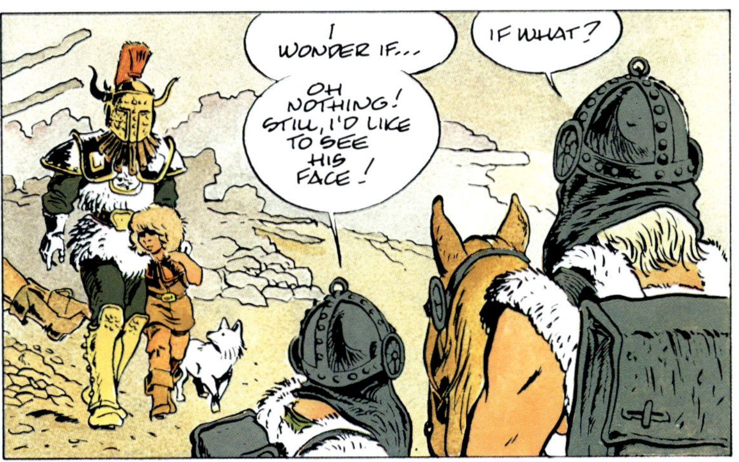
I WONDER IF...
IF WHAT?
OH NOTHING! STILL, I'D LIKE TO SEE HIS FACE!
17

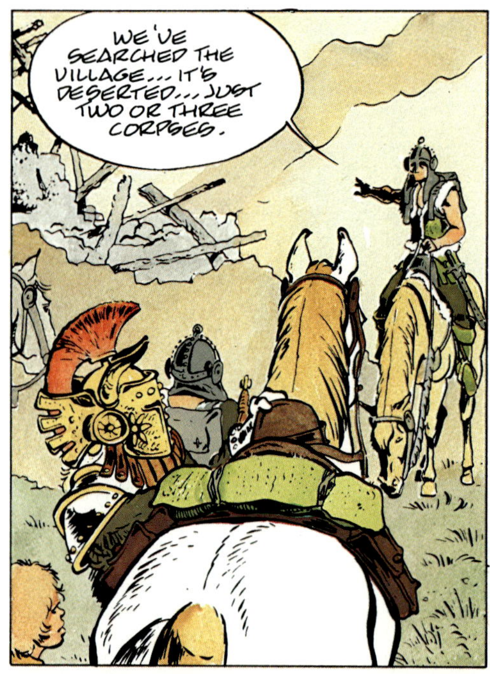

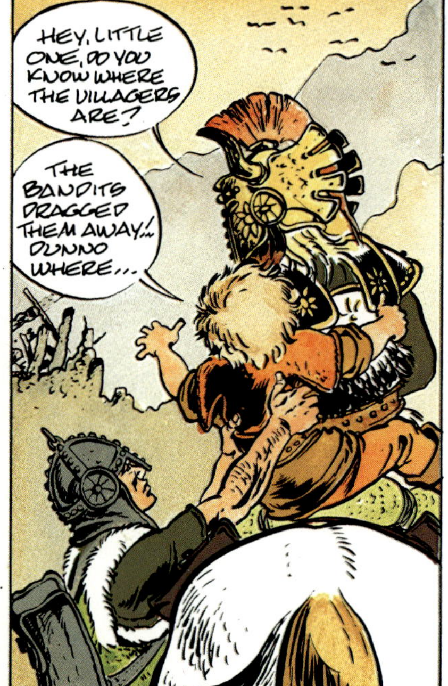

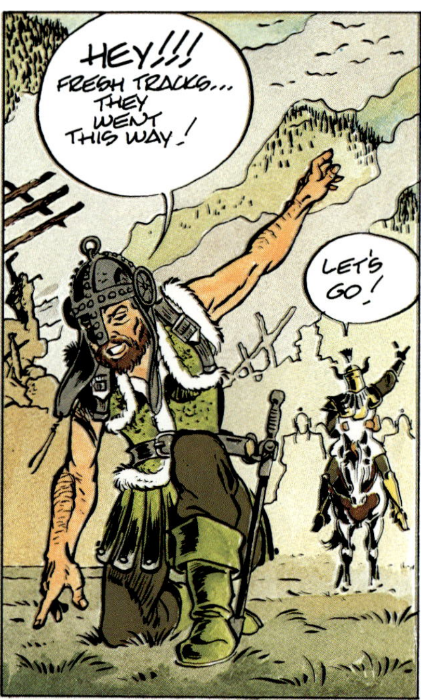

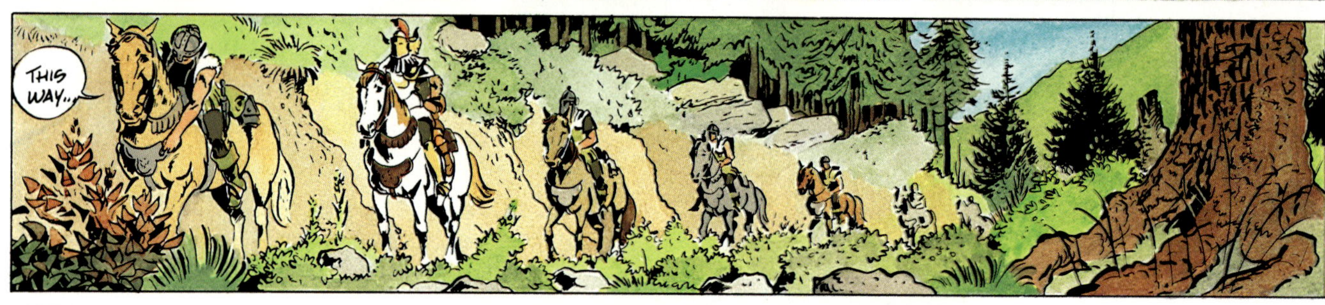

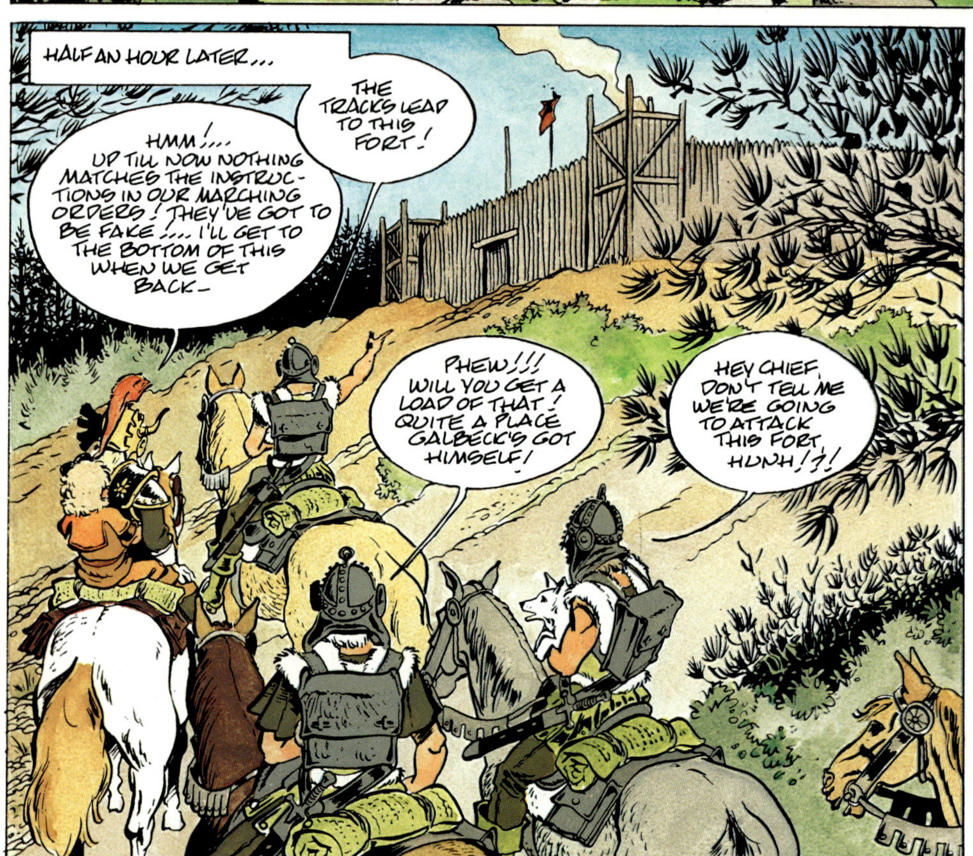

AND WHY NOT?... I'VE GOT A PLAN... WHICH DOES CALL FOR A LITTLE PREPARATION...

MEANWHILE LET'S PULL BACK INTO THE WOODS...

AND MAKE SOME WELL-CAMOUFLAGED SHELTERS!

18

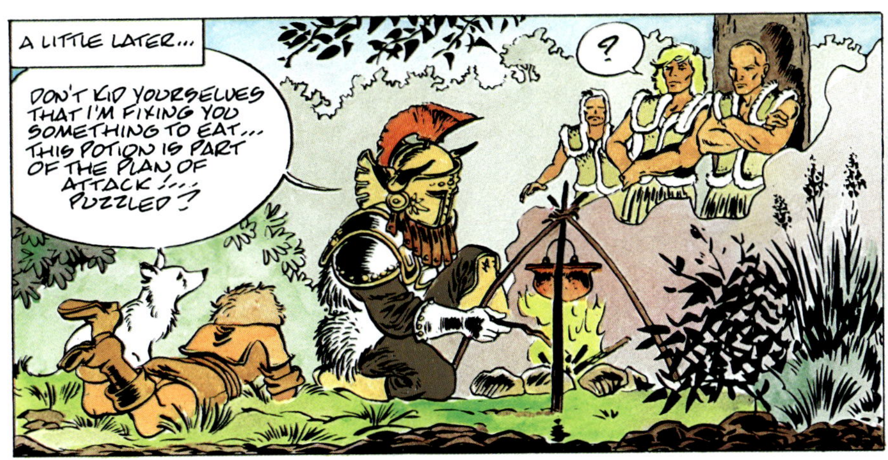
A LITTLE LATER...
DON'T KID YOURSELVES THAT I'M FIXING YOU SOMETHING TO EAT... THIS POTION IS PART OF THE PLAN OF ATTACK!... PUZZLED?
?

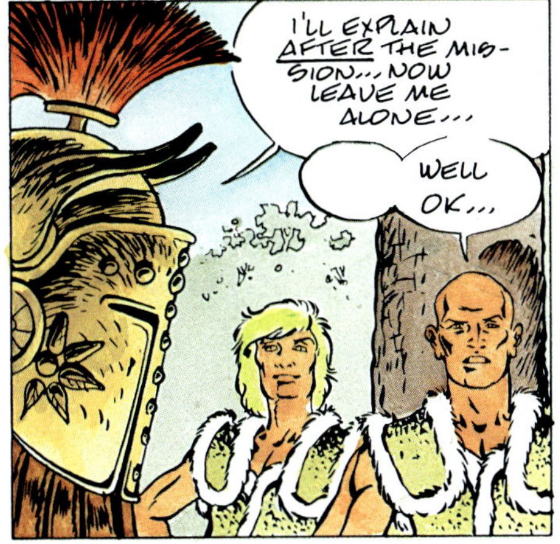
I'LL EXPLAIN AFTER THE MISSION... NOW LEAVE ME ALONE...
WELL OK...

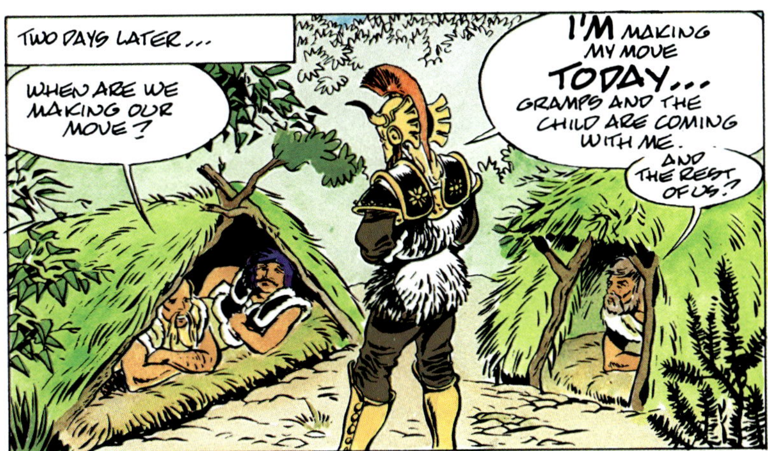
TWO DAYS LATER...
WHEN ARE WE MAKING OUR MOVE?
I'M MAKING MY MOVE TODAY... GRAMPS AND THE CHILD ARE COMING WITH ME.
AND THE REST OF US?

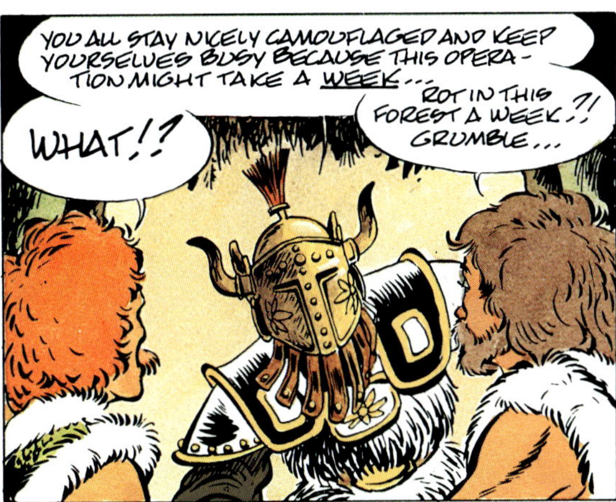
YOU ALL STAY NICELY CAMOUFLAGED AND KEEP YOURSELVES BUSY BECAUSE THIS OPERATION MIGHT TAKE A WEEK...
WHAT!?
ROT IN THIS FOREST A WEEK?! GRUMBLE...

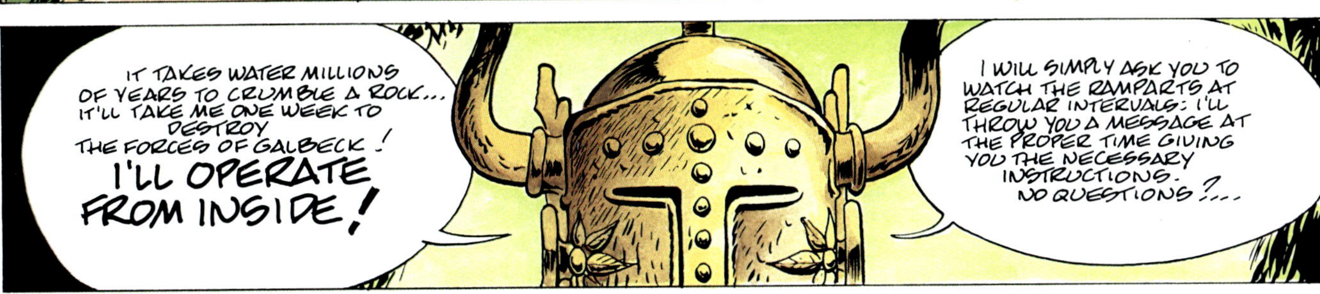
IT TAKES WATER MILLIONS OF YEARS TO CRUMBLE A ROCK... IT'LL TAKE ME ONE WEEK TO DESTROY THE FORCES OF GALBECK! I'LL OPERATE FROM INSIDE!
I WILL SIMPLY ASK YOU TO WATCH THE RAMPARTS AT REGULAR INTERVALS: I'LL THROW YOU A MESSAGE AT THE PROPER TIME GIVING YOU THE NECESSARY INSTRUCTIONS. NO QUESTIONS?...

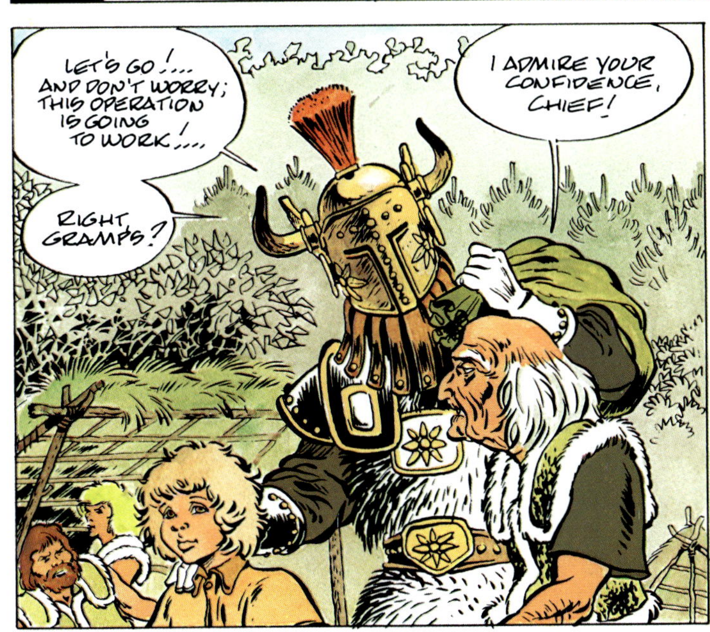
LET'S GO!... AND DON'T WORRY; THIS OPERATION IS GOING TO WORK!...
RIGHT, GRAMPS?
I ADMIRE YOUR CONFIDENCE, CHIEF!

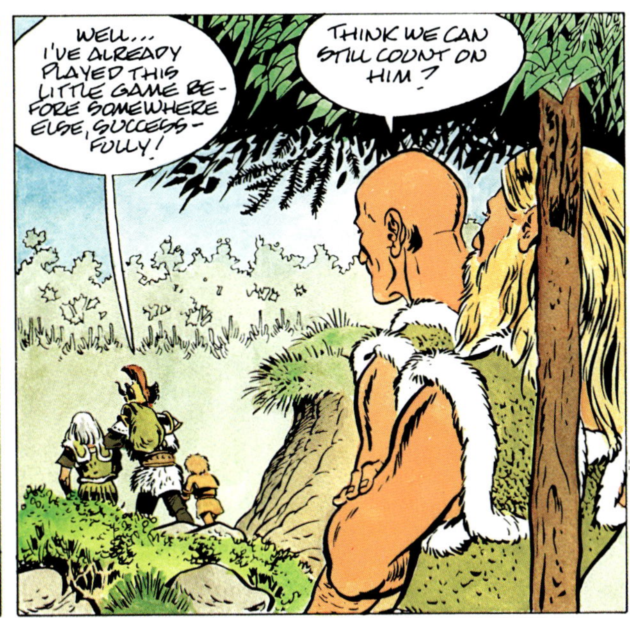
WELL... I'VE ALREADY PLAYED THIS LITTLE GAME BEFORE SOMEWHERE ELSE, SUCCESSFULLY!
THINK WE CAN STILL COUNT ON HIM?
19

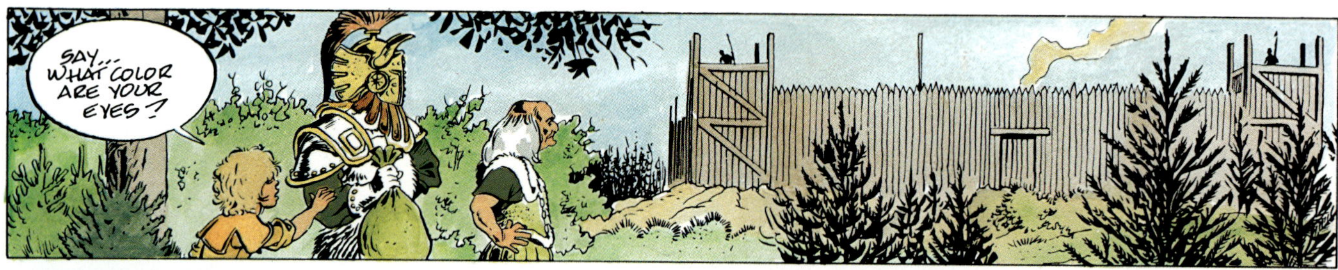
SAY... WHAT COLOR ARE YOUR EYES?

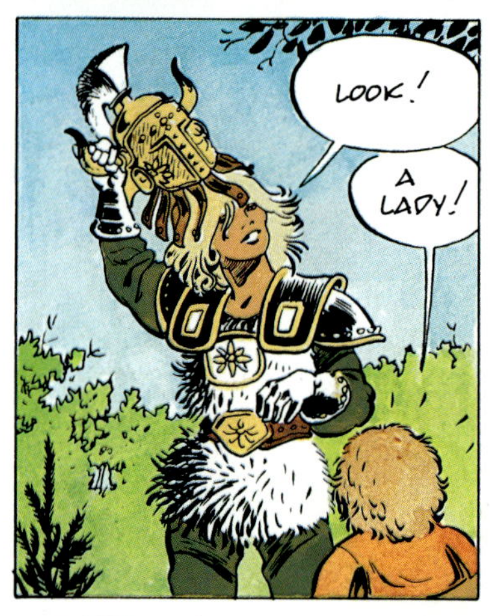
LOOK!
A LADY!

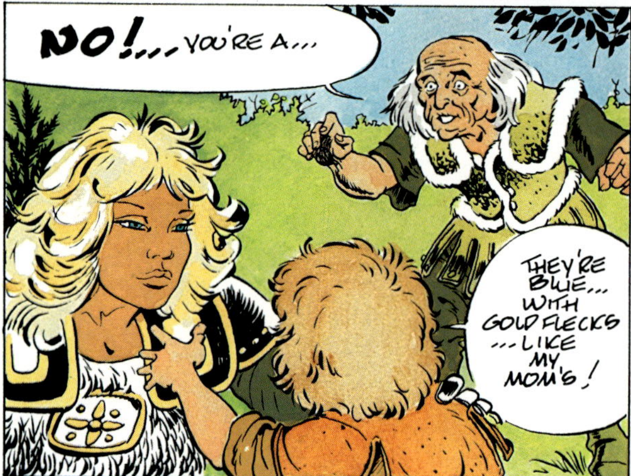
NO!... YOU'RE A...
THEY'RE BLUE... WITH GOLD FLECKS ...LIKE MY MOM'S!

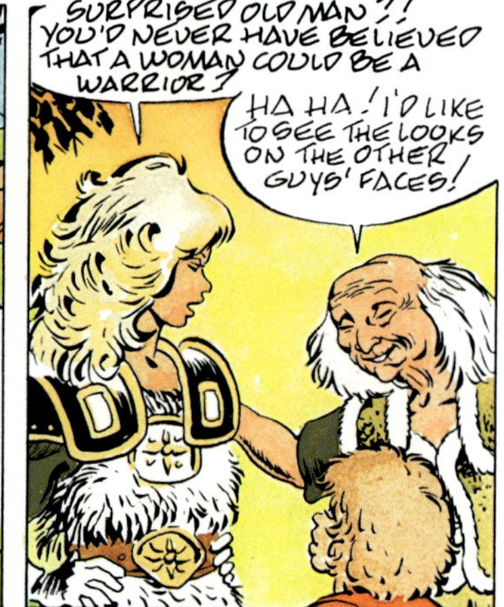
SURPRISED OLD MAN?! YOU'D NEVER HAVE BELIEVED THAT A WOMAN COULD BE A WARRIOR?
HA HA! I'D LIKE TO SEE THE LOOKS ON THE OTHER GUYS' FACES!

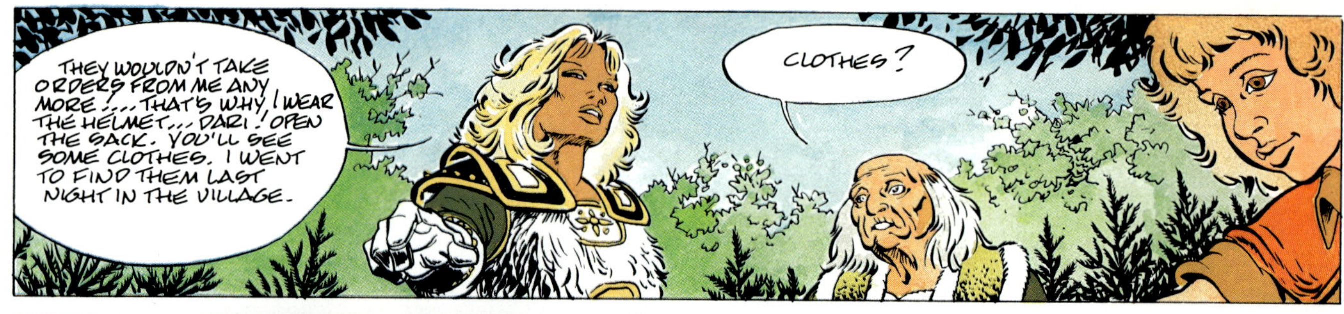
THEY WOULDN'T TAKE ORDERS FROM ME ANY MORE... THAT'S WHY I WEAR THE HELMET... DARI! OPEN THE SACK. YOU'LL SEE SOME CLOTHES. I WENT TO FIND THEM LAST NIGHT IN THE VILLAGE.
CLOTHES?

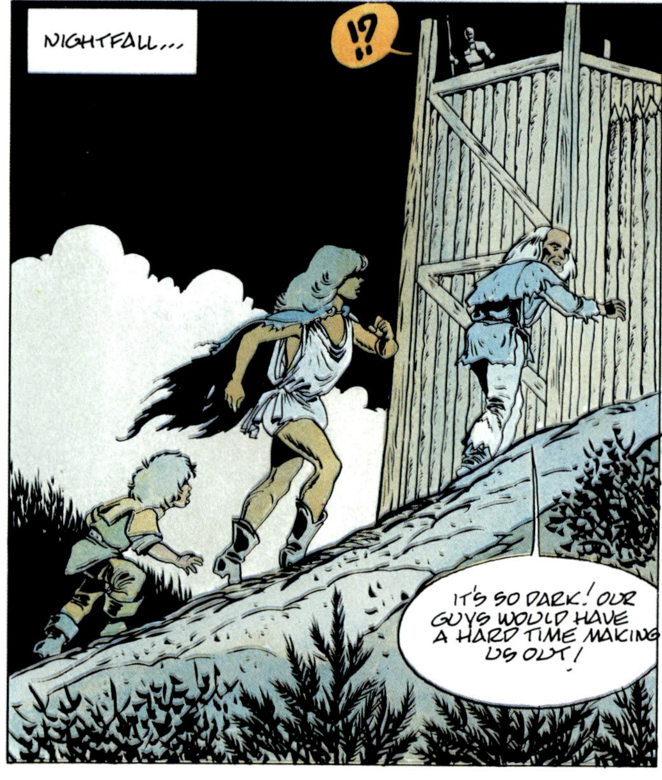
NIGHTFALL...
!?
IT'S SO DARK! OUR GUYS WOULD HAVE A HARD TIME MAKING US OUT!

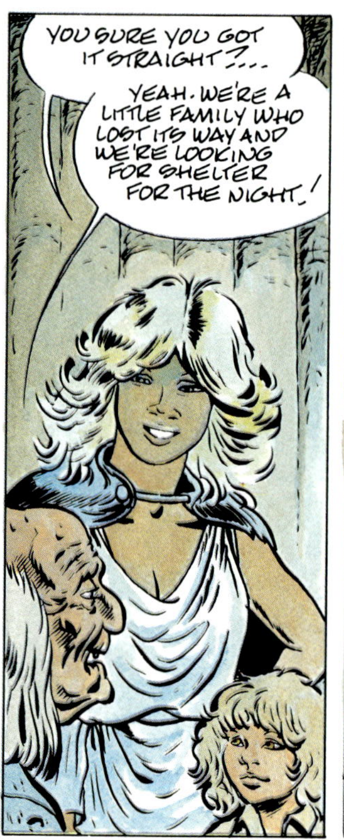
YOU SURE YOU GOT IT STRAIGHT?...
YEAH. WE'RE A LITTLE FAMILY WHO LOST ITS WAY AND WE'RE LOOKING FOR SHELTER FOR THE NIGHT!

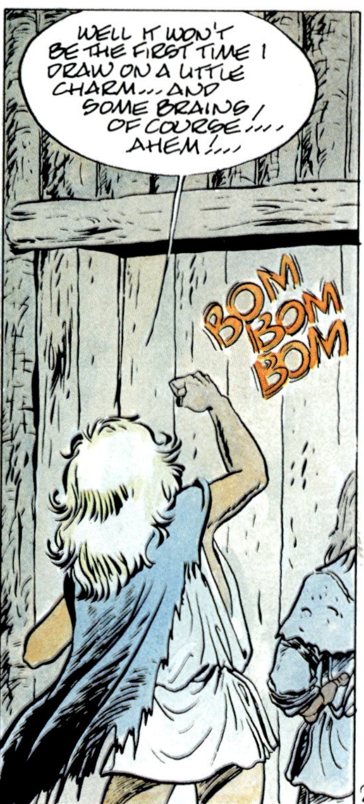
WELL IT WON'T BE THE FIRST TIME I DRAW ON A LITTLE CHARM... AND SOME BRAINS! OF COURSE... AHEM!...
BOM BOM BOM
20

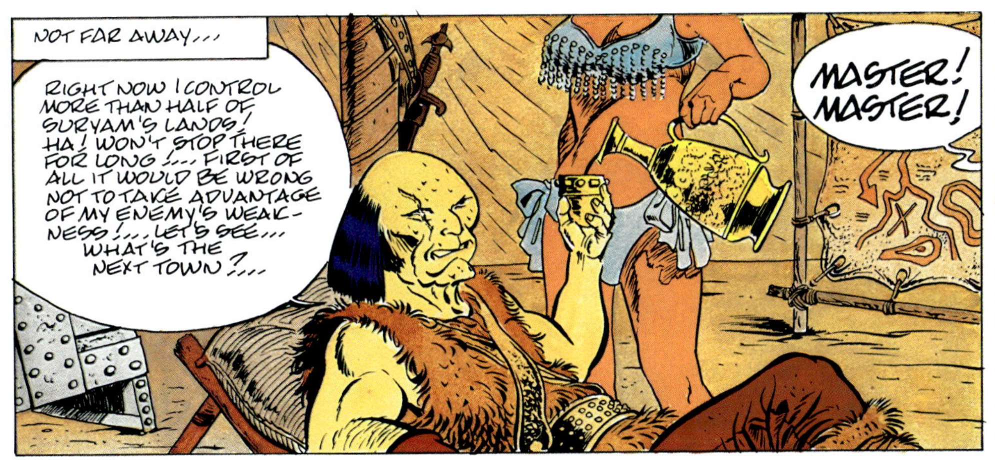
NOT FAR AWAY...
RIGHT NOW I CONTROL MORE THAN HALF OF SURYAM'S LANDS! HA! WON'T STOP THERE FOR LONG!... FIRST OF ALL IT WOULD BE WRONG NOT TO TAKE ADVANTAGE OF MY ENEMY'S WEAKNESS!... LET'S SEE... WHAT'S THE NEXT TOWN?...
MASTER! MASTER!
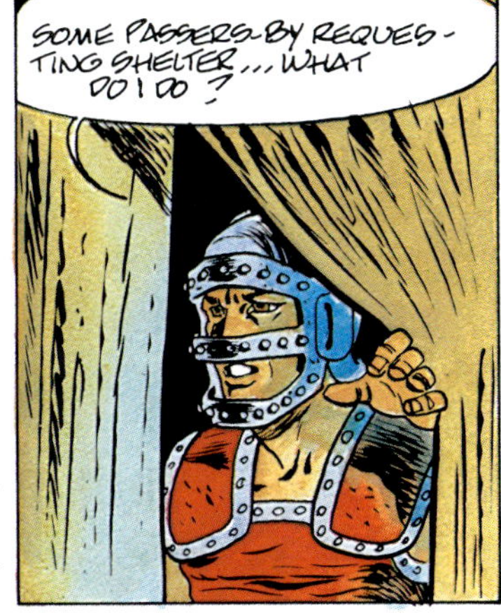
SOME PASSERS-BY REQUESTING SHELTER... WHAT DO I DO?
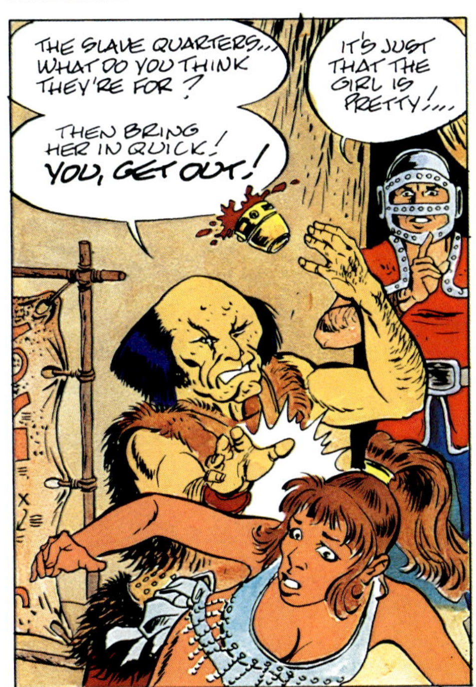
THE SLAVE QUARTERS... WHAT DO YOU THINK THEY'RE FOR?
IT'S JUST THAT THE GIRL IS PRETTY!...
THEN BRING HER IN QUICK! YOU, GET OUT!
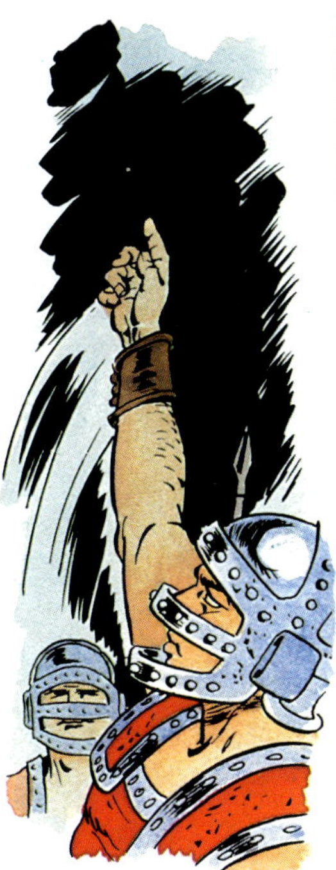
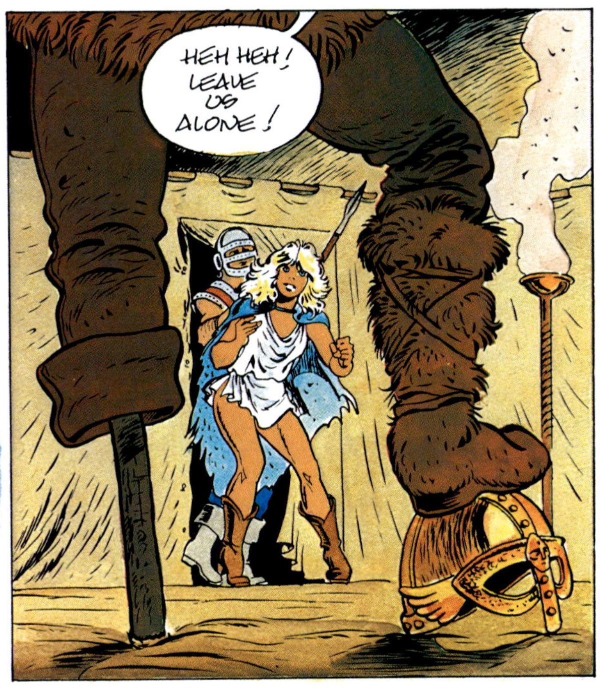
HEH HEH! LEAVE US ALONE!
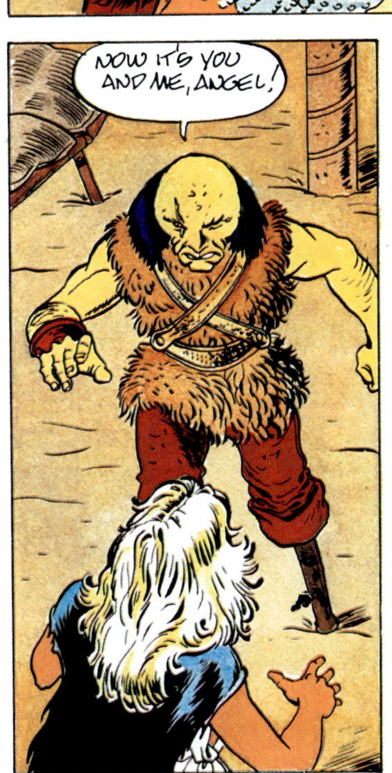
NOW IT'S YOU AND ME, ANGEL!
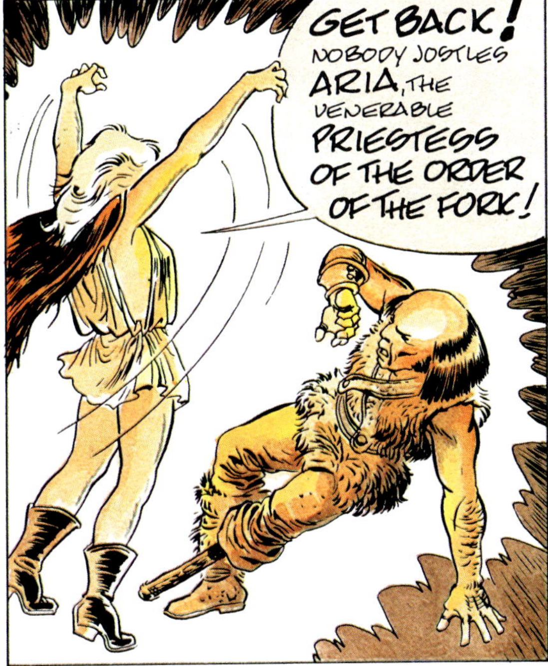
GET BACK! NOBODY JOSTLES ARIA, THE VENERABLE PRIESTESS OF THE ORDER OF THE FORK!
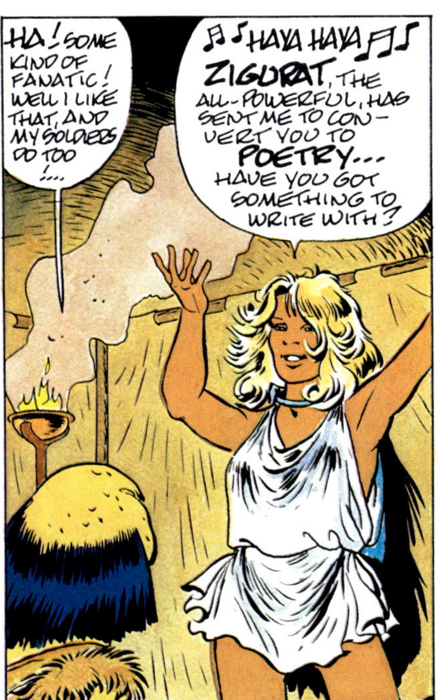
HA! SOME KIND OF FANATIC! WELL I LIKE THAT, AND MY SOLDIERS DO TOO!...
HAYA HAYA
ZIGURAT, THE ALL-POWERFUL, HAS SENT ME TO CONVERT YOU TO POETRY... HAVE YOU GOT SOMETHING TO WRITE WITH?
21

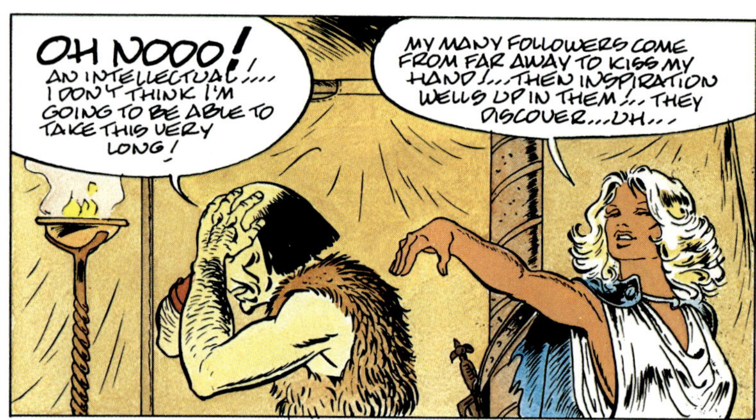
OH NOOO! AN INTELLECTUAL!... I DON'T THINK I'M GOING TO BE ABLE TO TAKE THIS VERY LONG!
MY MANY FOLLOWERS COME FROM FAR AWAY TO KISS MY HAND!... THEN INSPIRATION WELLS UP IN THEM!... THEY DISCOVER... UH...

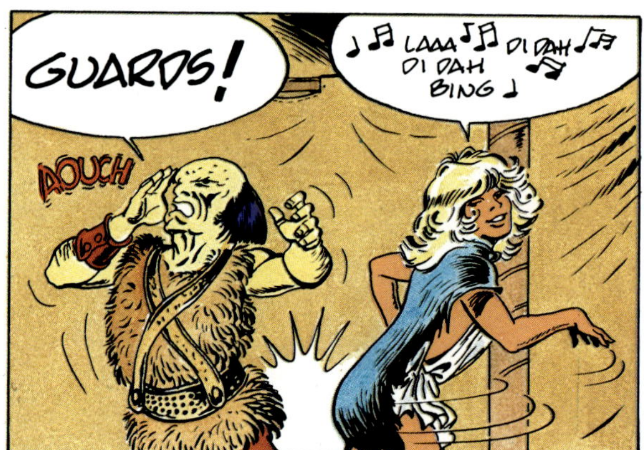
GUARDS!
AOUCH
LAAA DI DAH DI DAH BING

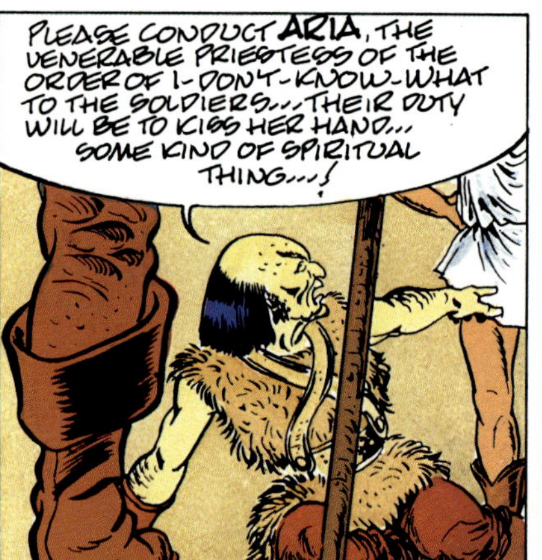
PLEASE CONDUCT ARIA, THE VENERABLE PRIESTESS OF THE ORDER OF I-DON'T-KNOW-WHAT TO THE SOLDIERS... THEIR DUTY WILL BE TO KISS HER HAND... SOME KIND OF SPIRITUAL THING...!

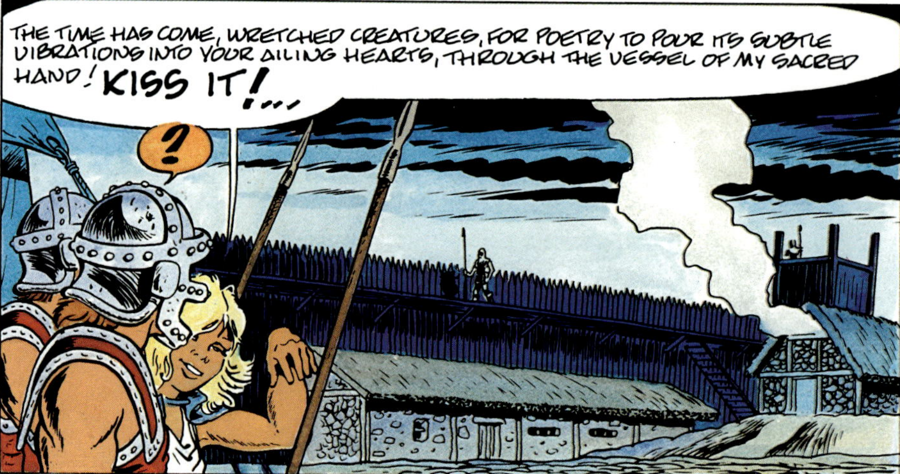
THE TIME HAS COME, WRETCHED CREATURES, FOR POETRY TO POUR ITS SUBTLE VIBRATIONS INTO YOUR AILING HEARTS, THROUGH THE VESSEL OF MY SACRED HAND! KISS IT!...
?

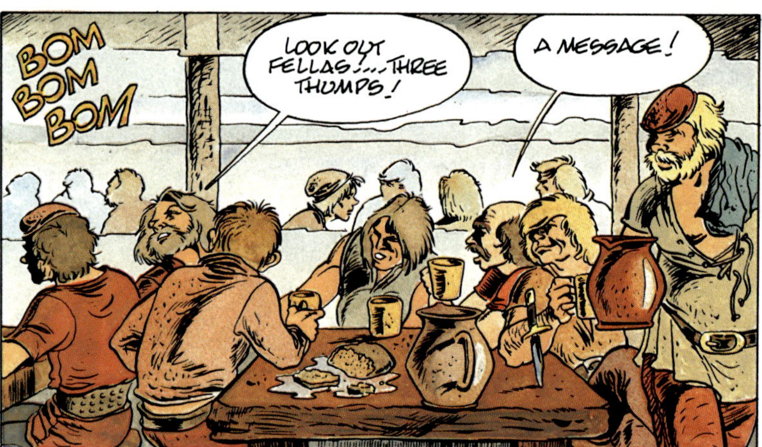
BOM BOM BOM
LOOK OUT FELLAS!... THREE THUMPS!
A MESSAGE!

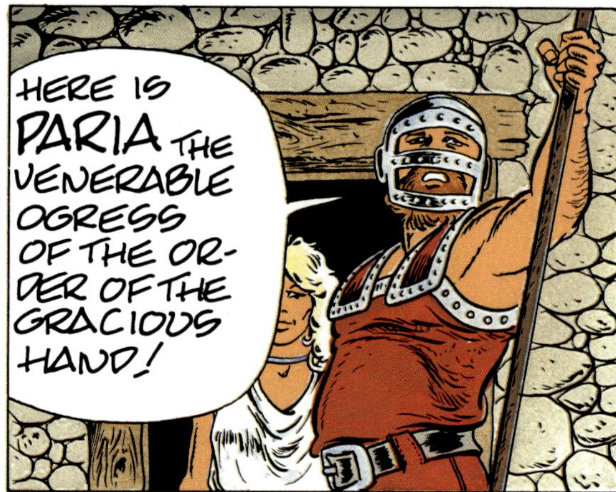
HERE IS PARIA THE VENERABLE OGRESS OF THE ORDER OF THE GRACIOUS HAND!

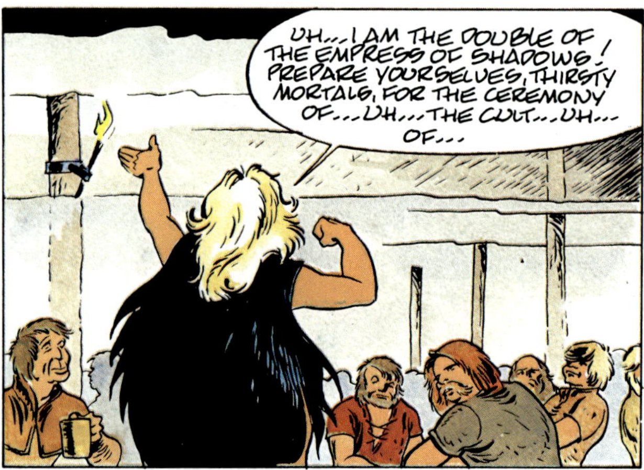
UH... I AM THE DOUBLE OF THE EMPRESS OF SHADOWS! PREPARE YOURSELVES, THIRSTY MORTALS, FOR THE CEREMONY OF... UH... THE CULT... UH... OF...

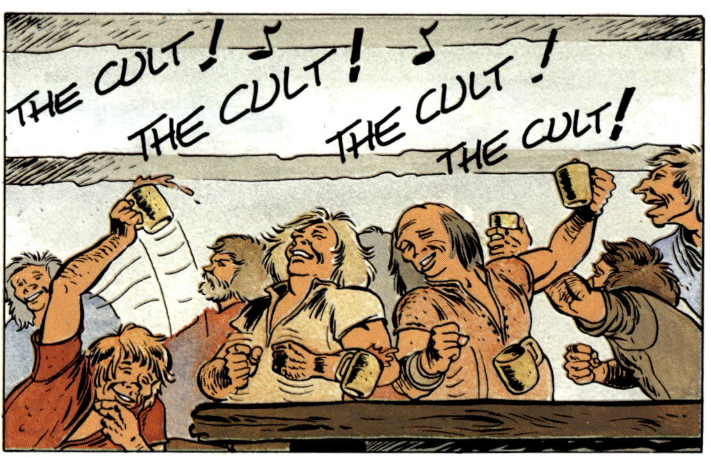
THE CULT!
THE CULT!
THE CULT!
THE CULT!
22

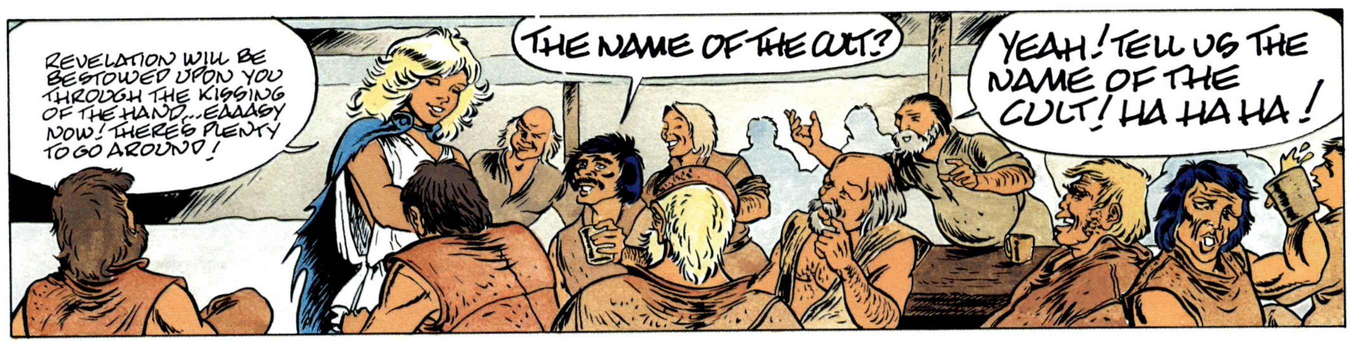
REVELATION WILL BE BESTOWED UPON YOU THROUGH THE KISSING OF THE HAND... EAAASY NOW! THERE'S PLENTY TO GO AROUND!
THE NAME OF THE CULT?
YEAH! TELL US THE NAME OF THE CULT! HA HA HA!

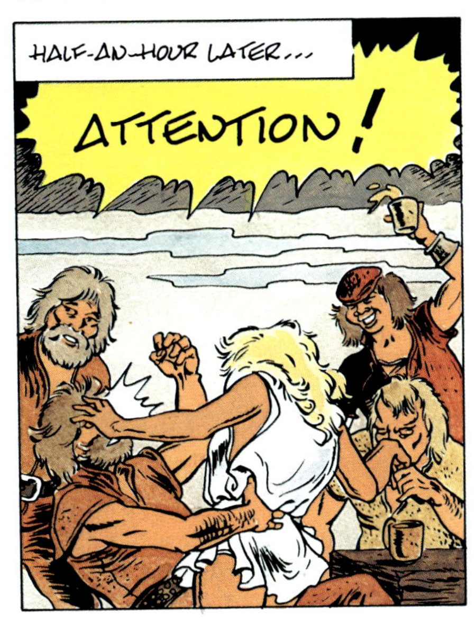
HALF-AN-HOUR LATER...
ATTENTION!

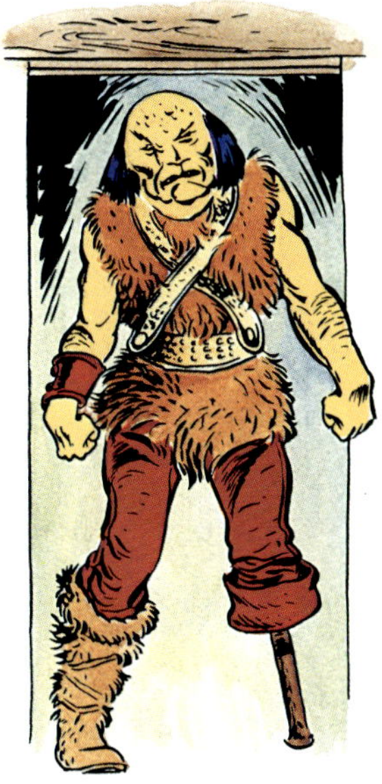

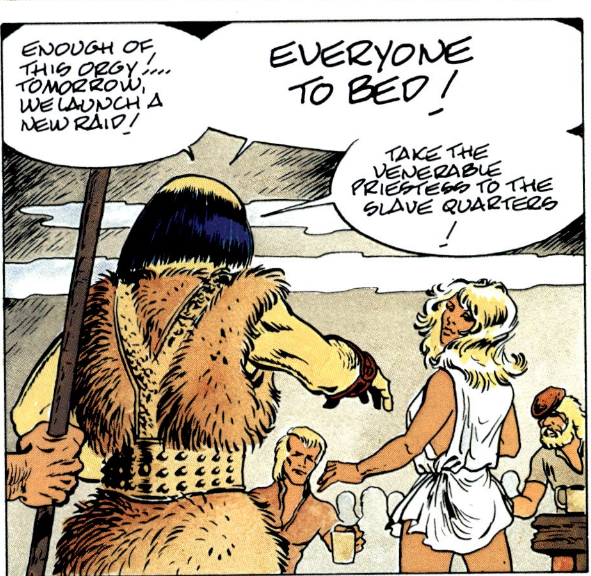
ENOUGH OF THIS ORGY!... TOMORROW, WE LAUNCH A NEW RAID!
EVERYONE TO BED!
TAKE THE VENERABLE PRIESTESS TO THE SLAVE QUARTERS!

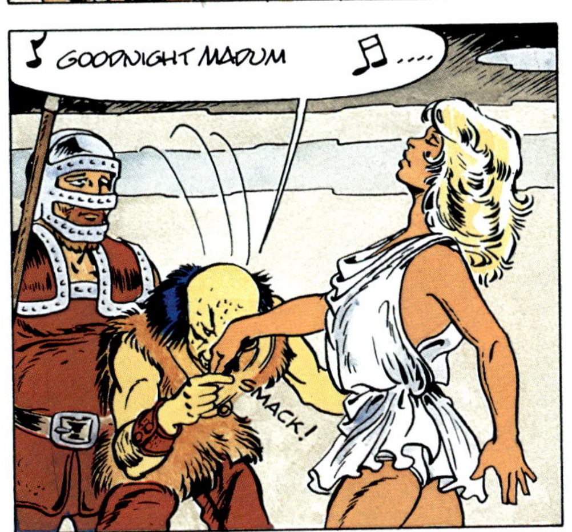
GOODNIGHT MADUM ....
SMACK!

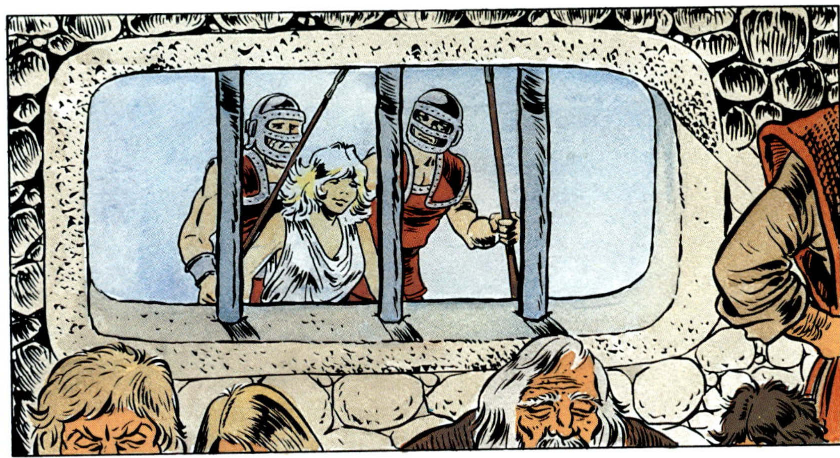

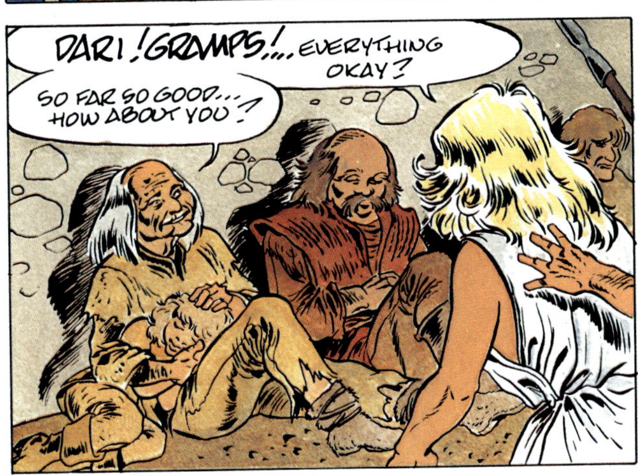
DARI! GRAMPS!... EVERYTHING OKAY?
SO FAR SO GOOD... HOW ABOUT YOU?

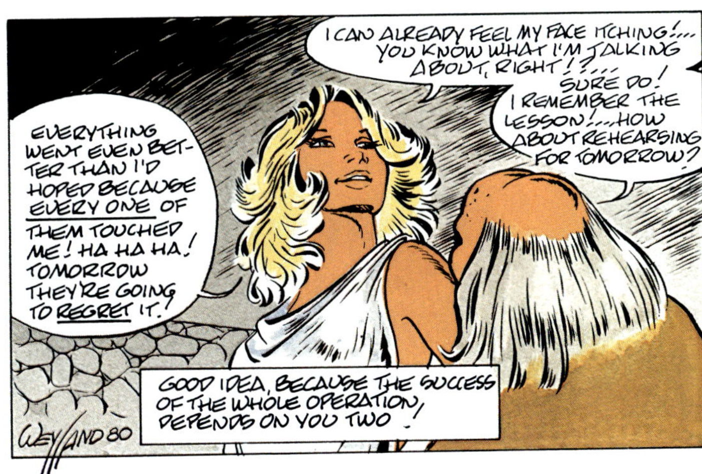
EVERYTHING WENT EVEN BETTER THAN I'D HOPED BECAUSE EVERY ONE OF THEM TOUCHED ME! HA HA HA! TOMORROW THEY'RE GOING TO REGRET IT.
I CAN ALREADY FEEL MY FACE ITCHING!... YOU KNOW WHAT I'M TALKING ABOUT, RIGHT!?...
SURE DO! I REMEMBER THE LESSON!... HOW ABOUT REHEARSING FOR TOMORROW?
GOOD IDEA, BECAUSE THE SUCCESS OF THE WHOLE OPERATION DEPENDS ON YOU TWO!
WEYLAND 80

23

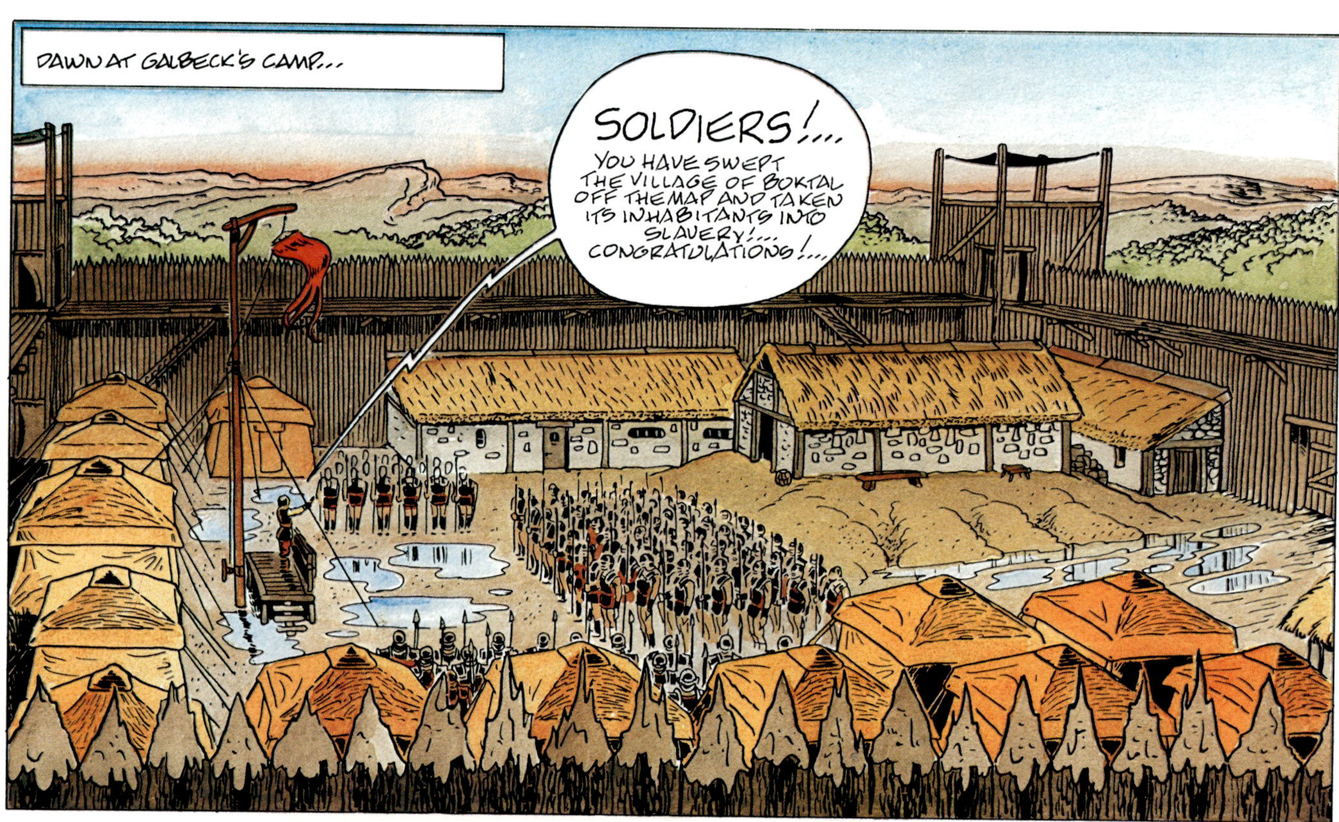
DAWN AT GALBECK'S CAMP...
SOLDIERS!...
YOU HAVE SWEPT THE VILLAGE OF BOKTAL OFF THE MAP AND TAKEN ITS INHABITANTS INTO SLAVERY!... CONGRATULATIONS!...

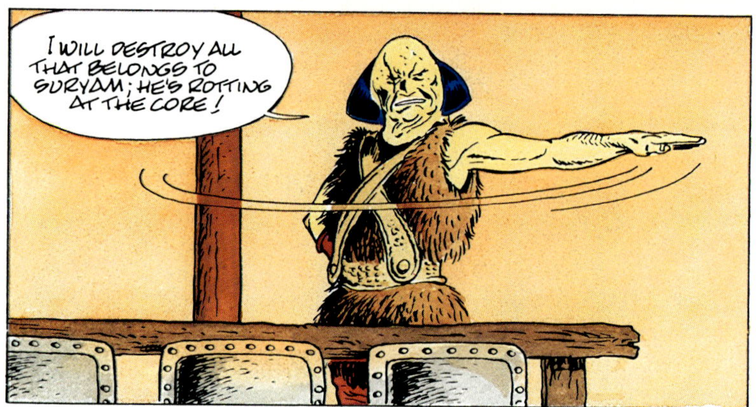
I WILL DESTROY ALL THAT BELONGS TO SURYAM; HE'S ROTTING AT THE CORE!

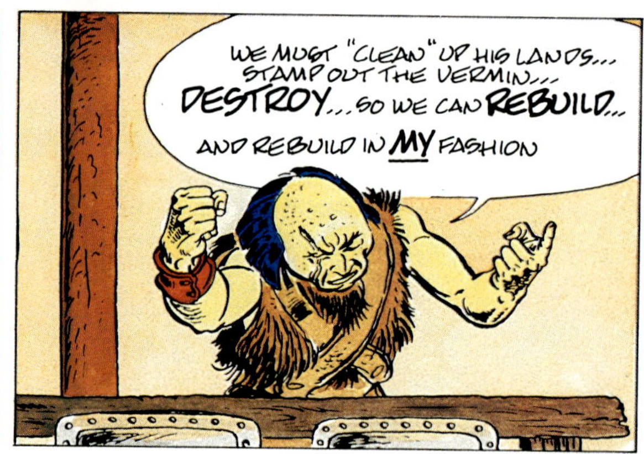
WE MUST "CLEAN" UP HIS LANDS... STAMP OUT THE VERMIN... DESTROY... SO WE CAN REBUILD... AND REBUILD IN MY FASHION

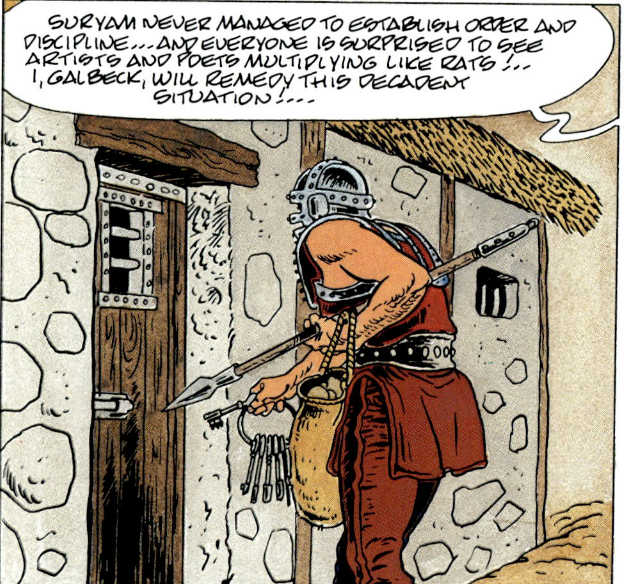
SURYAM NEVER MANAGED TO ESTABLISH ORDER AND DISCIPLINE... AND EVERYONE IS SURPRISED TO SEE ARTISTS AND POETS MULTIPLYING LIKE RATS!... I, GALBECK, WILL REMEDY THIS DECADENT SITUATION!...

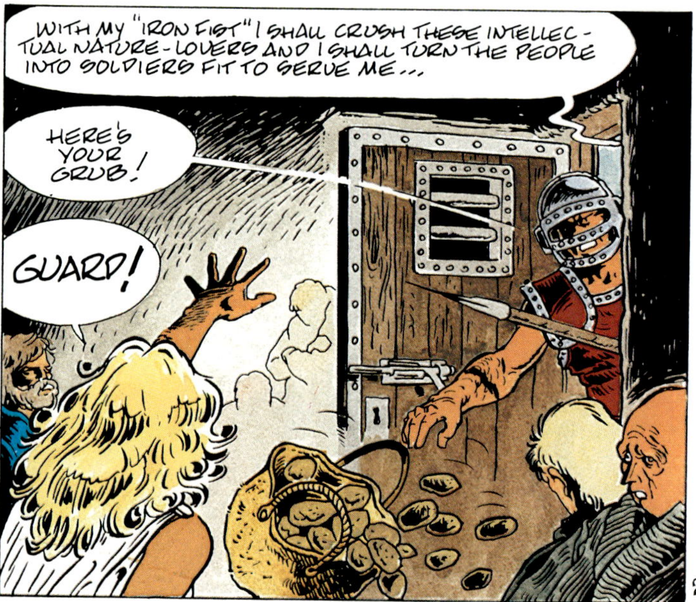
WITH MY "IRON FIST" I SHALL CRUSH THESE INTELLEC-TUAL NATURE-LOVERS AND I SHALL TURN THE PEOPLE INTO SOLDIERS FIT TO SERVE ME...
HERE'S YOUR GRUB!
GUARD!
24

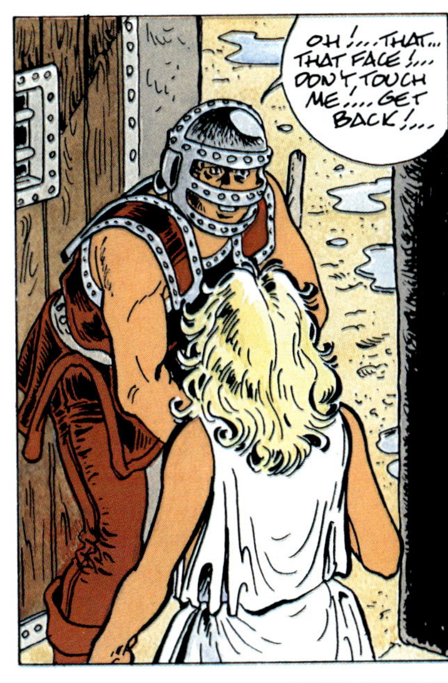
OH!... THAT... THAT FACE!... DON'T TOUCH ME!... GET BACK!...
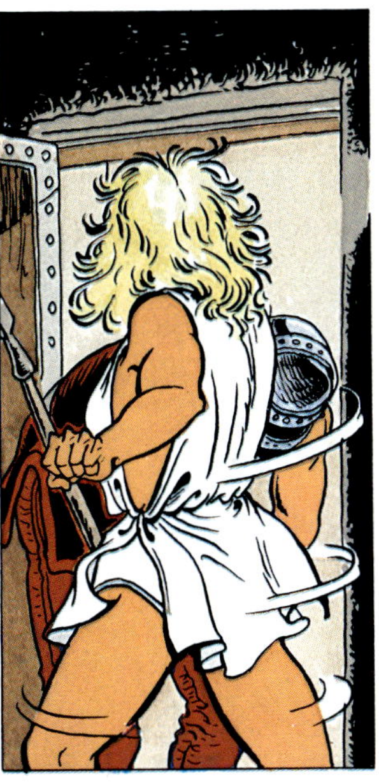
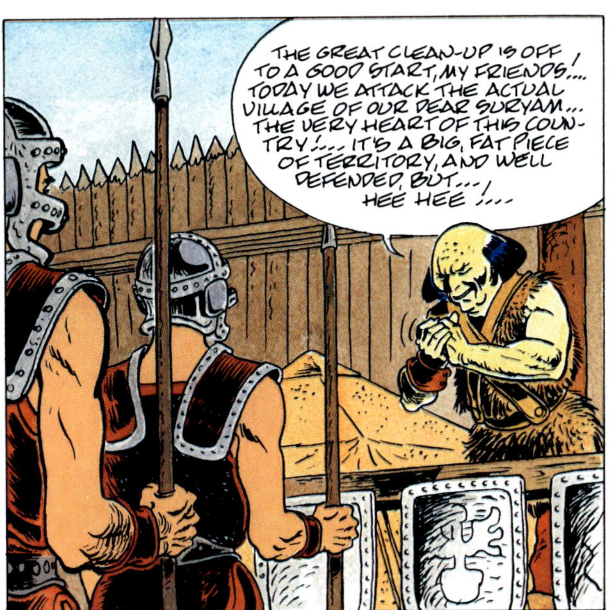
THE GREAT CLEAN-UP IS OFF TO A GOOD START, MY FRIENDS!... TODAY WE ATTACK THE ACTUAL VILLAGE OF OUR DEAR SURYAM... THE VERY HEART OF THIS COUNTRY!... IT'S A BIG, FAT PIECE OF TERRITORY, AND WELL DEFENDED, BUT...! HEE HEE!...
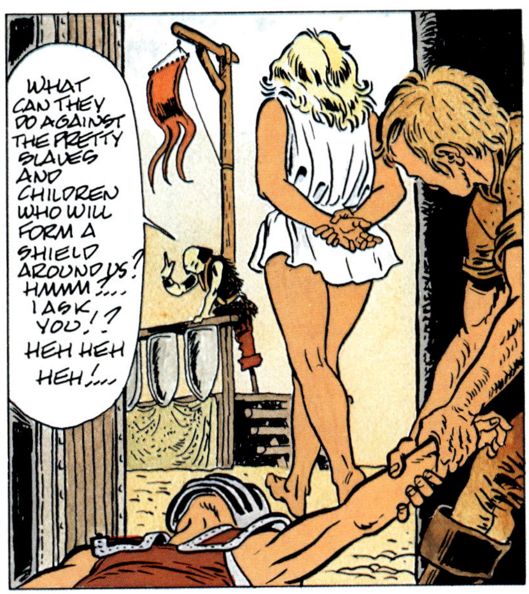
WHAT CAN THEY DO AGAINST THE PRETTY SLAVES AND CHILDREN WHO WILL FORM A SHIELD AROUND US? HMMM? I ASK YOU!? HEH HEH HEH!...
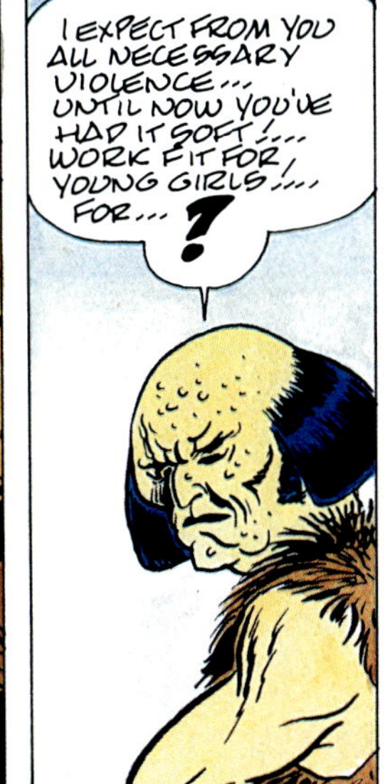
I EXPECT FROM YOU ALL NECESSARY VIOLENCE... UNTIL NOW YOU'VE HAD IT SOFT!... WORK FIT FOR YOUNG GIRLS!... FOR... ?
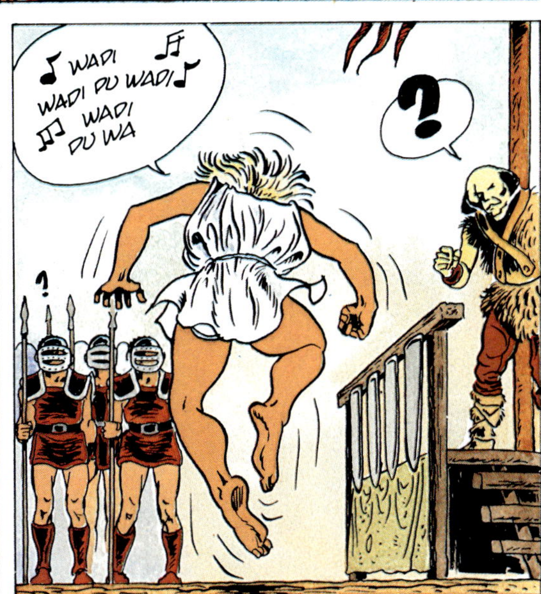
♪ WADI ♫
WADI DU WADI ♪
♫ WADI DU WA
?
?
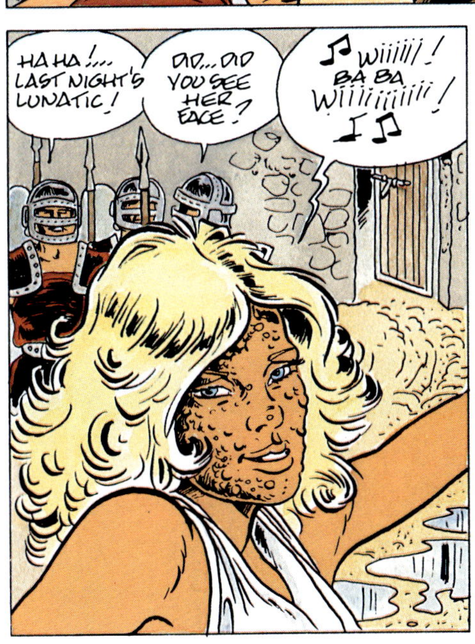
HA HA!... LAST NIGHT'S LUNATIC!
DID... DID YOU SEE HER FACE?
♪ Wiiiii! BA BA Wiiiiiiiiii! ♪♫
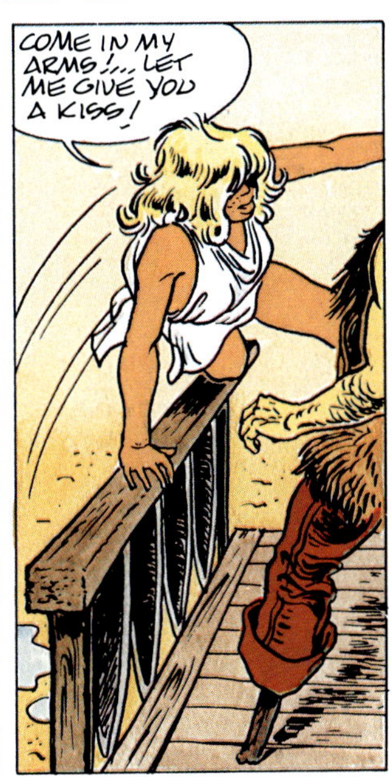
COME IN MY ARMS!... LET ME GIVE YOU A KISS!
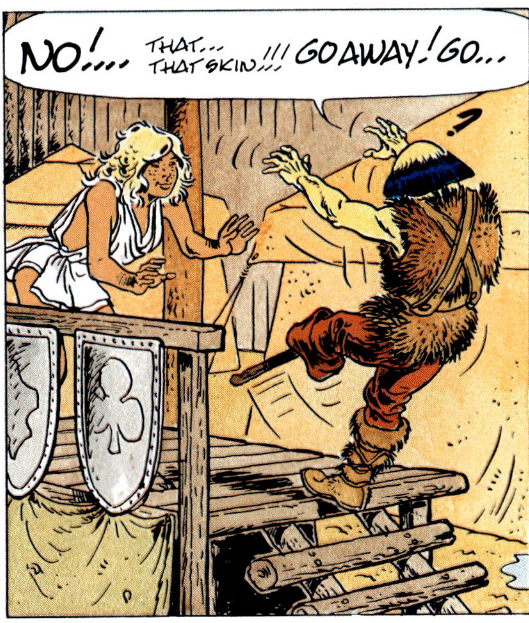
NO!... THAT... THAT SKIN!!! GO AWAY! GO...
?

25

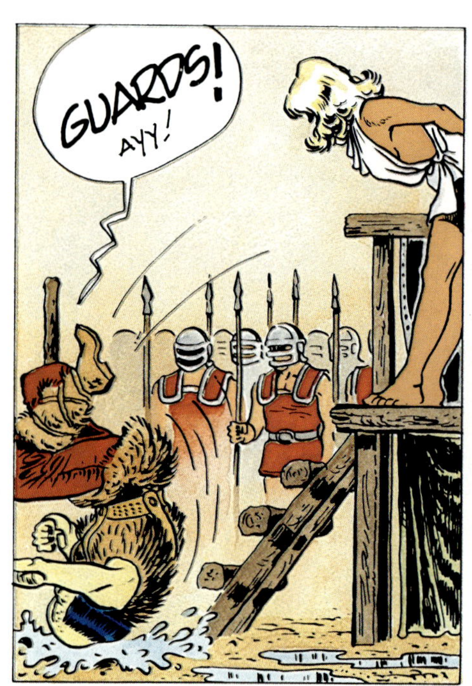
GUARDS!
AYY!

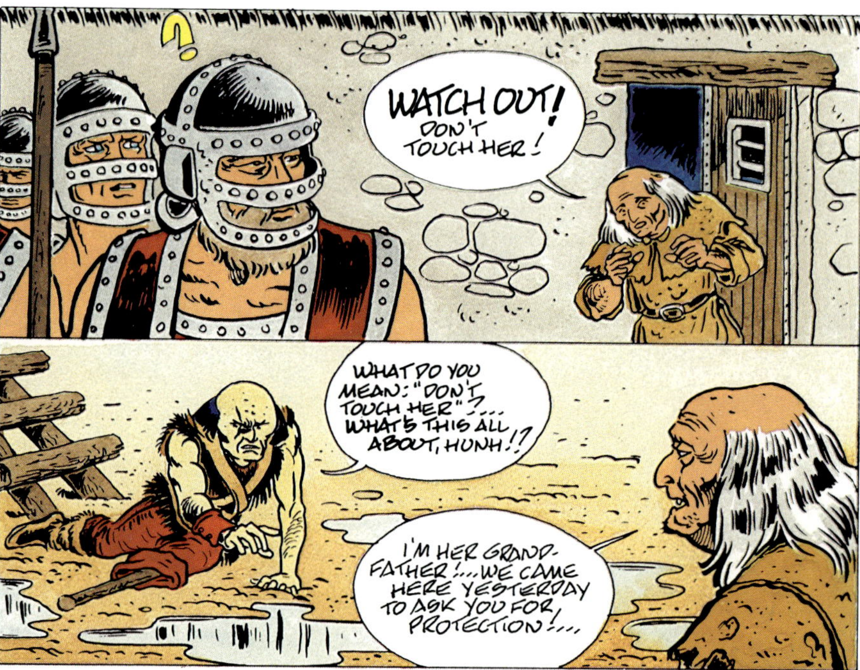
WATCH OUT! DON'T TOUCH HER!
WHAT DO YOU MEAN: "DON'T TOUCH HER"?... WHAT'S THIS ALL ABOUT, HUNH!?
I'M HER GRANDFATHER!... WE CAME HERE YESTERDAY TO ASK YOU FOR PROTECTION!...

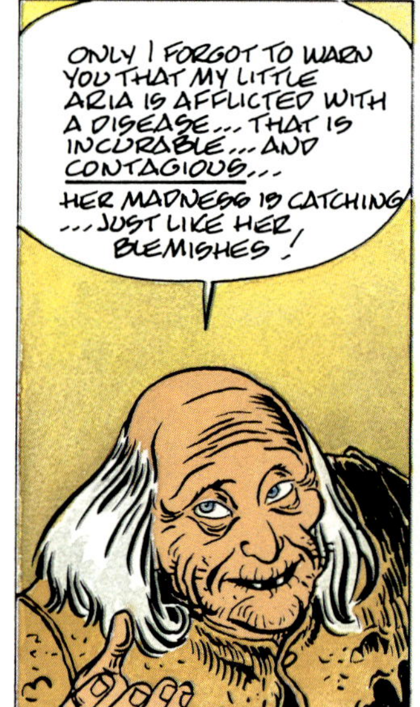
ONLY I FORGOT TO WARN YOU THAT MY LITTLE ARIA IS AFFLICTED WITH A DISEASE... THAT IS INCURABLE... AND CONTAGIOUS... HER MADNESS IS CATCHING... JUST LIKE HER BLEMISHES!

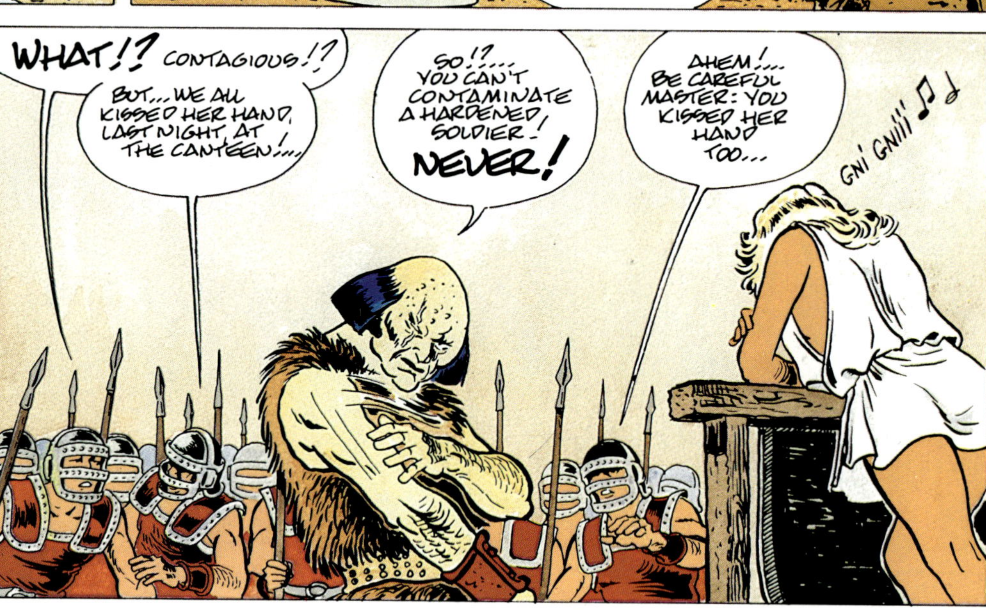
WHAT!? CONTAGIOUS!?
BUT... WE ALL KISSED HER HAND, LAST NIGHT, AT THE CANTEEN!...
SO!?... YOU CAN'T CONTAMINATE A HARDENED SOLDIER! NEVER!
AHEM!... BE CAREFUL MASTER: YOU KISSED HER HAND TOO...
GNI GNII!

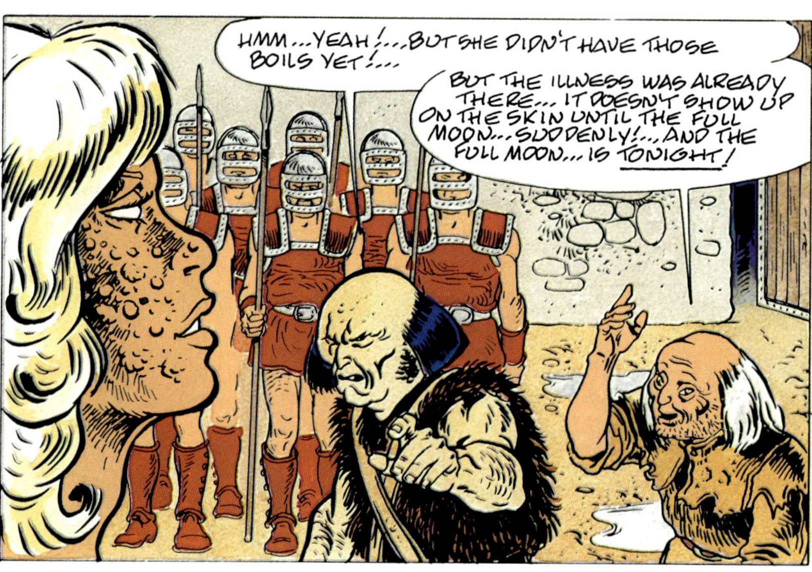
HMM... YEAH!... BUT SHE DIDN'T HAVE THOSE BOILS YET!...
BUT THE ILLNESS WAS ALREADY THERE... IT DOESN'T SHOW UP ON THE SKIN UNTIL THE FULL MOON... SUDDENLY!... AND THE FULL MOON... IS TONIGHT!

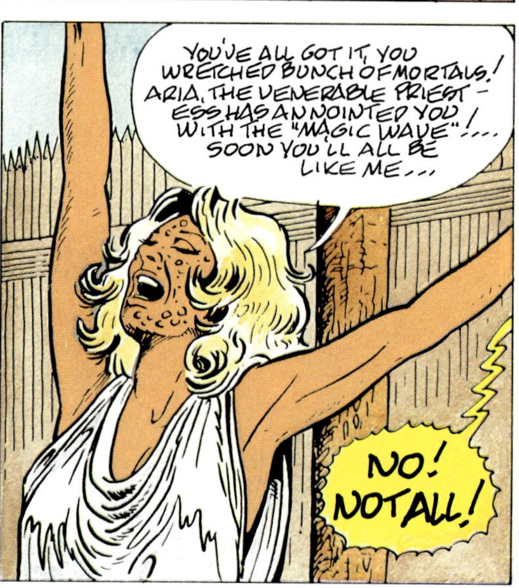
YOU'VE ALL GOT IT, YOU WRETCHED BUNCH OF MORTALS! ARIA, THE VENERABLE PRIESTESS HAS ANNOINTED YOU WITH THE "MAGIC WAVE"!... SOON YOU'LL ALL BE LIKE ME...
NO! NOT ALL!

26

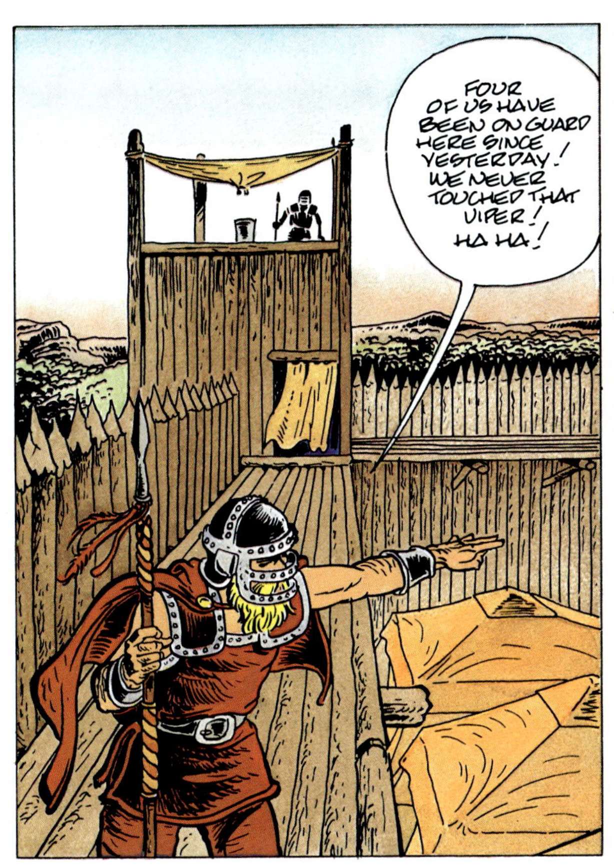
FOUR OF US HAVE BEEN ON GUARD HERE SINCE YESTERDAY! WE NEVER TOUCHED THAT VIPER! HA HA!

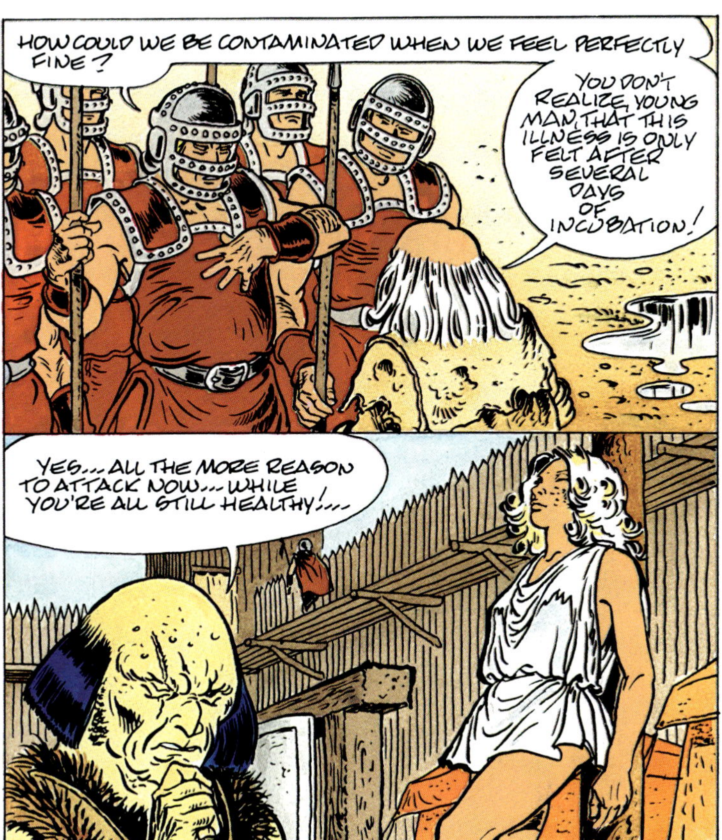
HOW COULD WE BE CONTAMINATED WHEN WE FEEL PERFECTLY FINE?
YOU DON'T REALIZE, YOUNG MAN, THAT THIS ILLNESS IS ONLY FELT AFTER SEVERAL DAYS OF INCUBATION!
YES... ALL THE MORE REASON TO ATTACK NOW... WHILE YOU'RE ALL STILL HEALTHY!...

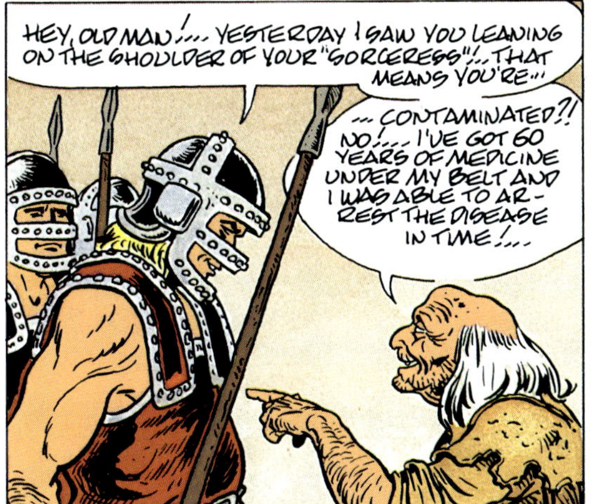
HEY, OLD MAN!... YESTERDAY I SAW YOU LEANING ON THE SHOULDER OF YOUR "SORCERESS"!.. THAT MEANS YOU'RE...
...CONTAMINATED?! NO!... I'VE GOT 60 YEARS OF MEDICINE UNDER MY BELT AND I WAS ABLE TO ARREST THE DISEASE IN TIME!...

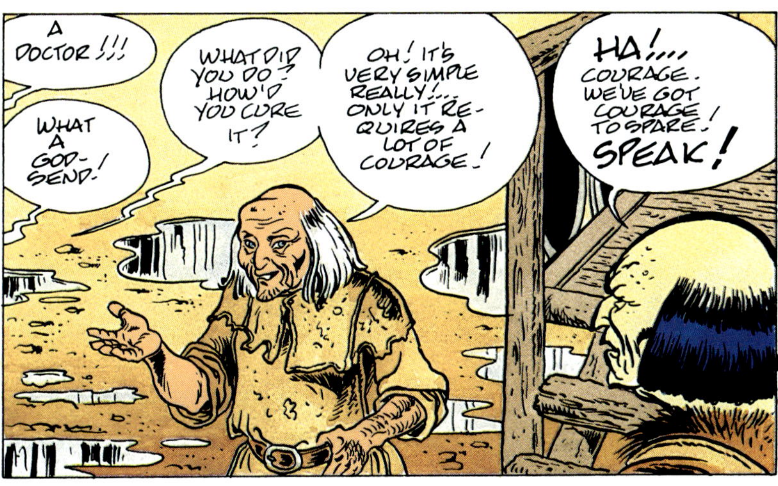
A DOCTOR!!!
WHAT A GOD-SEND!
WHAT DID YOU DO? HOW'D YOU CURE IT?
OH! IT'S VERY SIMPLE REALLY!... ONLY IT REQUIRES A LOT OF COURAGE!
HA!... COURAGE. WE'VE GOT COURAGE TO SPARE! SPEAK!

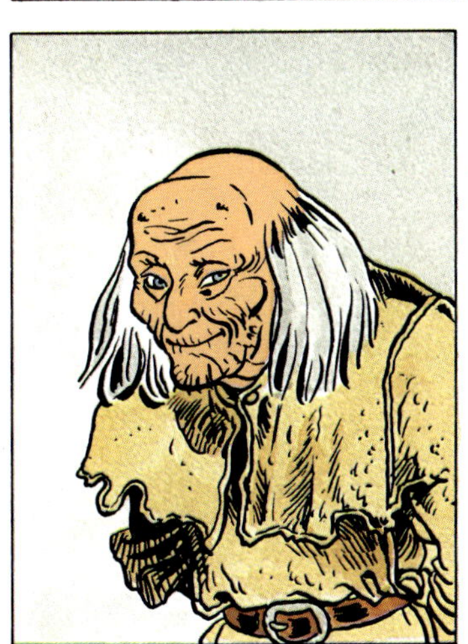

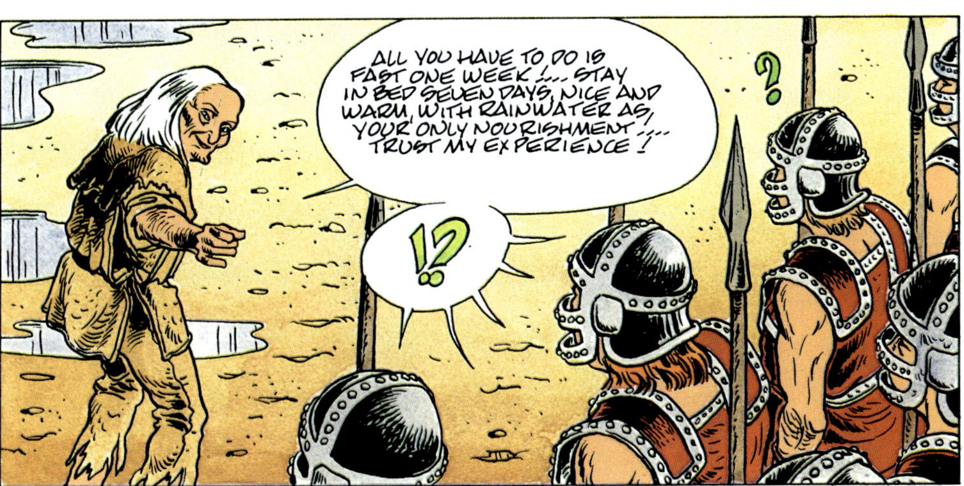
ALL YOU HAVE TO DO IS FAST ONE WEEK!... STAY IN BED SEVEN DAYS, NICE AND WARM, WITH RAINWATER AS YOUR ONLY NOURISHMENT!... TRUST MY EXPERIENCE!
?
!?
27

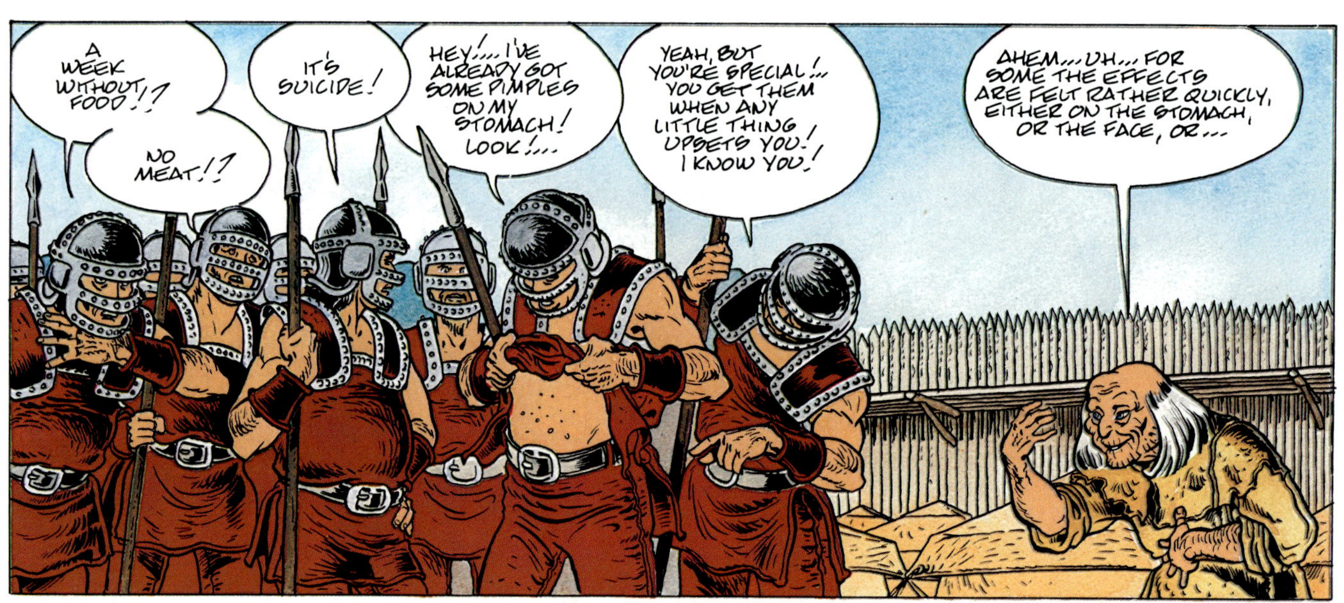
A WEEK WITHOUT FOOD!?
NO MEAT!?
IT'S SUICIDE!
HEY!... I'VE ALREADY GOT SOME PIMPLES ON MY STOMACH! LOOK!...
YEAH, BUT YOU'RE SPECIAL!.. YOU GET THEM WHEN ANY LITTLE THING UPSETS YOU!.. I KNOW YOU!
AHEM... UH... FOR SOME THE EFFECTS ARE FELT RATHER QUICKLY, EITHER ON THE STOMACH, OR THE FACE, OR...

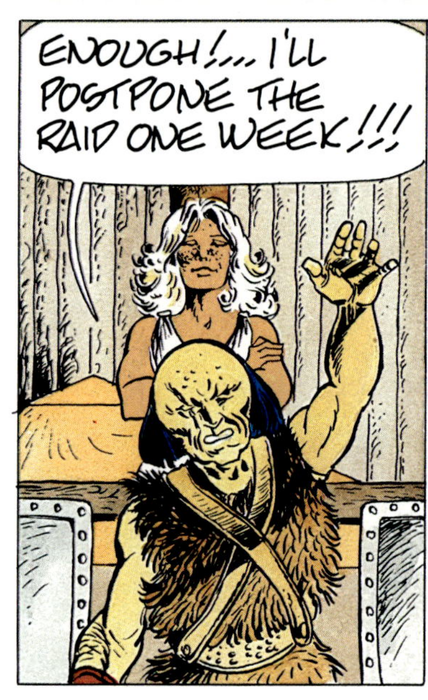
ENOUGH!... I'LL POSTPONE THE RAID ONE WEEK!!!

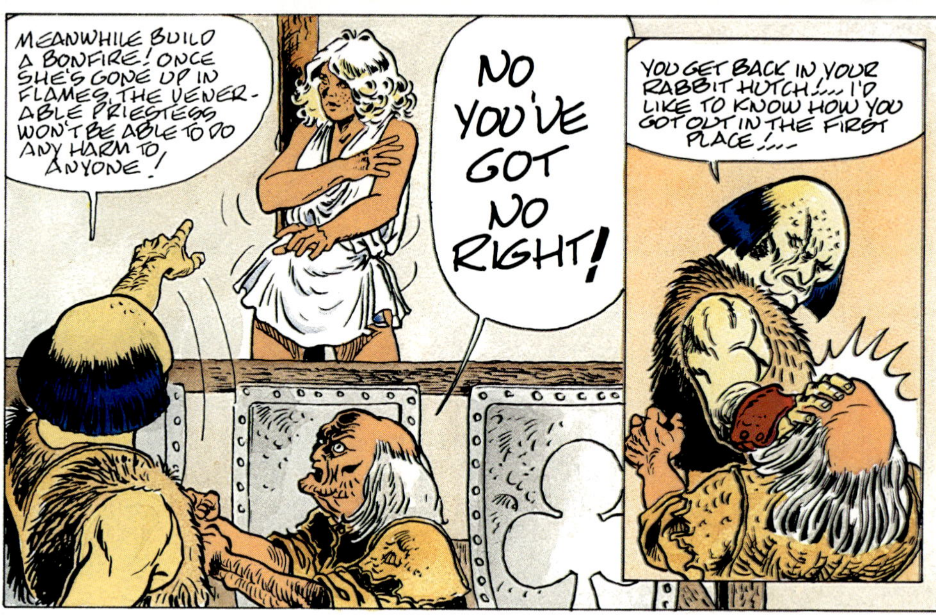
MEANWHILE BUILD A BONFIRE! ONCE SHE'S GONE UP IN FLAMES, THE VENERABLE PRIESTESS WON'T BE ABLE TO DO ANY HARM TO ANYONE!
NO YOU'VE GOT NO RIGHT!
YOU GET BACK IN YOUR RABBIT HUTCH!... I'D LIKE TO KNOW HOW YOU GOT OUT IN THE FIRST PLACE!...

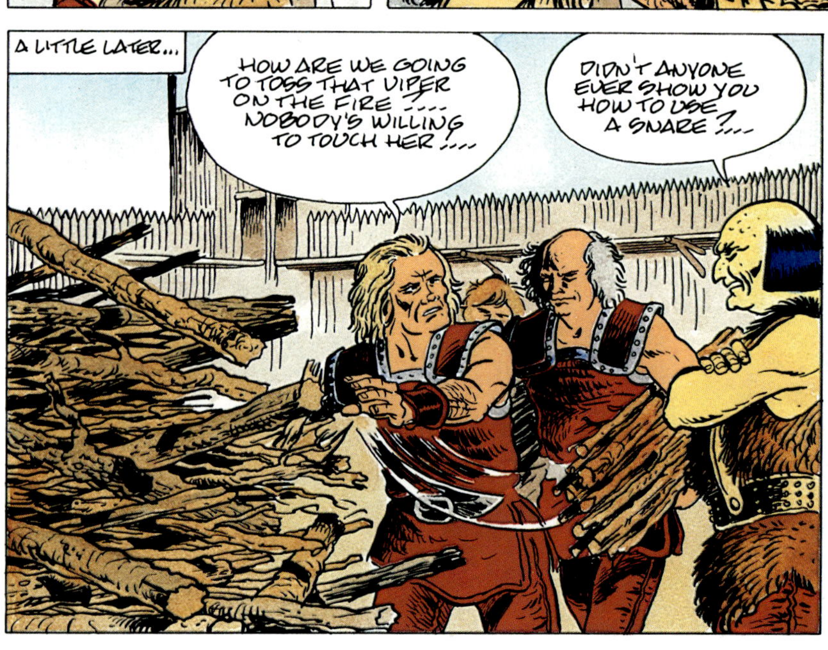
A LITTLE LATER...
HOW ARE WE GOING TO TOSS THAT VIPER ON THE FIRE.... NOBODY'S WILLING TO TOUCH HER!...
DIDN'T ANYONE EVER SHOW YOU HOW TO USE A SNARE?...

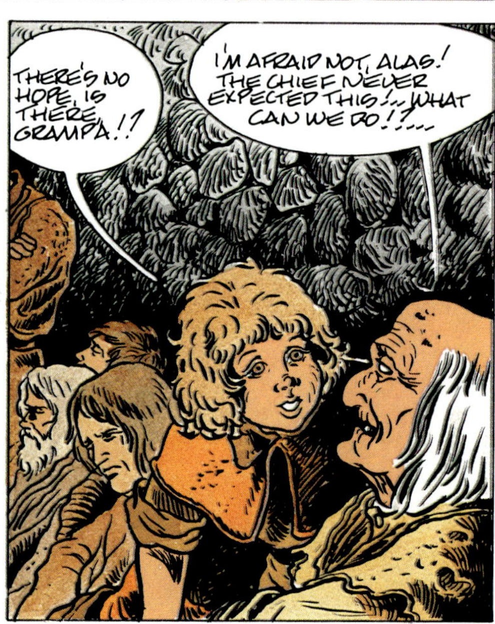
THERE'S NO HOPE, IS THERE, GRAMPA!?
I'M AFRAID NOT, ALAS! THE CHIEF NEVER EXPECTED THIS!.. WHAT CAN WE DO!?...

28

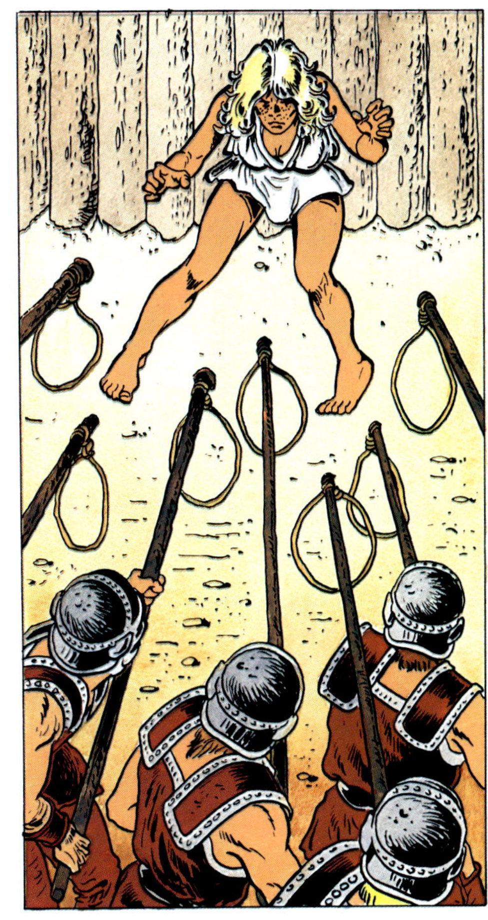
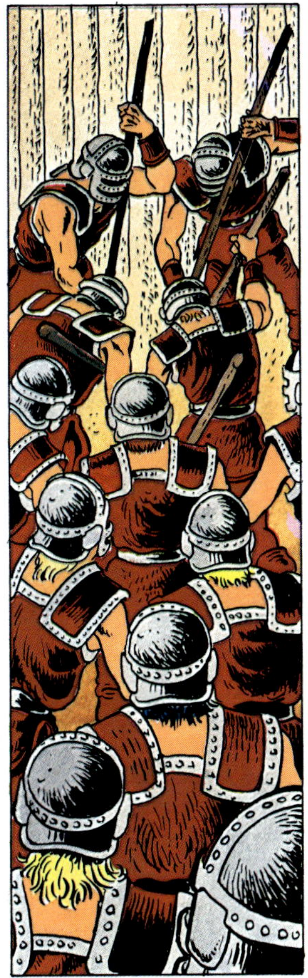
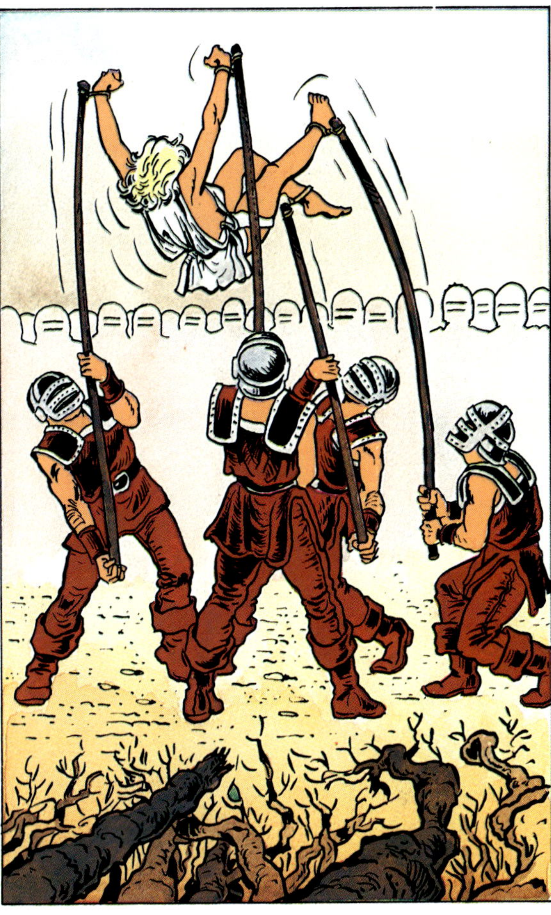
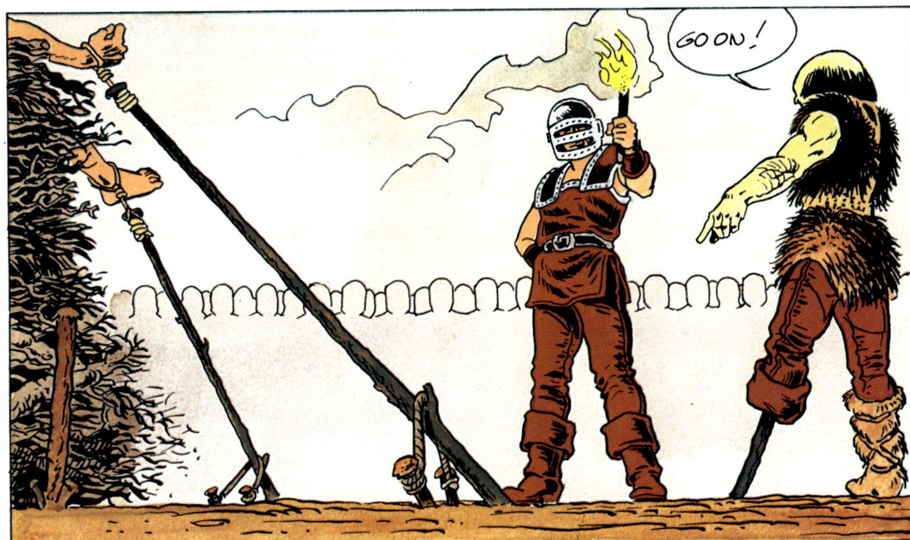
GO ON!
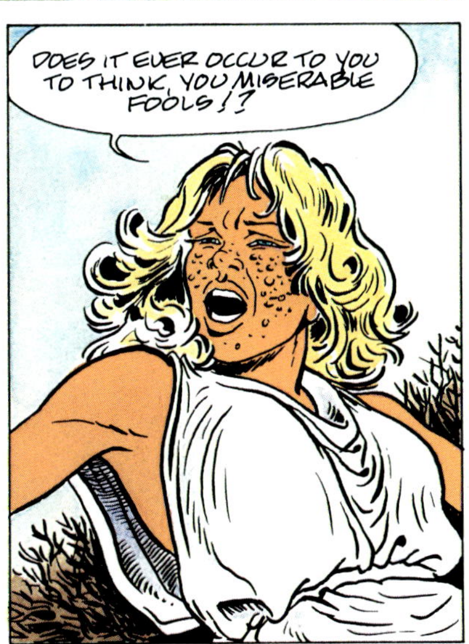
DOES IT EVER OCCUR TO YOU TO THINK, YOU MISERABLE FOOLS!?
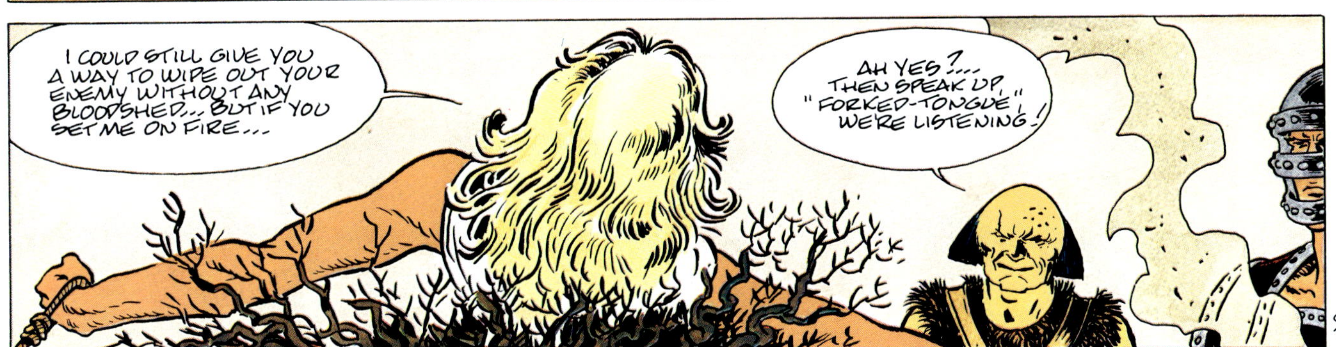
I COULD STILL GIVE YOU A WAY TO WIPE OUT YOUR ENEMY WITHOUT ANY BLOODSHED... BUT IF YOU SET ME ON FIRE...
AH YES?... THEN SPEAK UP, "FORKED-TONGUE"! WE'RE LISTENING!

29

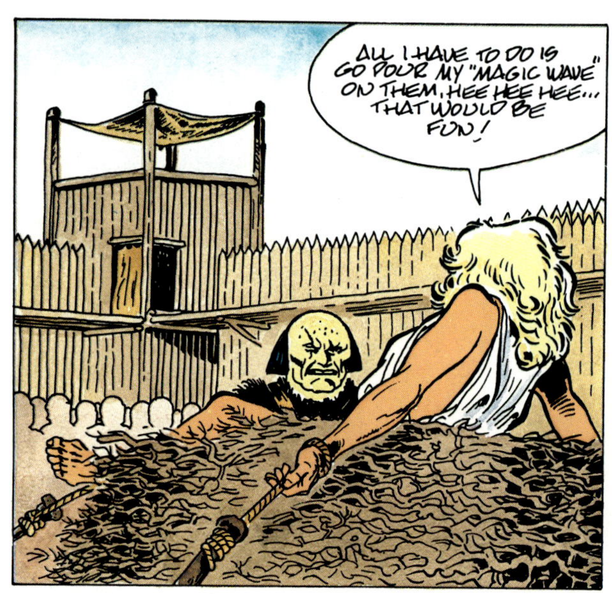

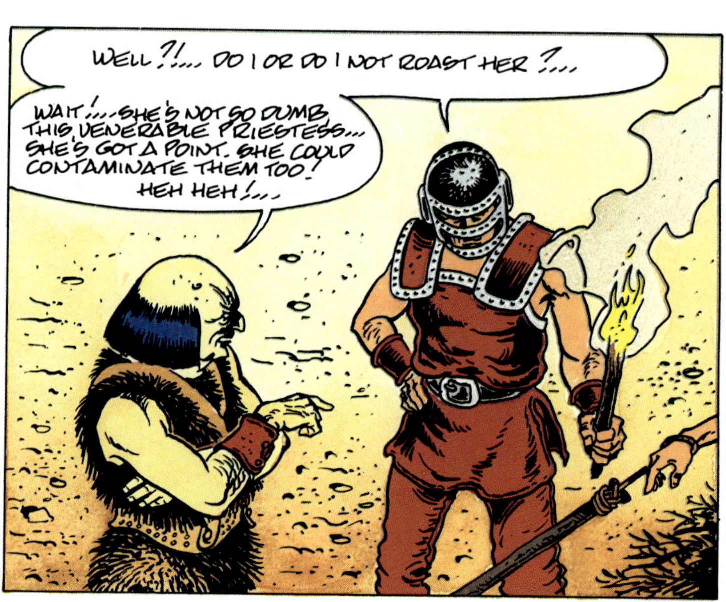

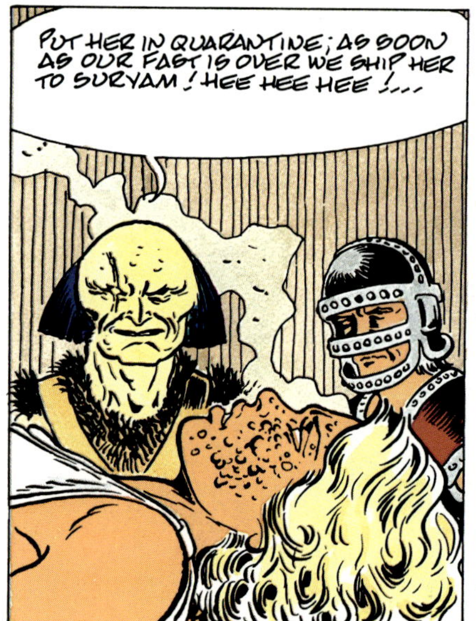

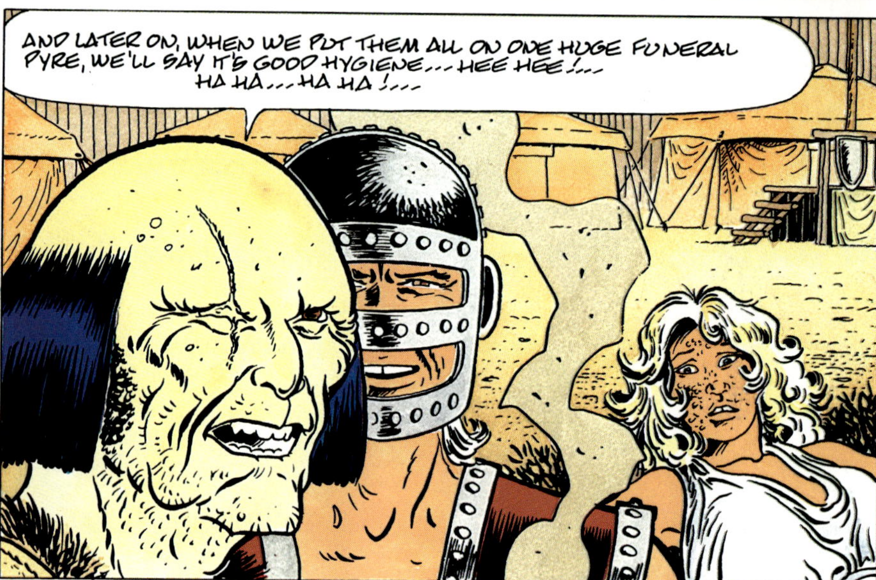

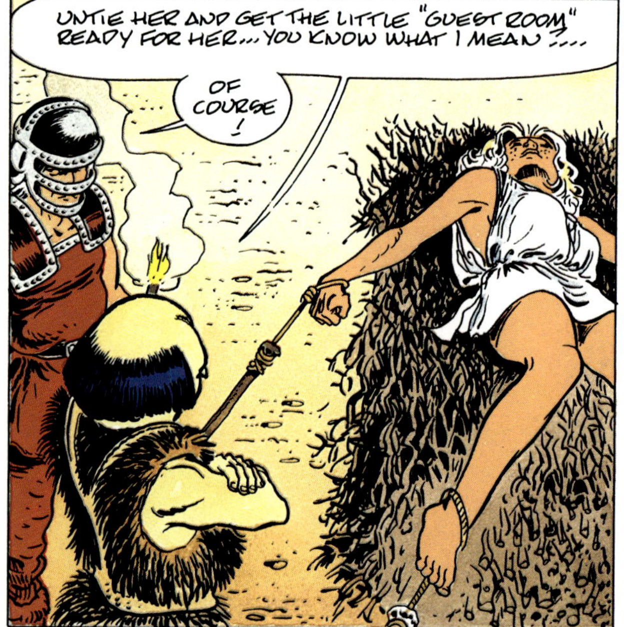

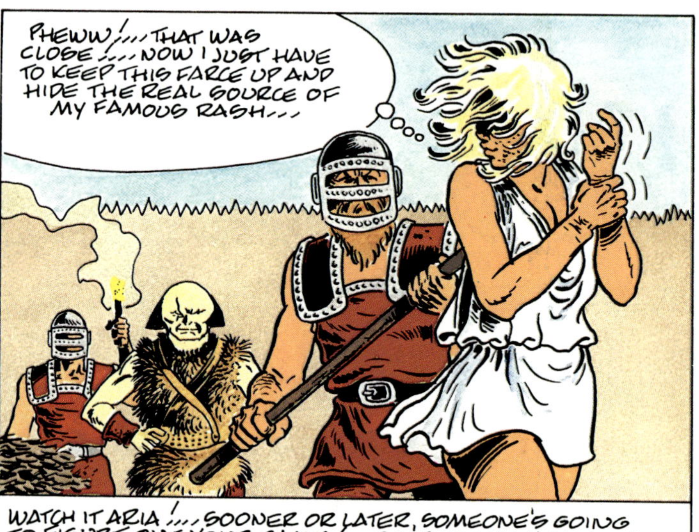

WATCH IT ARIA!... SOONER OR LATER, SOMEONE'S GOING TO FIGURE OUT YOUR GAME... SO IF YOU DON'T WANT TO FIND YOURSELF ON THAT BONFIRE AGAIN, BETTER LAUNCH YOUR PLAN OF ATTACK WITHOUT DELAY!...

WEYLAND 80. 30

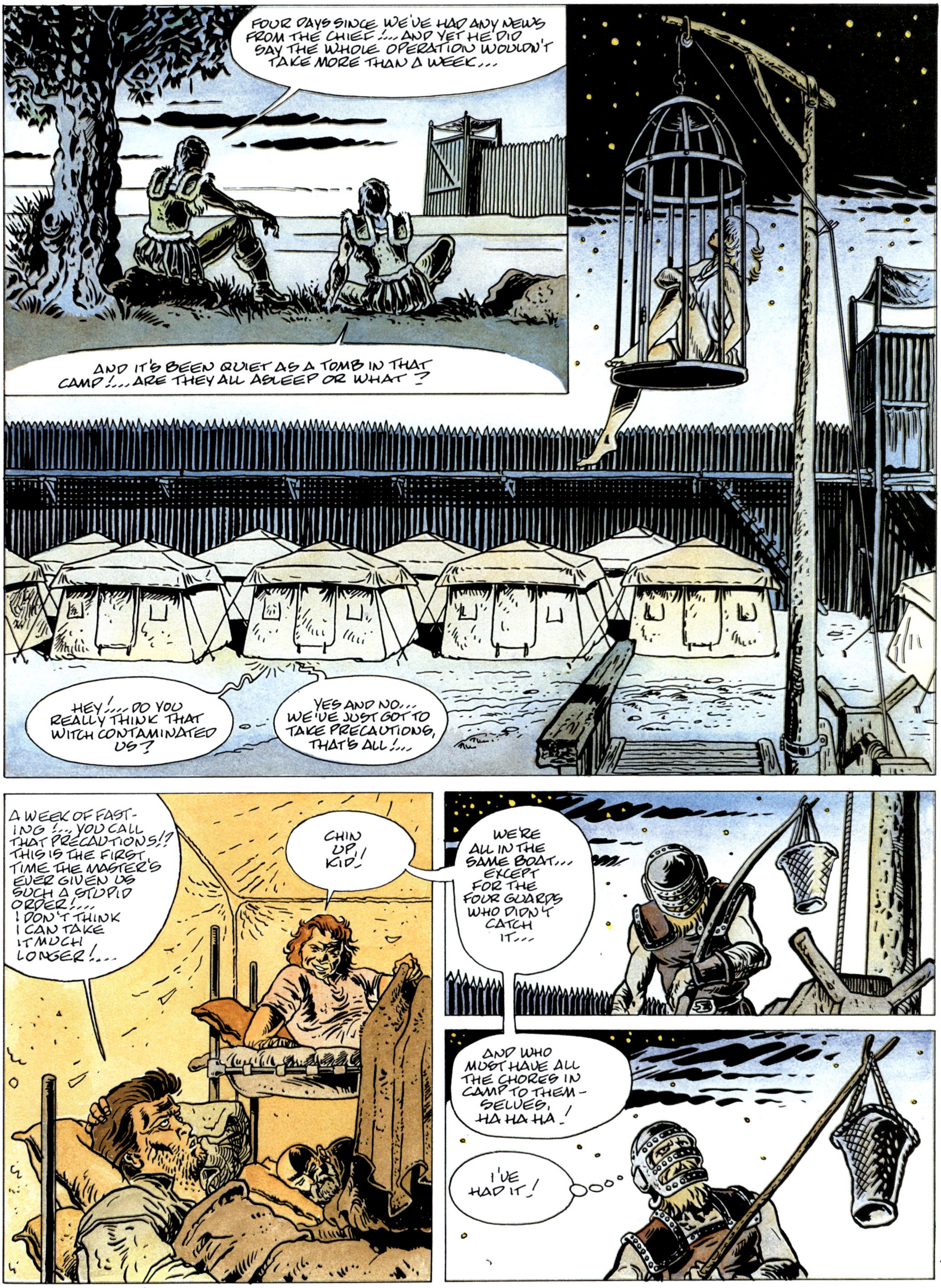

FOUR DAYS SINCE WE'VE HAD ANY NEWS FROM THE CHIEF !... AND YET HE DID SAY THE WHOLE OPERATION WOULDN'T TAKE MORE THAN A WEEK...

AND IT'S BEEN QUIET AS A TOMB IN THAT CAMP !... ARE THEY ALL ASLEEP OR WHAT ?

HEY !... DO YOU REALLY THINK THAT WITCH CONTAMINATED US ?

YES AND NO... WE'VE JUST GOT TO TAKE PRECAUTIONS, THAT'S ALL !...

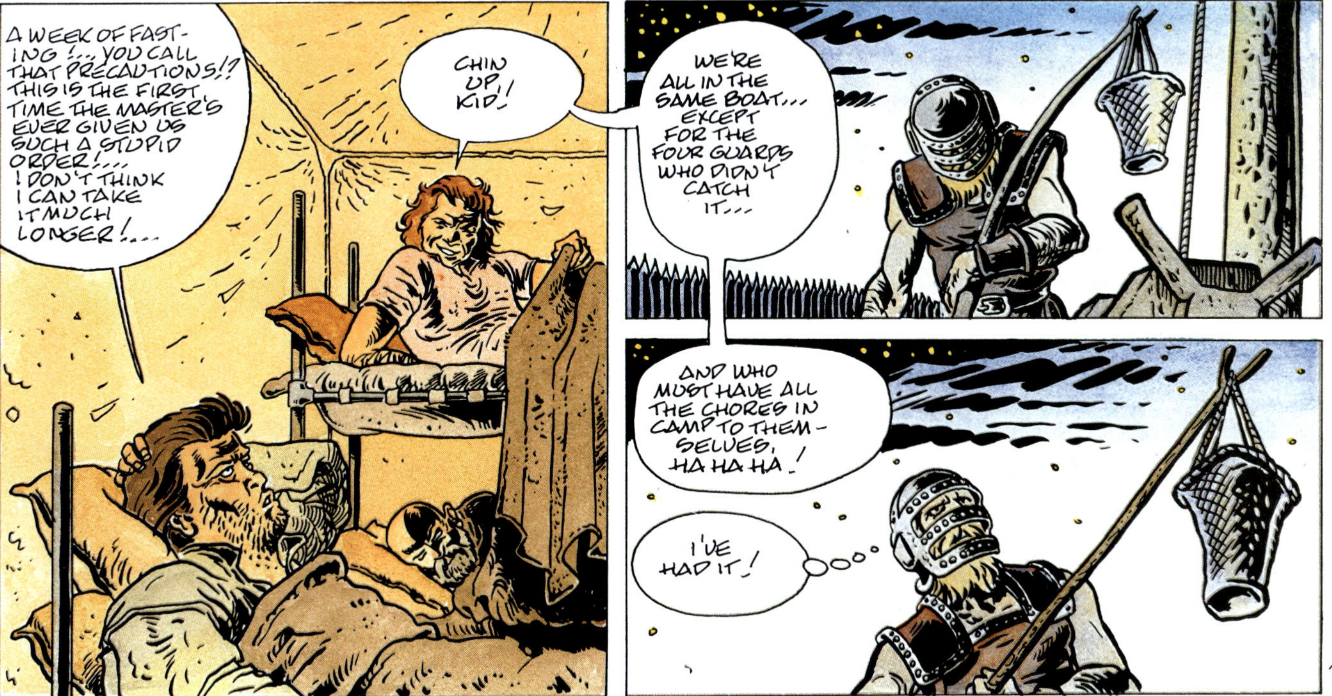

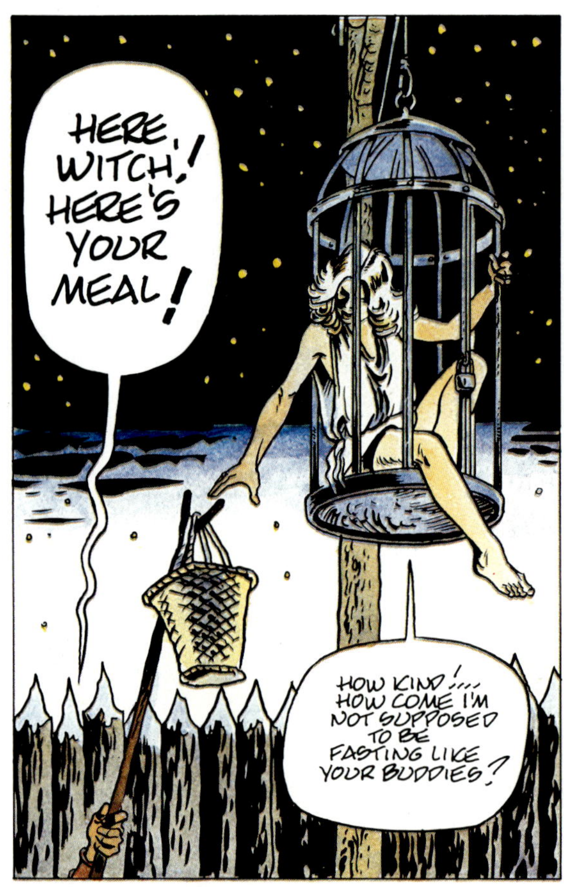
HERE, WITCH! HERE'S YOUR MEAL!
HOW KIND!... HOW COME I'M NOT SUPPOSED TO BE FASTING LIKE YOUR BUDDIES?

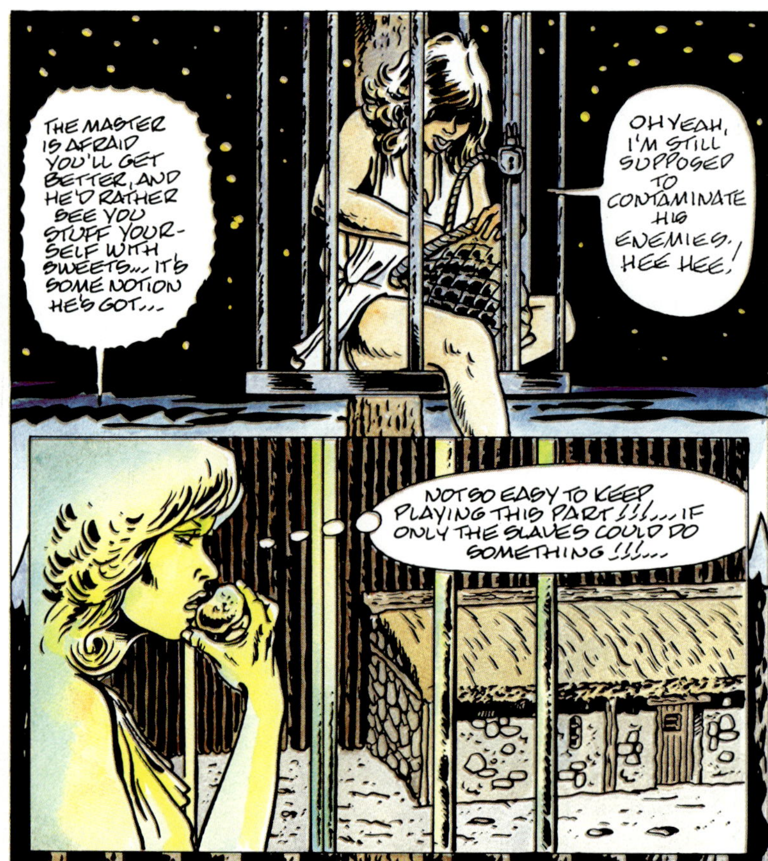
THE MASTER IS AFRAID YOU'LL GET BETTER, AND HE'D RATHER SEE YOU STUFF YOURSELF WITH SWEETS... IT'S SOME NOTION HE'S GOT...
OH YEAH, I'M STILL SUPPOSED TO CONTAMINATE HIS ENEMIES. HEE HEE!
NOT SO EASY TO KEEP PLAYING THIS PART!!!... IF ONLY THE SLAVES COULD DO SOMETHING!!!...

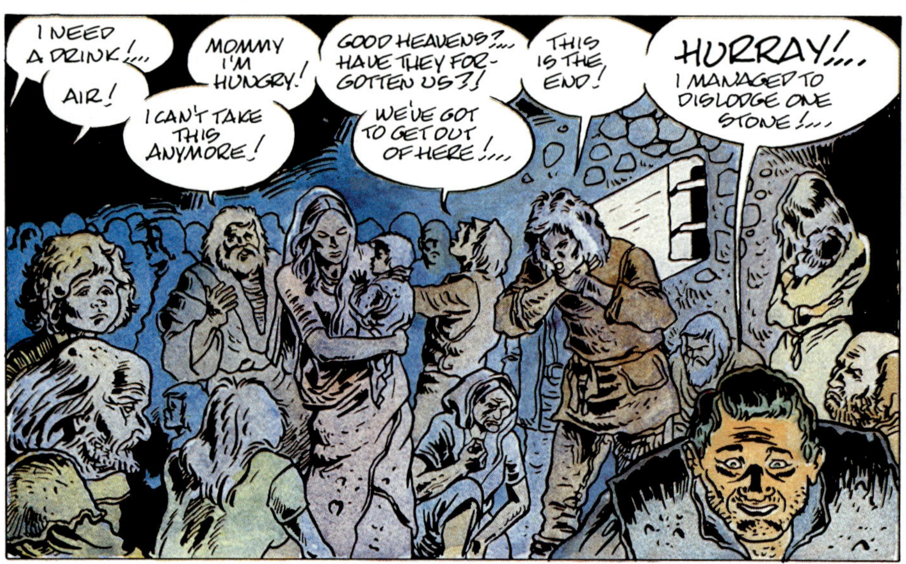
I NEED A DRINK!...
AIR!
MOMMY I'M HUNGRY!
I CAN'T TAKE THIS ANYMORE!
GOOD HEAVENS?! HAVE THEY FORGOTTEN US?!
WE'VE GOT TO GET OUT OF HERE!...
THIS IS THE END!
HURRAY!... I MANAGED TO DISLODGE ONE STONE!...

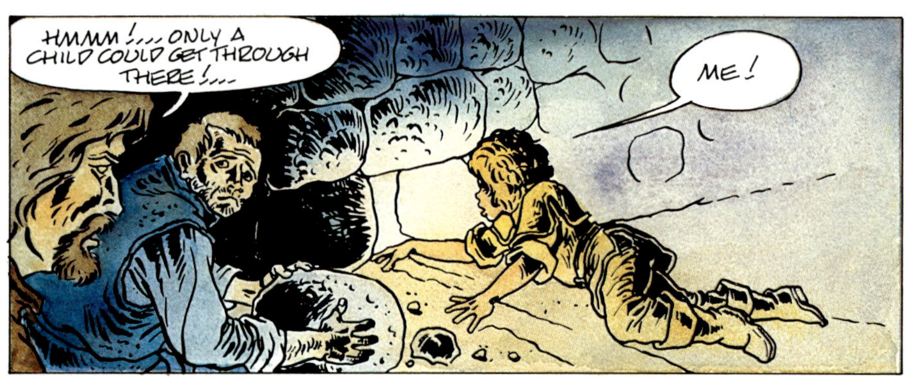
HMMM!... ONLY A CHILD COULD GET THROUGH THERE!...
ME!

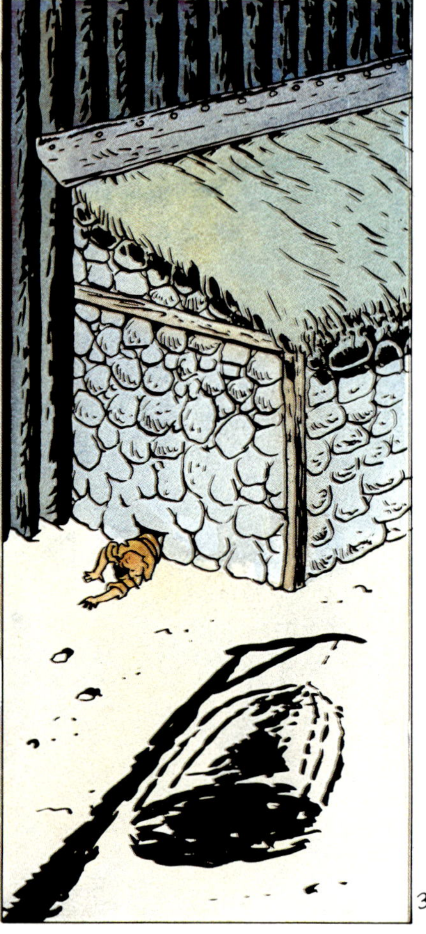

32

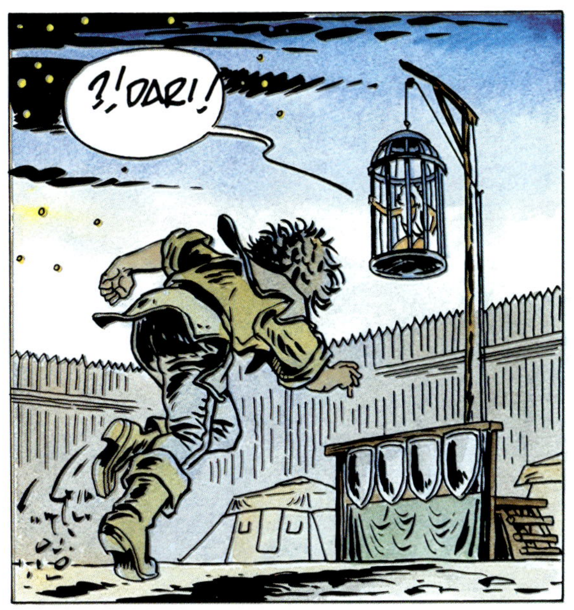
?! DARI!

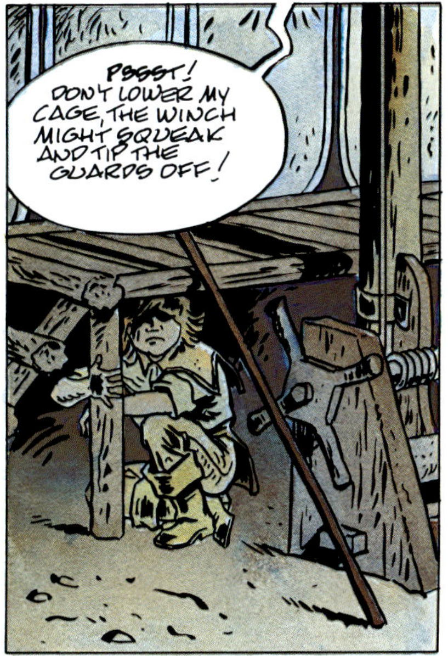
PSSST! DON'T LOWER MY CAGE, THE WINCH MIGHT SQUEAK AND TIP THE GUARDS OFF!

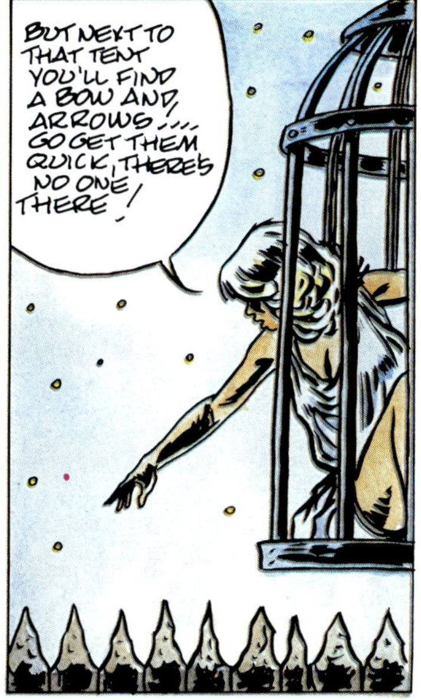
BUT NEXT TO THAT TENT YOU'LL FIND A BOW AND ARROWS.... GO GET THEM QUICK, THERE'S NO ONE THERE!

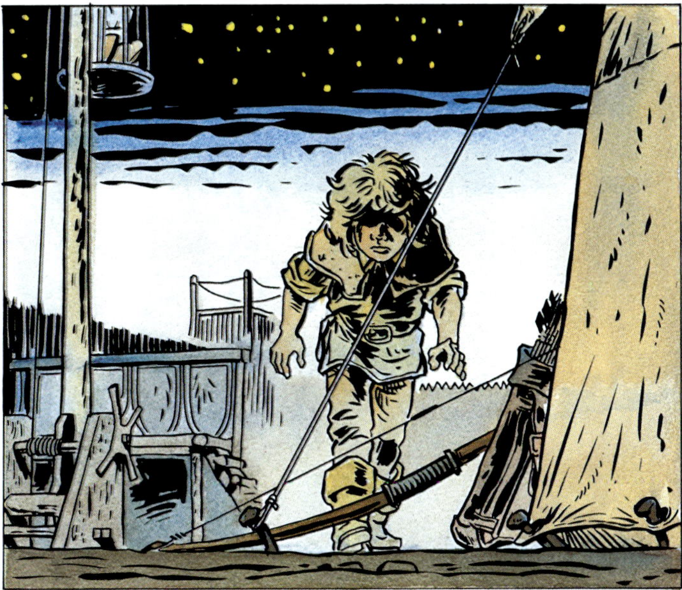

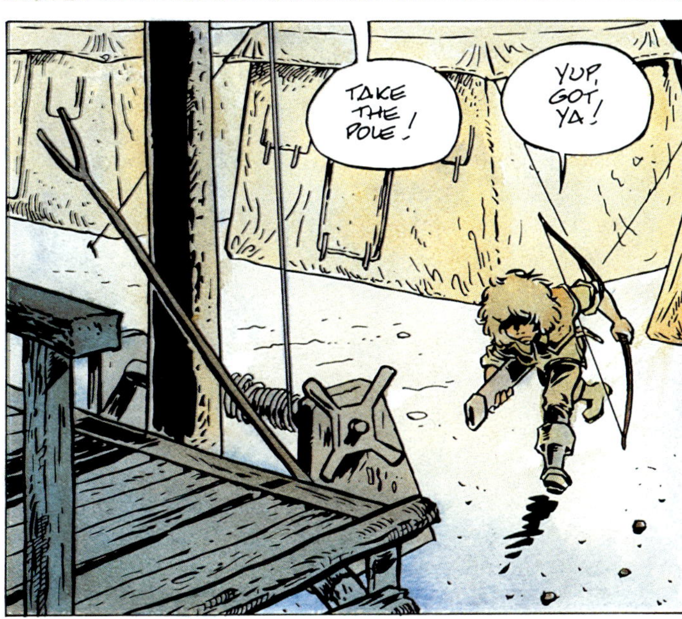
TAKE THE POLE!
YUP, GOT YA!

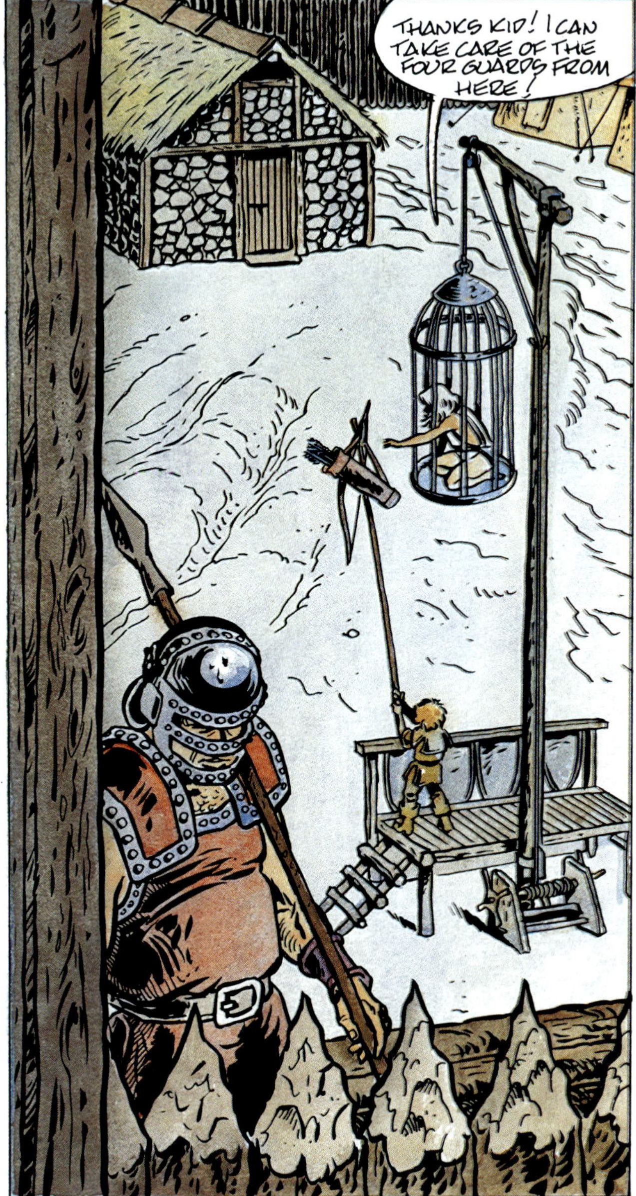
THANKS KID! I CAN TAKE CARE OF THE FOUR GUARDS FROM HERE!

33.

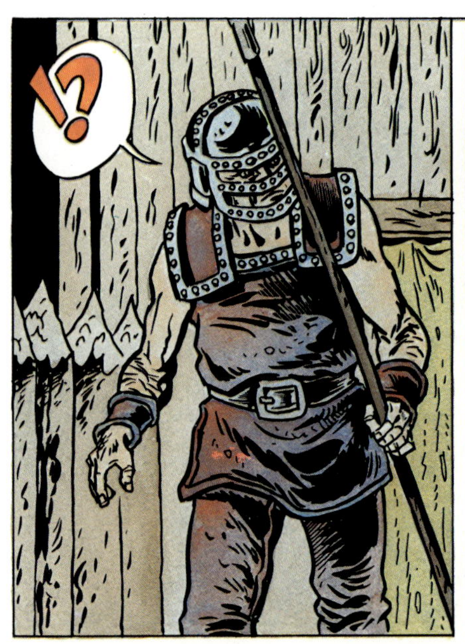
!?

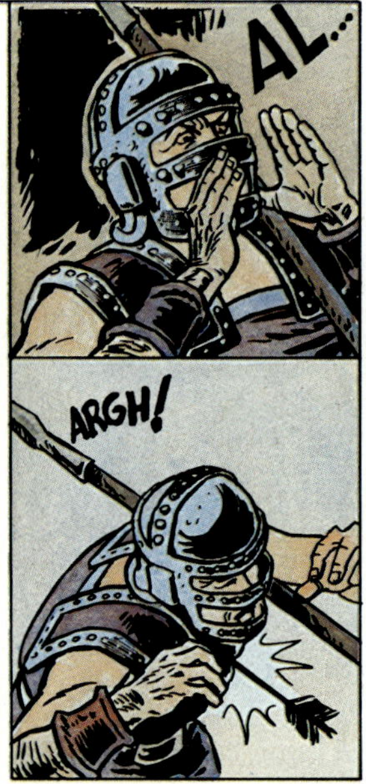
AL...
ARGH!

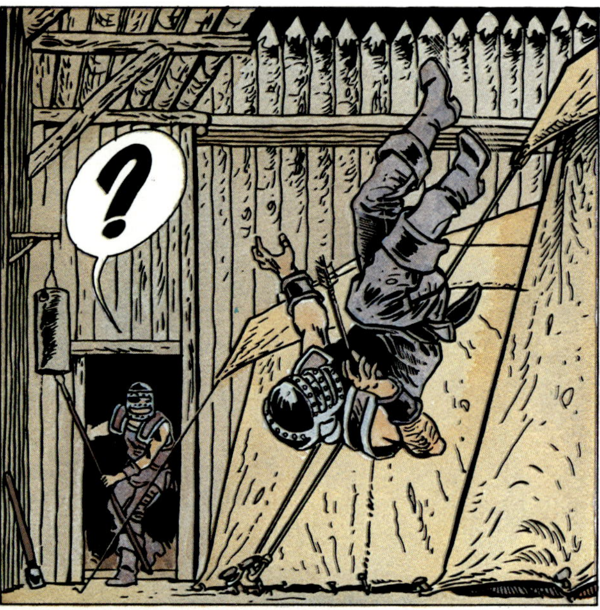
?

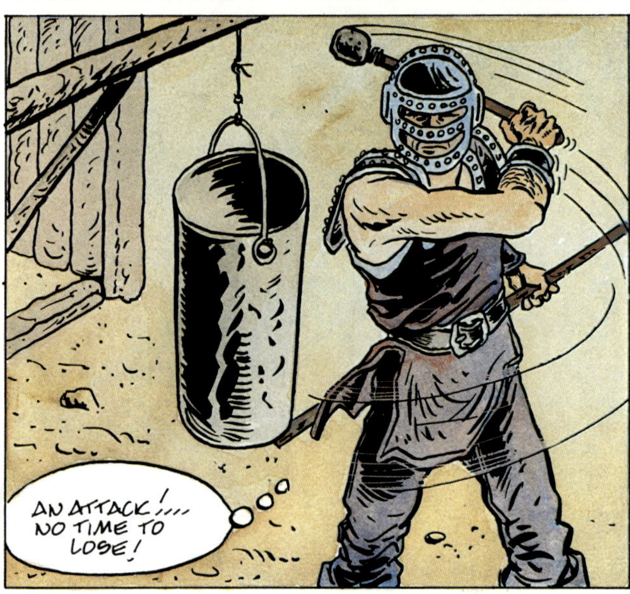
AN ATTACK!... NO TIME TO LOSE!

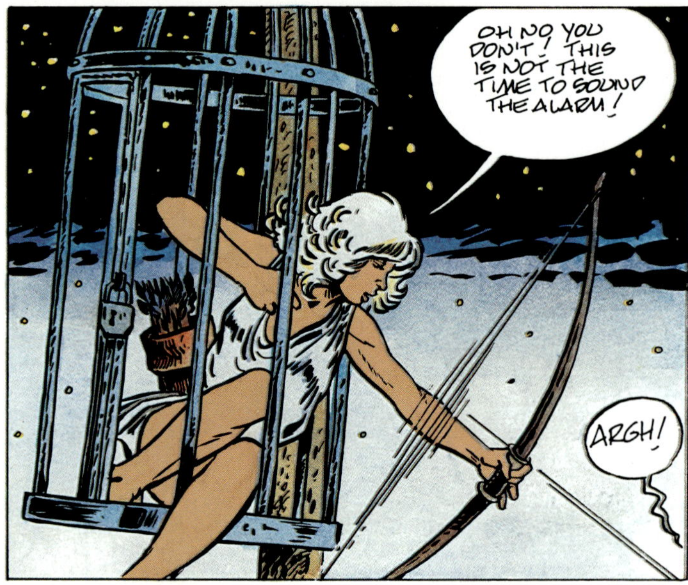
OH NO YOU DON'T! THIS IS NOT THE TIME TO SOUND THE ALARM!
ARGH!

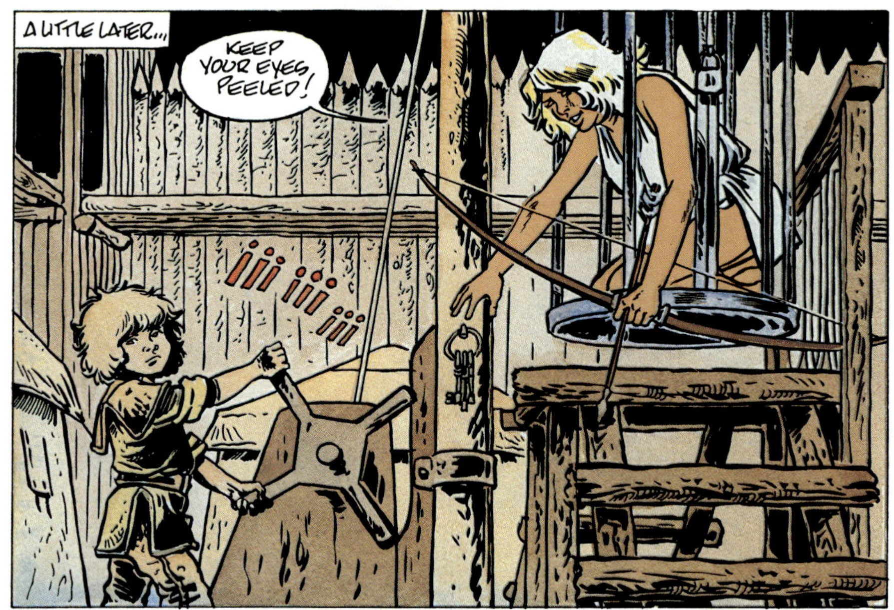
A LITTLE LATER...
KEEP YOUR EYES PEELED!
iii iii iii

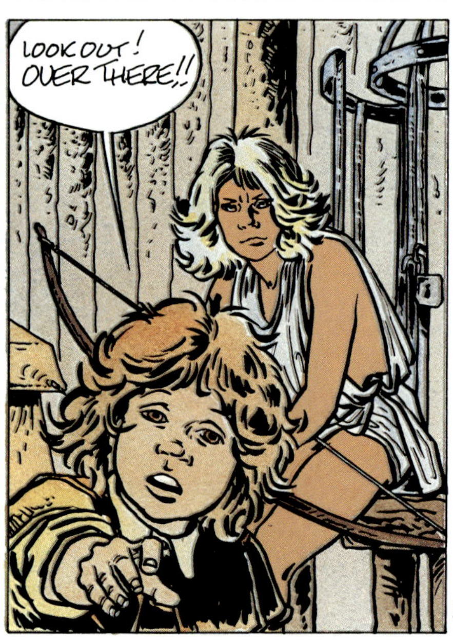
LOOK OUT! OVER THERE!!

34

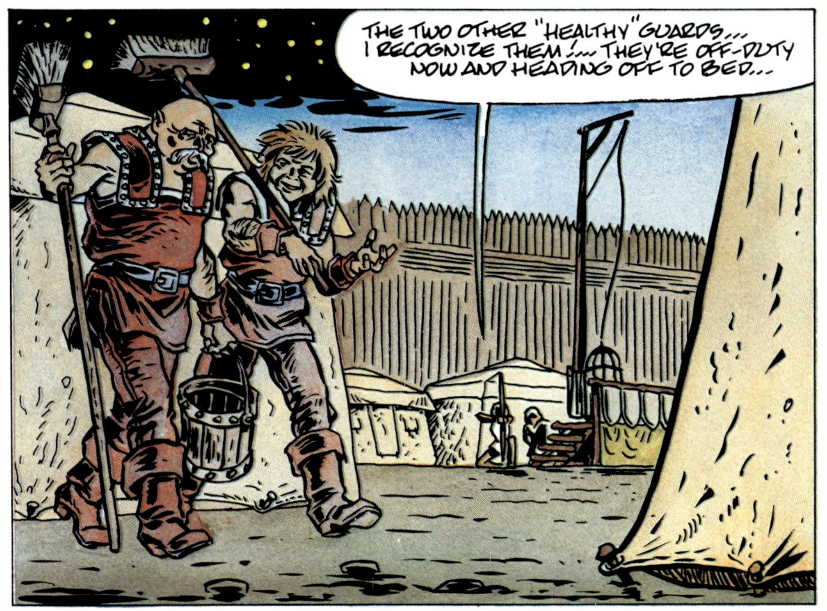
THE TWO OTHER "HEALTHY" GUARDS... I RECOGNIZE THEM!... THEY'RE OFF-DUTY NOW AND HEADING OFF TO BED...

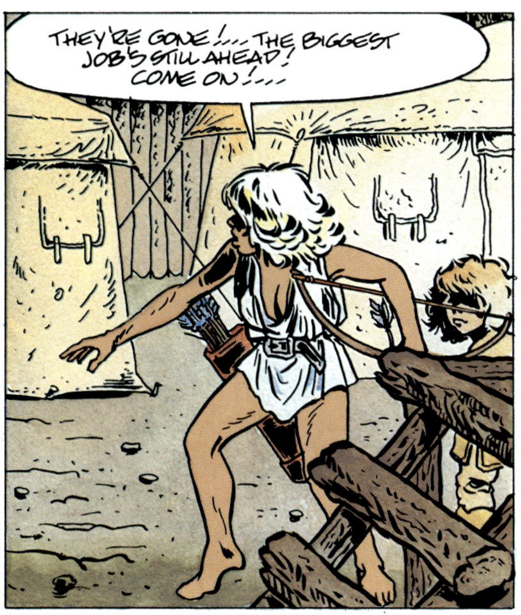
THEY'RE GONE!... THE BIGGEST JOB'S STILL AHEAD! COME ON!...

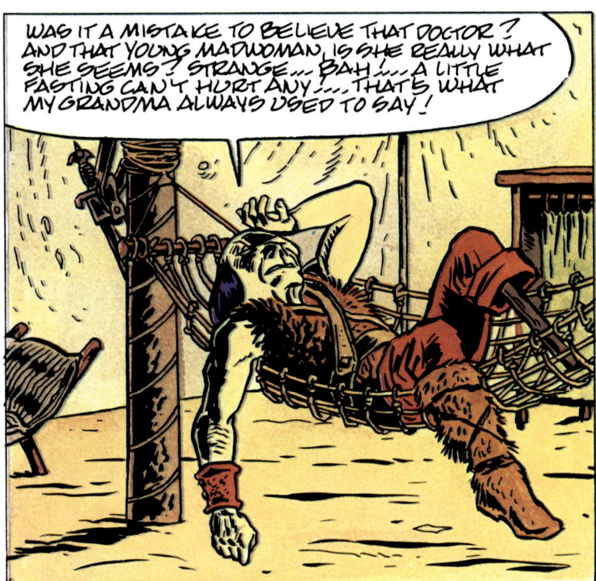
WAS IT A MISTAKE TO BELIEVE THAT DOCTOR? AND THAT YOUNG MADWOMAN, IS SHE REALLY WHAT SHE SEEMS? STRANGE... BAH!... A LITTLE FASTING CAN'T HURT ANY!... THAT'S WHAT MY GRANDMA ALWAYS USED TO SAY!

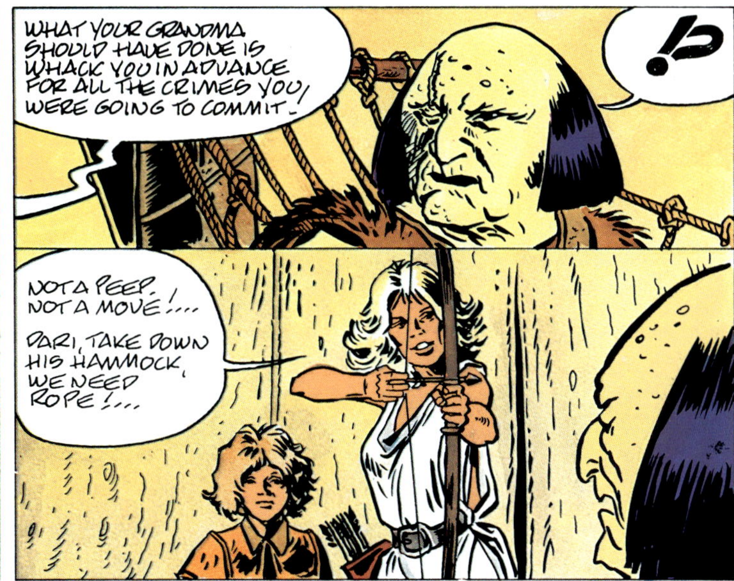
WHAT YOUR GRANDMA SHOULD HAVE DONE IS WHACK YOU IN ADVANCE FOR ALL THE CRIMES YOU WERE GOING TO COMMIT!
!?
NOT A PEEP. NOT A MOVE!...
DARI, TAKE DOWN HIS HAMMOCK, WE NEED ROPE!...

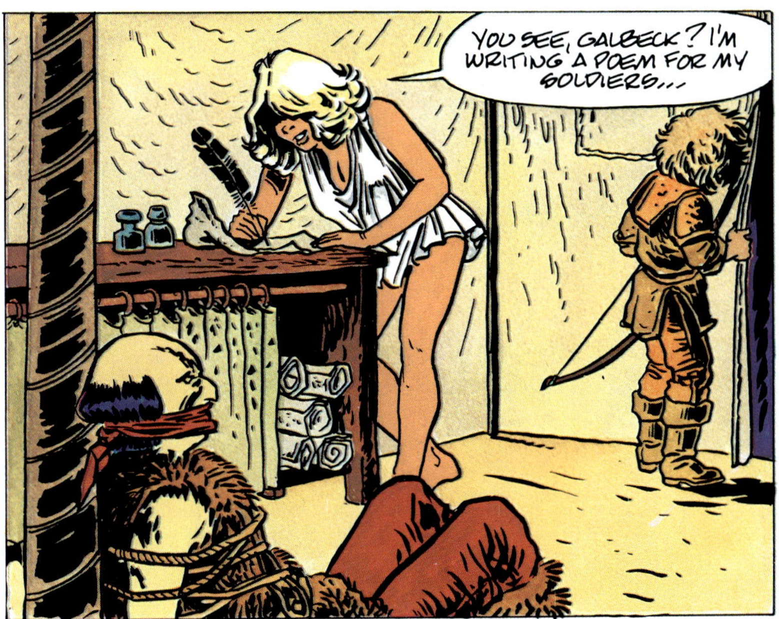
YOU SEE, GALBECK? I'M WRITING A POEM FOR MY SOLDIERS...

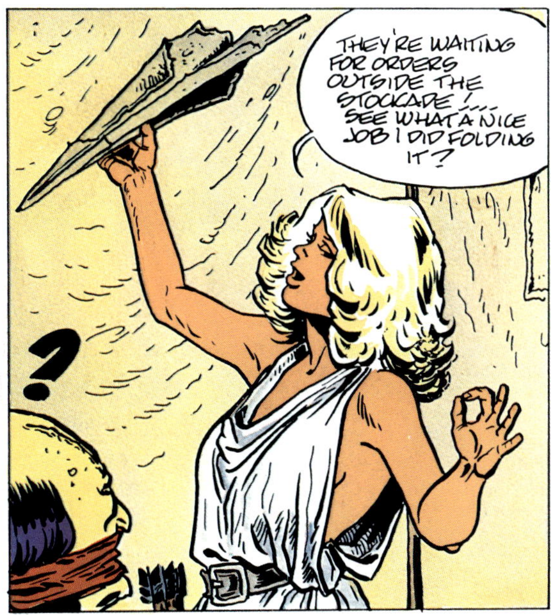
THEY'RE WAITING FOR ORDERS OUTSIDE THE STOCKADE!... SEE WHAT A NICE JOB I DID FOLDING IT?
?

35

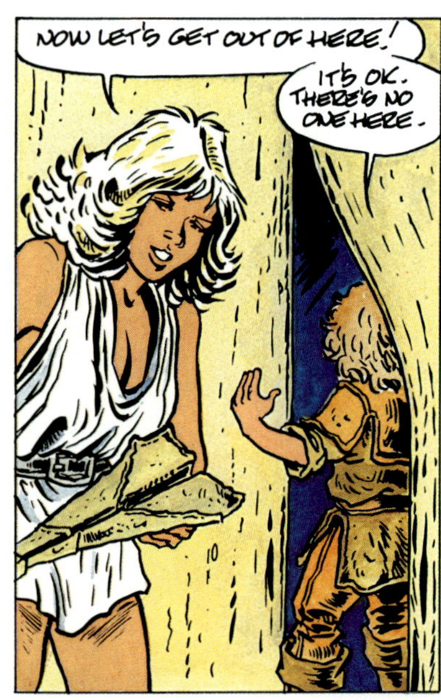
NOW LET'S GET OUT OF HERE!
IT'S OK. THERE'S NO ONE HERE.

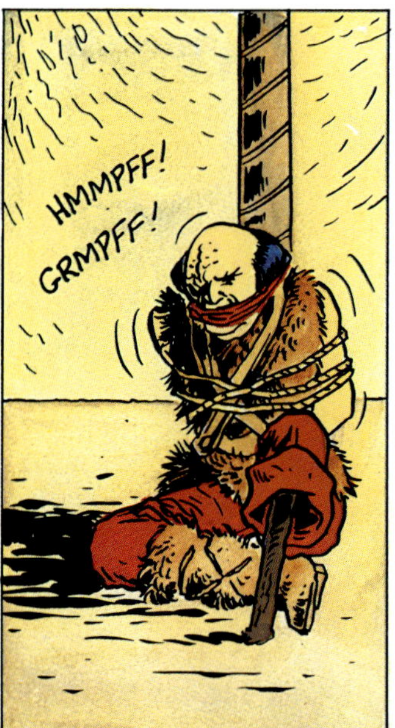
HMMPFF!
GRMPFF!

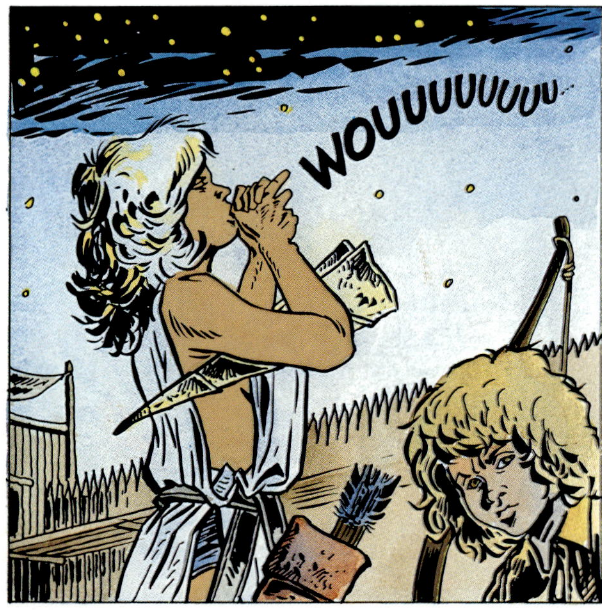
WOUUUUUUUU...

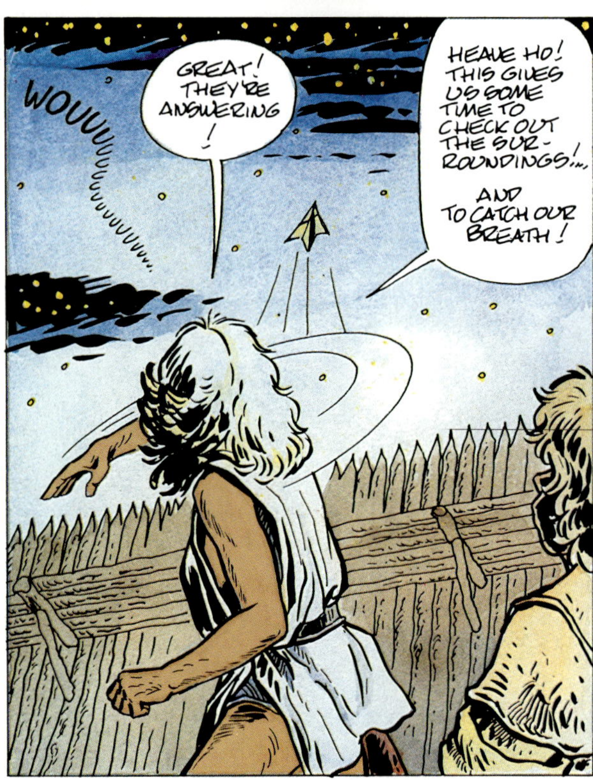
WOUUUUUUUUU...
GREAT! THEY'RE ANSWERING!
HEAVE HO! THIS GIVES US SOME TIME TO CHECK OUT THE SURROUNDINGS!...
AND TO CATCH OUR BREATH!

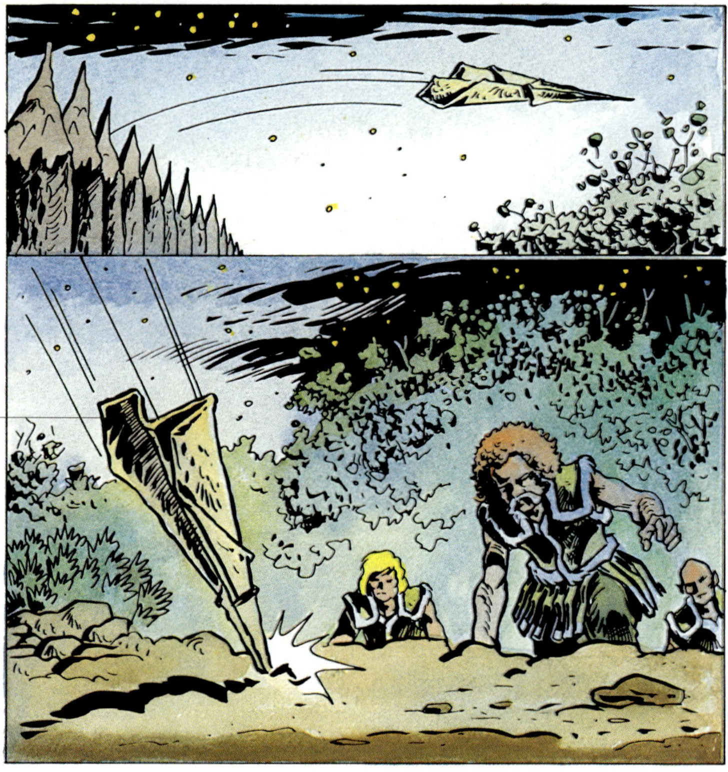

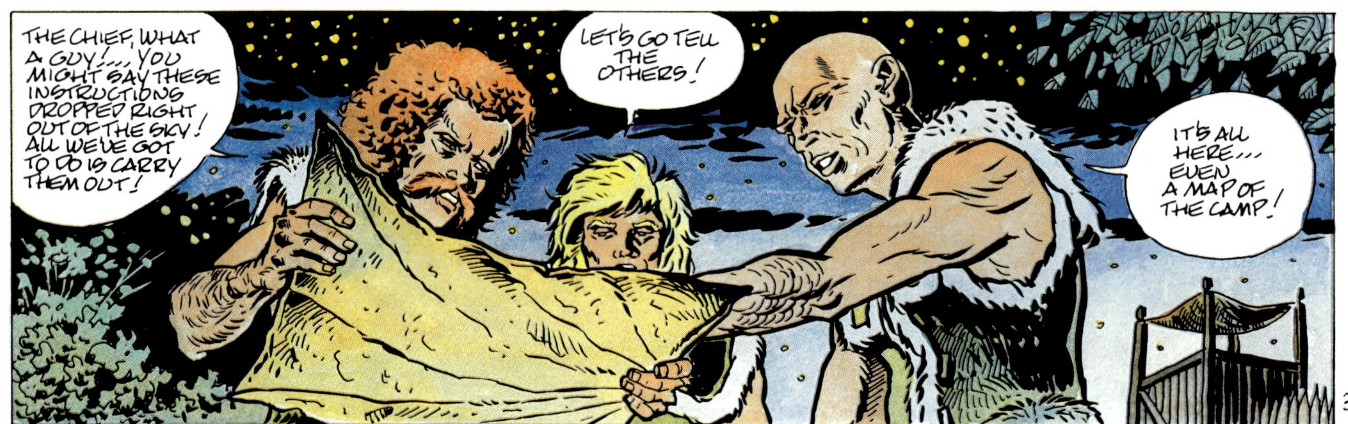
THE CHIEF, WHAT A GUY!... YOU MIGHT SAY THESE INSTRUCTIONS DROPPED RIGHT OUT OF THE SKY! ALL WE'VE GOT TO DO IS CARRY THEM OUT!
LET'S GO TELL THE OTHERS!
IT'S ALL HERE... EVEN A MAP OF THE CAMP!
36.

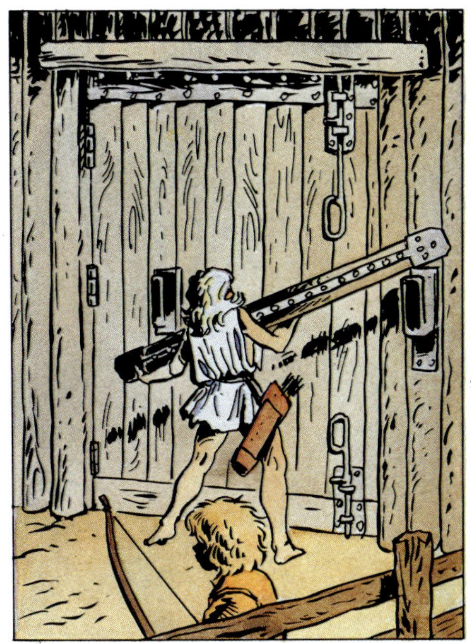

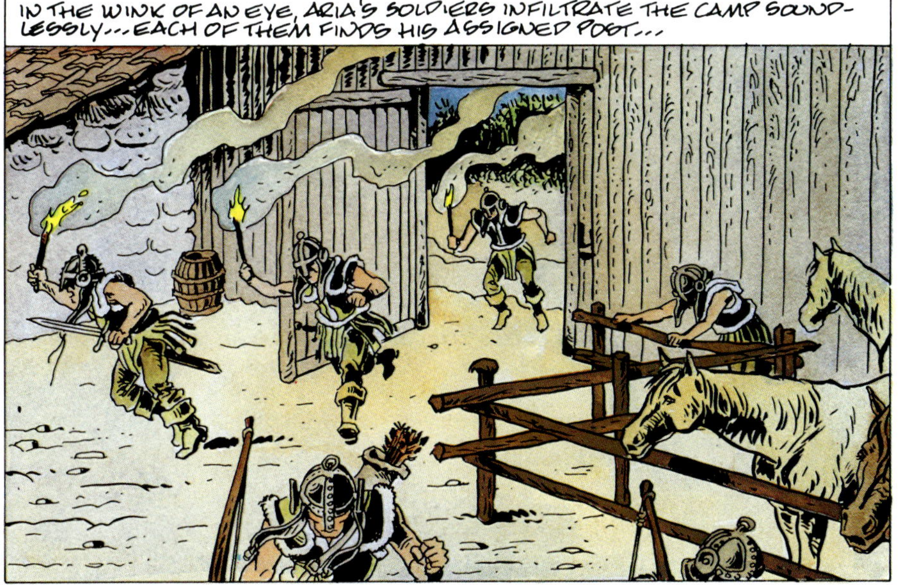
IN THE WINK OF AN EYE, ARIA'S SOLDIERS INFILTRATE THE CAMP SOUND-LESSLY... EACH OF THEM FINDS HIS ASSIGNED POST...

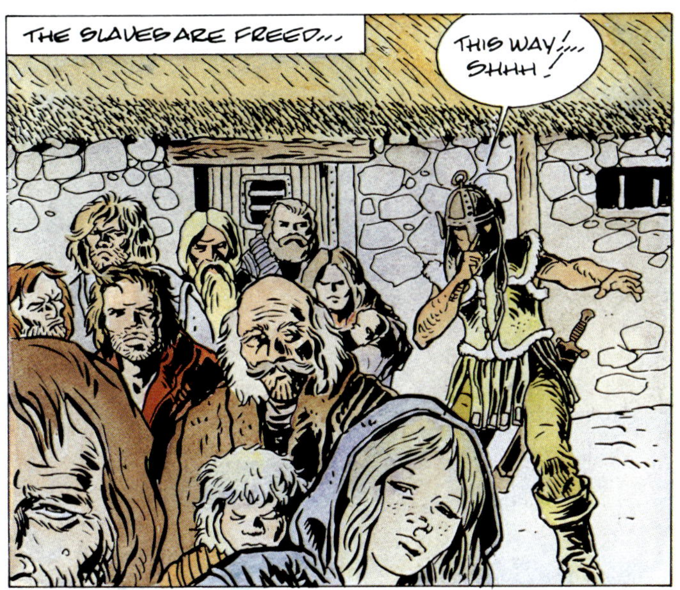
THE SLAVES ARE FREED...
THIS WAY!... SHHH!

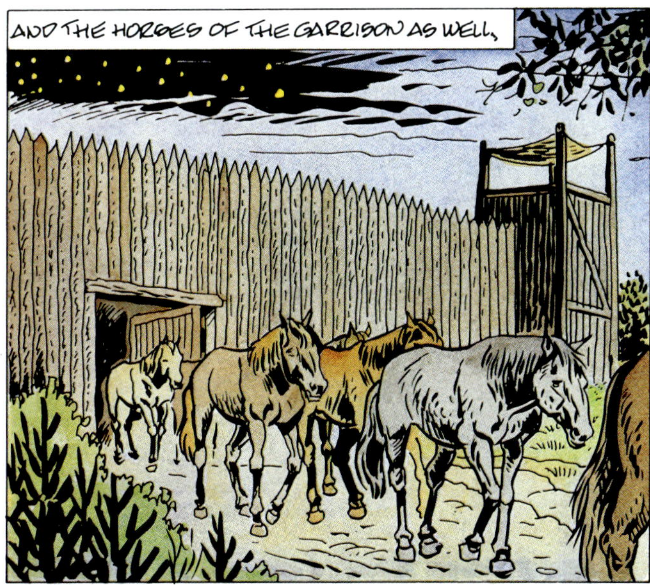
AND THE HORSES OF THE GARRISON AS WELL,

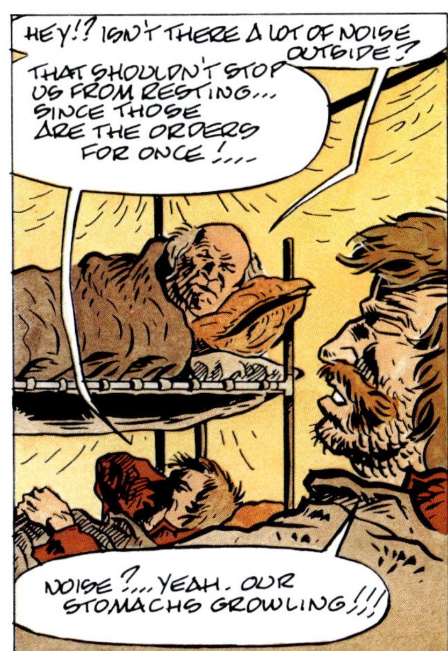
HEY!? ISN'T THERE A LOT OF NOISE OUTSIDE?
THAT SHOULDN'T STOP US FROM RESTING... SINCE THOSE ARE THE ORDERS FOR ONCE!...
NOISE?... YEAH. OUR STOMACHS GROWLING!!!

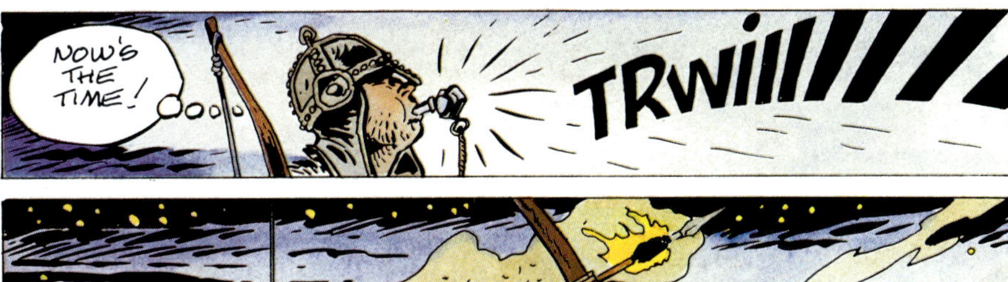
NOW'S THE TIME!
TRWIII

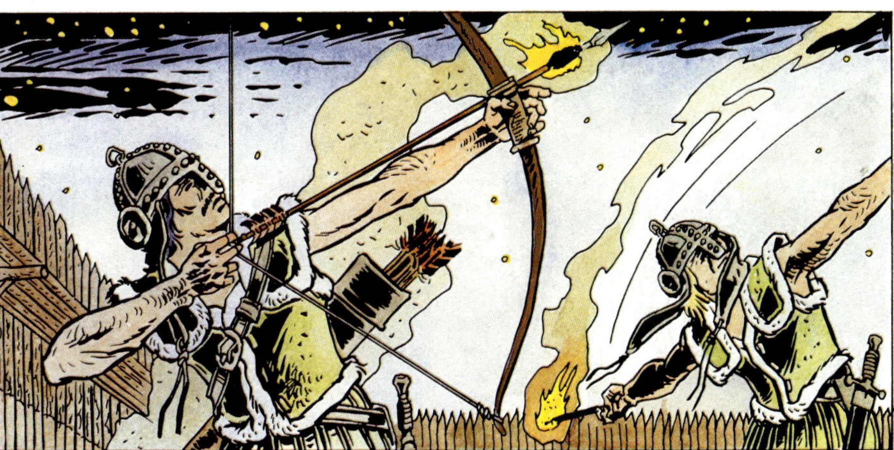

37.

IN TEN MINUTES, THE CAMP IS REDUCED TO A ROARING BLAZE. THE SLAVES AND ARIA'S SOLDIERS GATHER AT THE FOOT OF THE HILL...

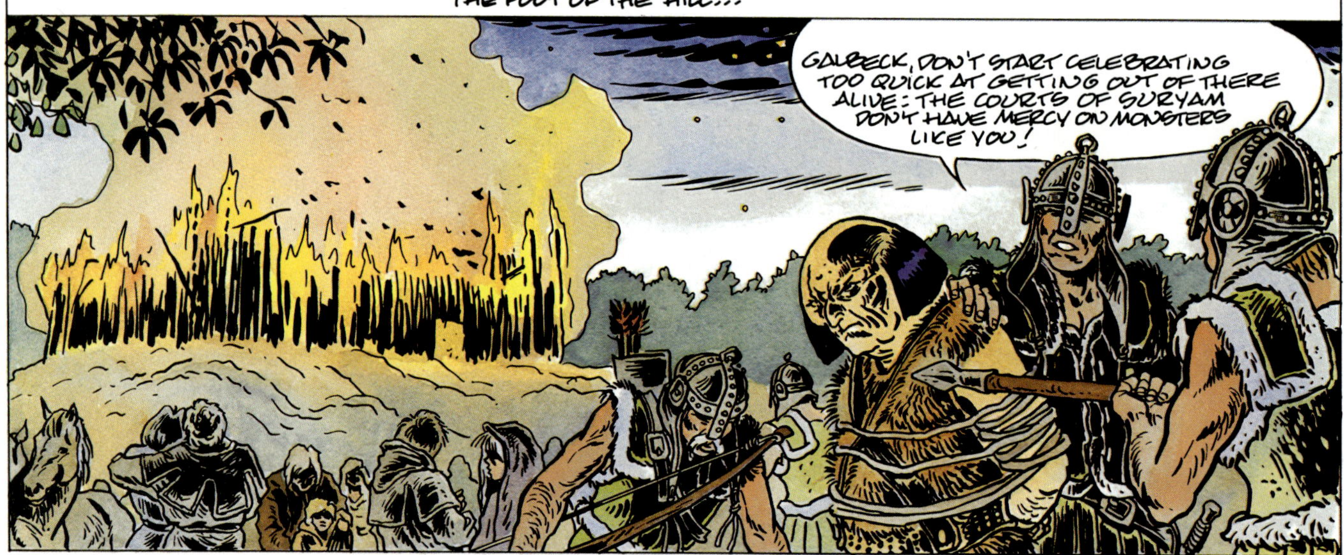

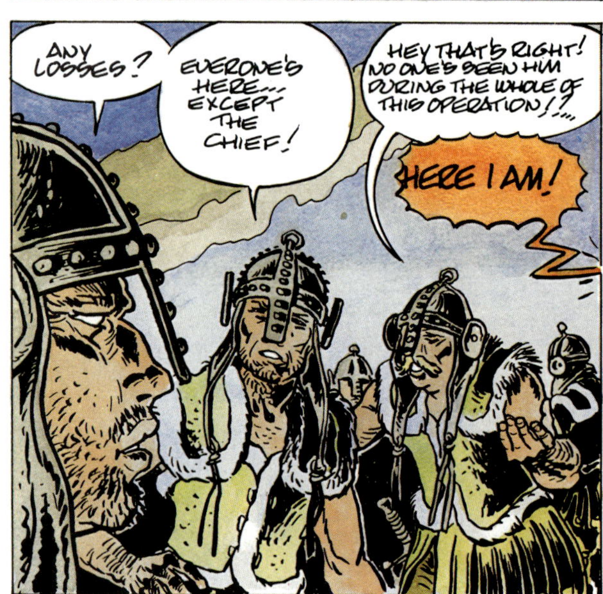

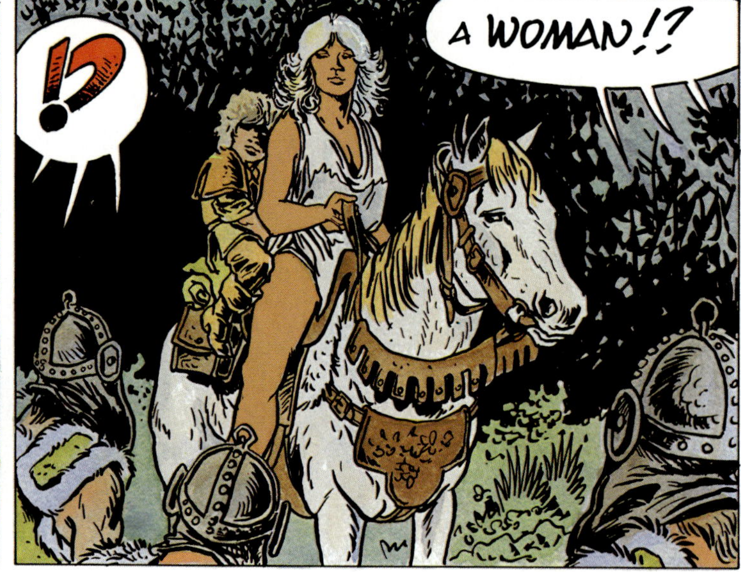

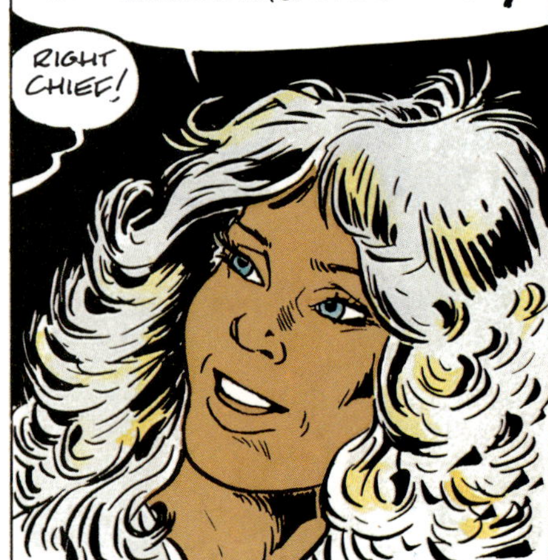

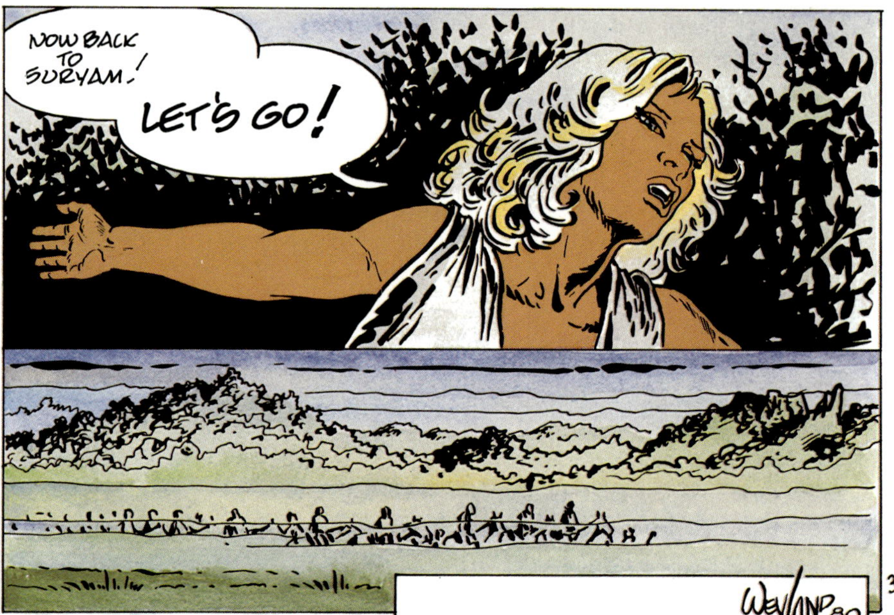

38

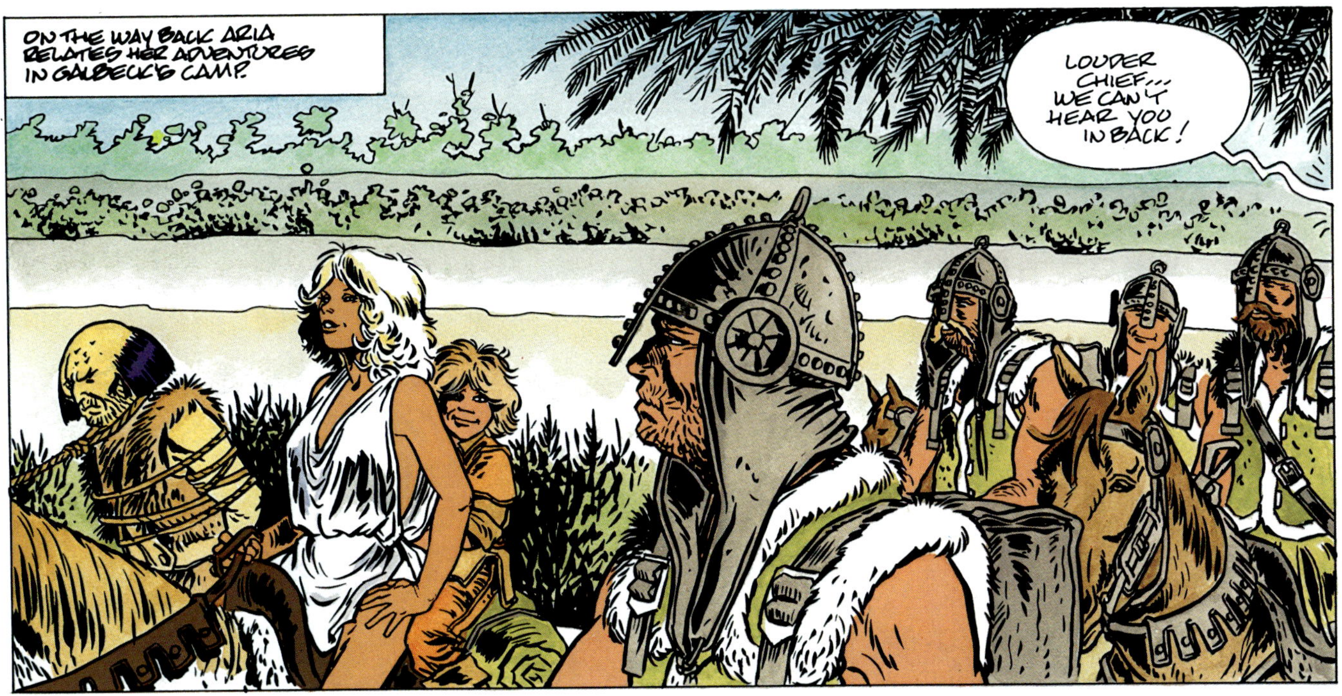

ON THE WAY BACK ARIA RELATES HER ADVENTURES IN GALBECK'S CAMP.
LOUDER CHIEF... WE CAN'T HEAR YOU IN BACK!

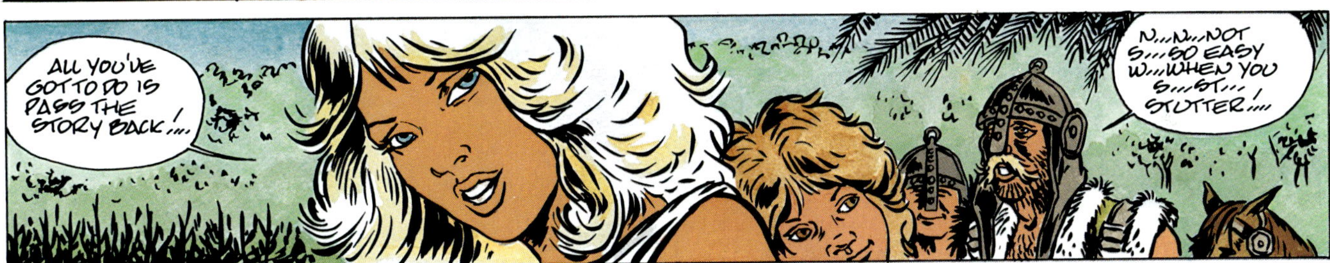

ALL YOU'VE GOT TO DO IS PASS THE STORY BACK!...
N...N...NOT S...SO EASY W...WHEN YOU S...ST... STUTTER!...

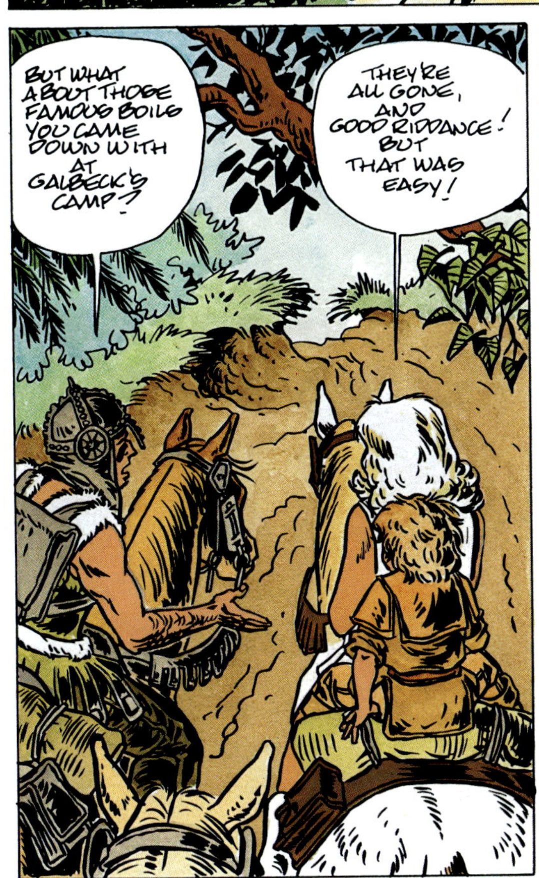

BUT WHAT ABOUT THOSE FAMOUS BOILS YOU CAME DOWN WITH AT GALBECK'S CAMP?
THEY'RE ALL GONE, AND GOOD RIDDANCE! BUT THAT WAS EASY!

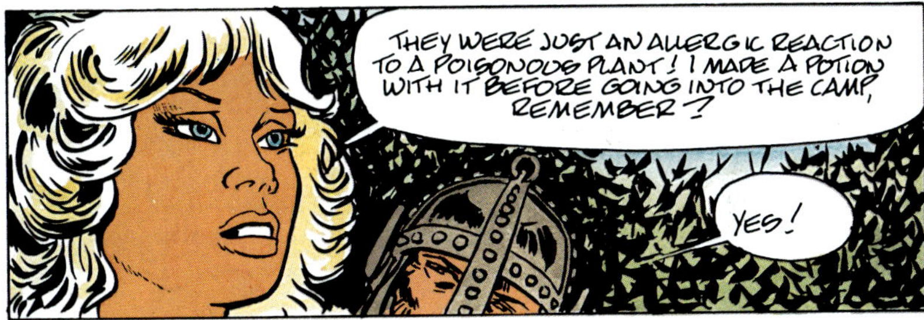

THEY WERE JUST AN ALLERGIC REACTION TO A POISONOUS PLANT! I MADE A POTION WITH IT BEFORE GOING INTO THE CAMP, REMEMBER?
YES!

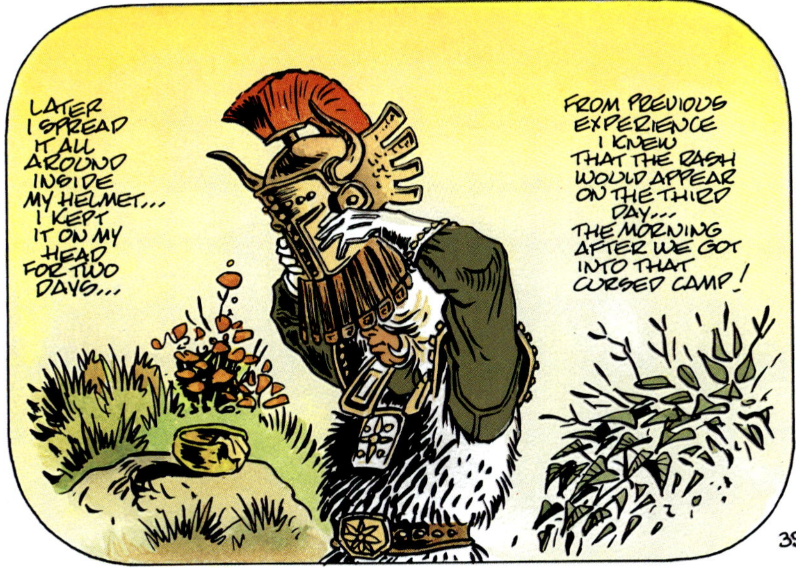

LATER I SPREAD IT ALL AROUND INSIDE MY HELMET... I KEPT IT ON MY HEAD FOR TWO DAYS...
FROM PREVIOUS EXPERIENCE I KNEW THAT THE RASH WOULD APPEAR ON THE THIRD DAY... THE MORNING AFTER WE GOT INTO THAT CURSED CAMP!

39.

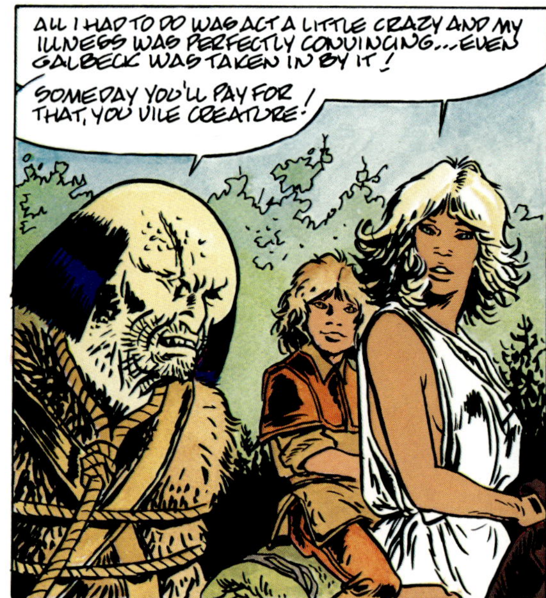
ALL I HAD TO DO WAS ACT A LITTLE CRAZY AND MY ILLNESS WAS PERFECTLY CONVINCING... EVEN GALBECK WAS TAKEN IN BY IT!
SOMEDAY YOU'LL PAY FOR THAT, YOU VILE CREATURE!

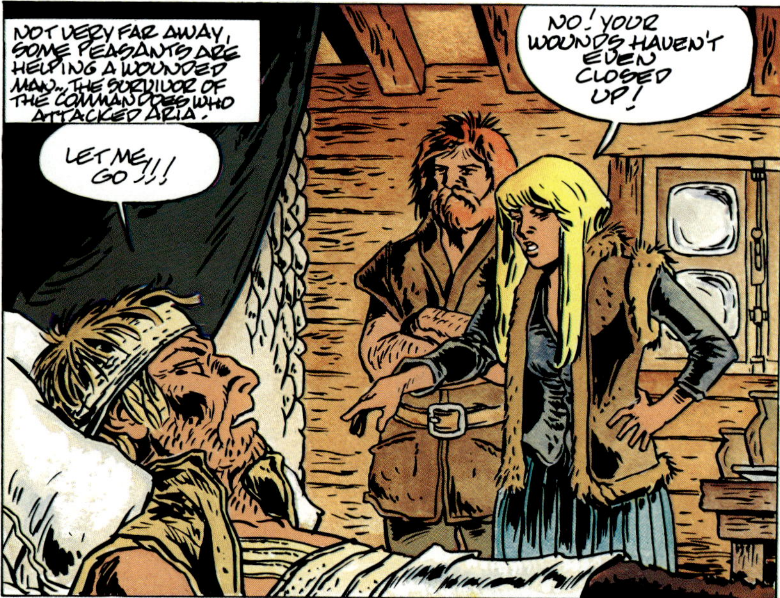
NOT VERY FAR AWAY, SOME PEASANTS ARE HELPING A WOUNDED MAN... THE SURVIVOR OF THE COMMANDOES WHO ATTACKED ARIA.
LET ME GO!!!
NO! YOUR WOUNDS HAVEN'T EVEN CLOSED UP!

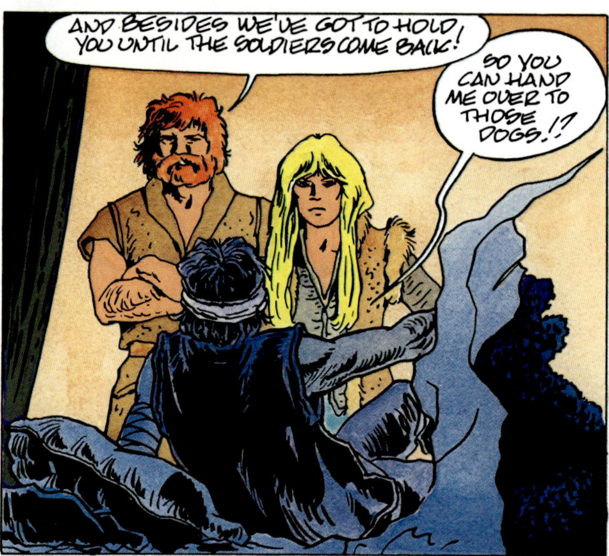
AND BESIDES WE'VE GOT TO HOLD YOU UNTIL THE SOLDIERS COME BACK!
SO YOU CAN HAND ME OVER TO THOSE DOGS!?

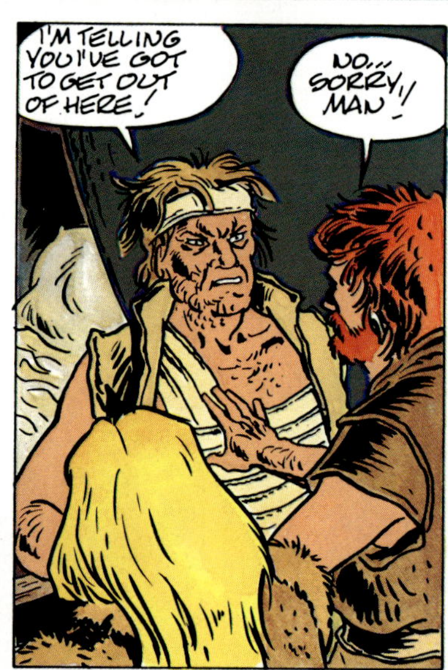
I'M TELLING YOU I'VE GOT TO GET OUT OF HERE!
NO... SORRY, MAN!

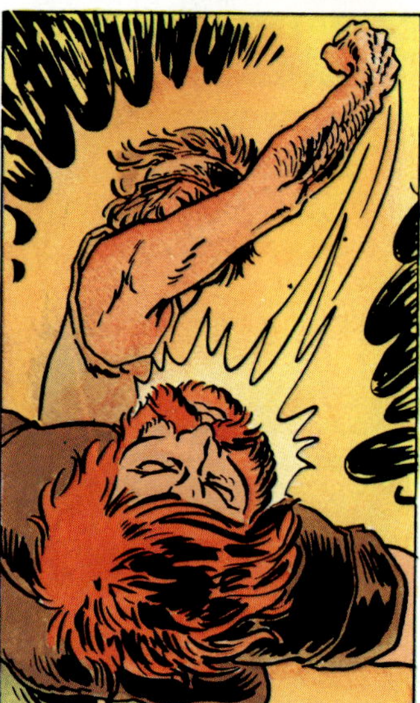

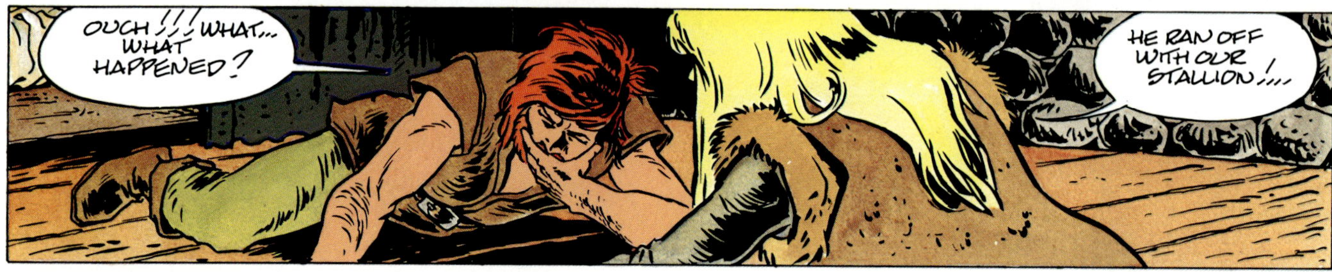
OUCH!!! WHAT... WHAT HAPPENED?
HE RAN OFF WITH OUR STALLION!...

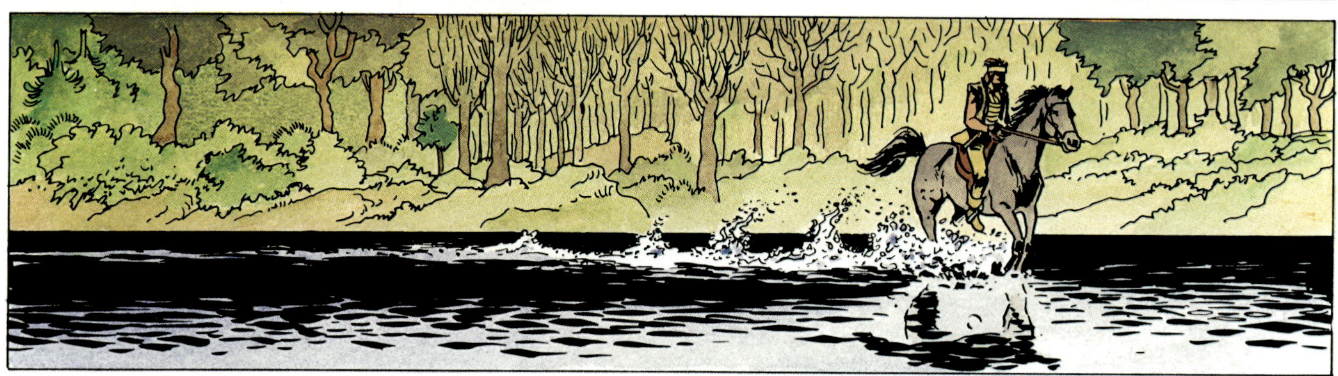
40.

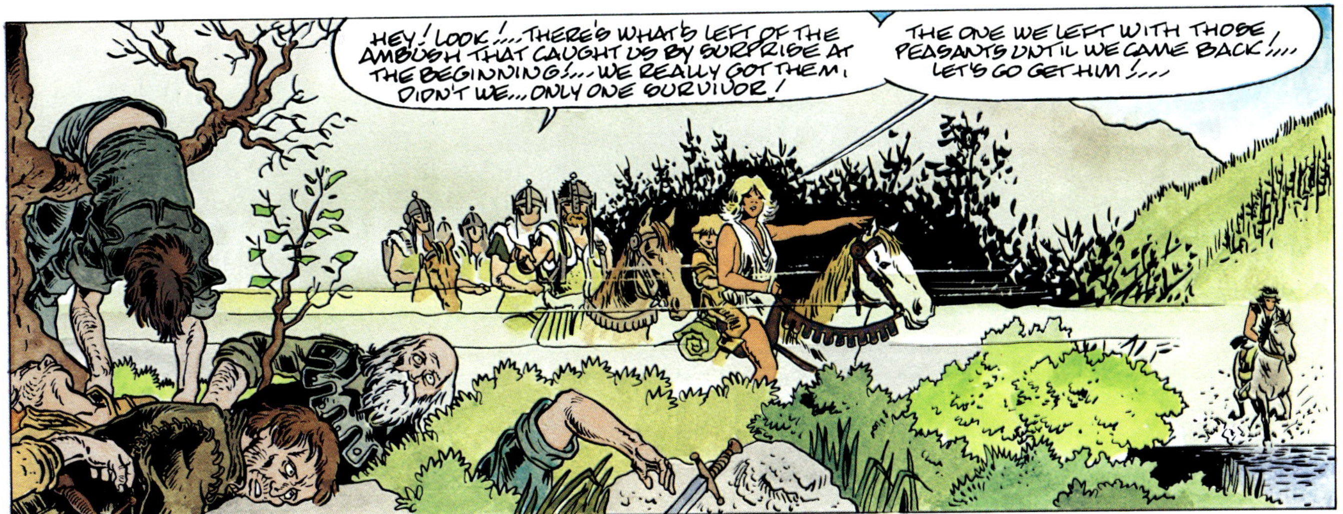
HEY! LOOK!... THERE'S WHAT'S LEFT OF THE AMBUSH THAT CAUGHT US BY SURPRISE AT THE BEGINNING!... WE REALLY GOT THEM, DIDN'T WE... ONLY ONE SURVIVOR!
THE ONE WE LEFT WITH THOSE PEASANTS UNTIL WE CAME BACK!... LET'S GO GET HIM!...

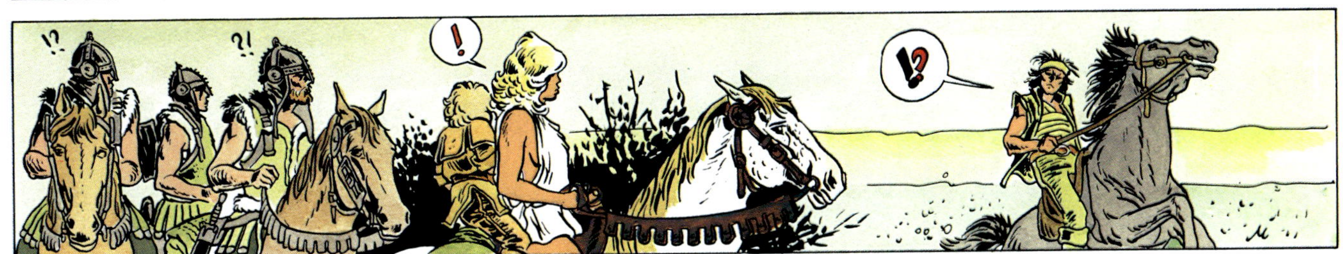
!?
?!
!
!?

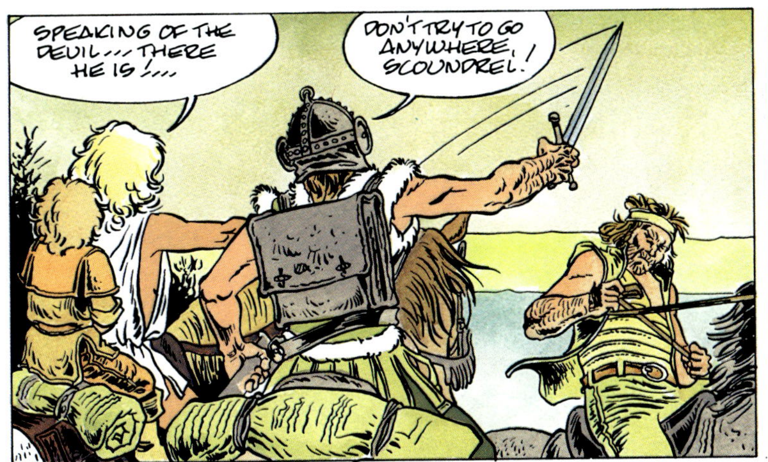
SPEAKING OF THE DEVIL... THERE HE IS!...
DON'T TRY TO GO ANYWHERE, SCOUNDREL!

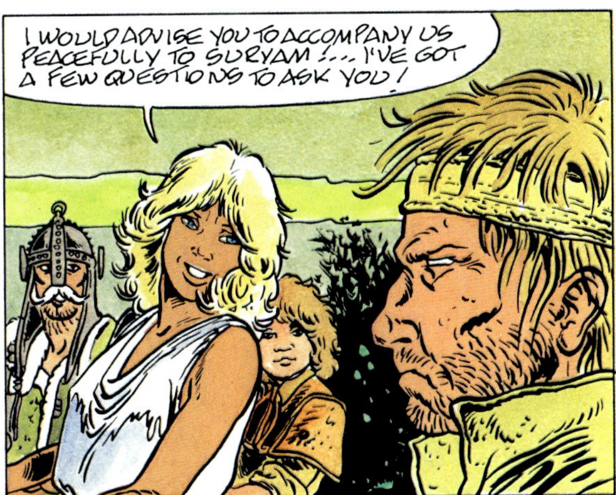
I WOULD ADVISE YOU TO ACCOMPANY US PEACEFULLY TO SURYAM!... I'VE GOT A FEW QUESTIONS TO ASK YOU!

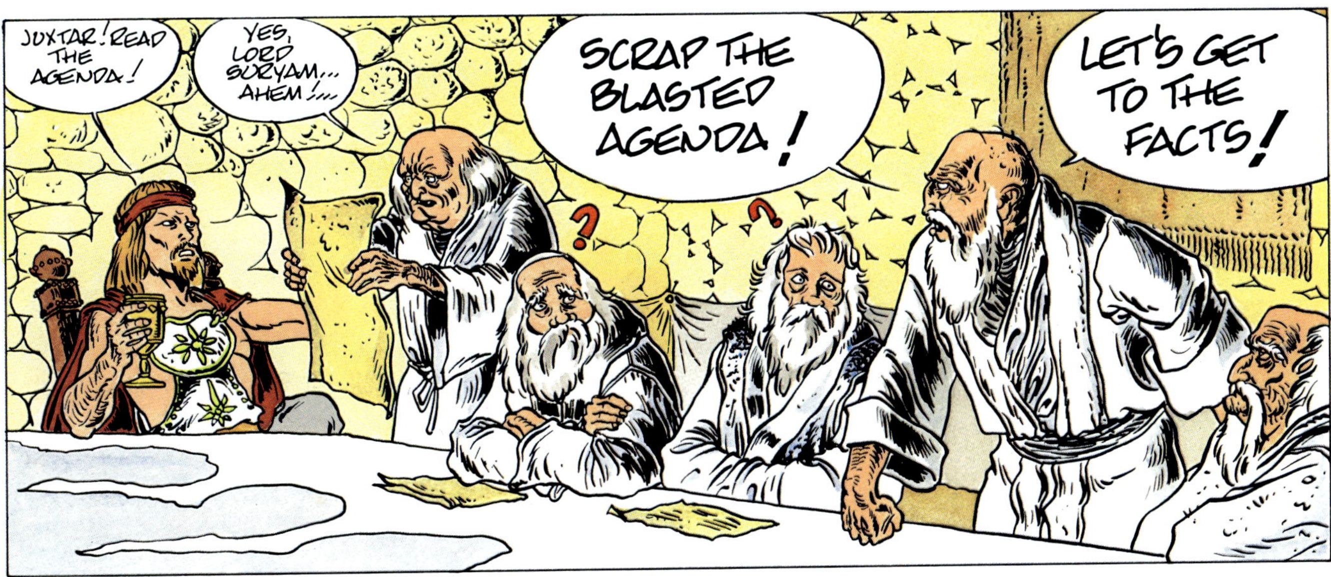
JUXTAR! READ THE AGENDA!
YES, LORD SURYAM... AHEM!...
SCRAP THE BLASTED AGENDA!
LET'S GET TO THE FACTS!
?
?
41

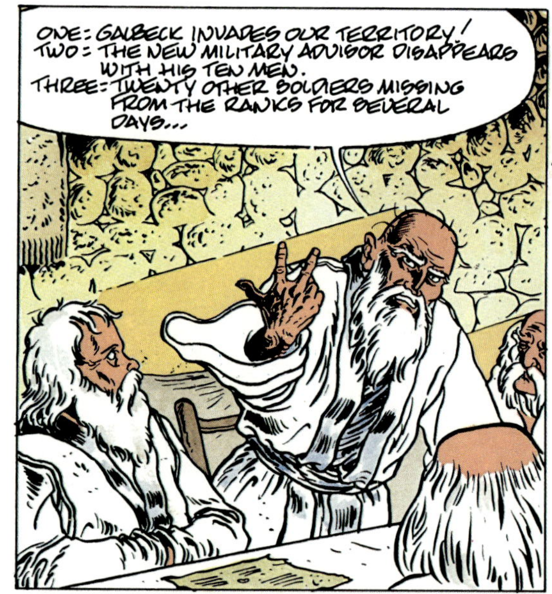
ONE: GALBECK INVADES OUR TERRITORY! TWO: THE NEW MILITARY ADVISOR DISAPPEARS WITH HIS TEN MEN. THREE: TWENTY OTHER SOLDIERS MISSING FROM THE RANKS FOR SEVERAL DAYS...

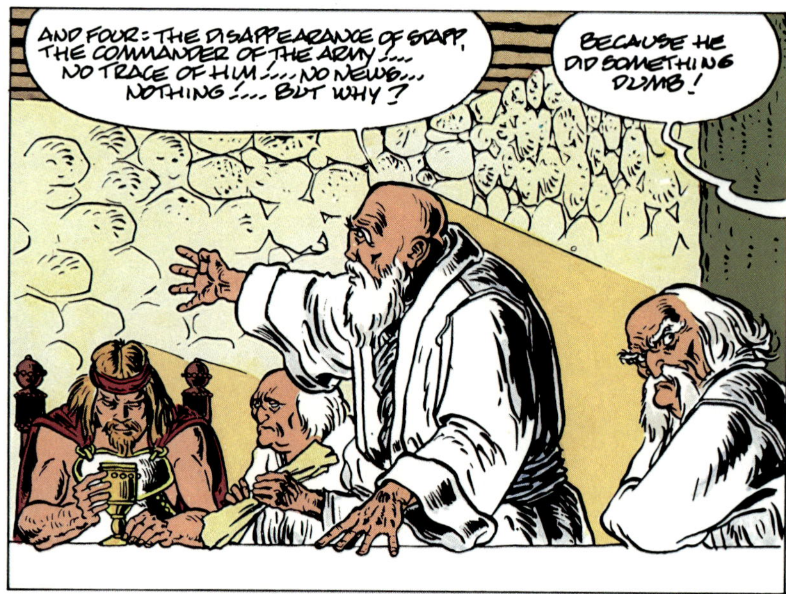
AND FOUR: THE DISAPPEARANCE OF STAPP, THE COMMANDER OF THE ARMY!... NO TRACE OF HIM!... NO NEWS... NOTHING!... BUT WHY?
BECAUSE HE DID SOMETHING DUMB!

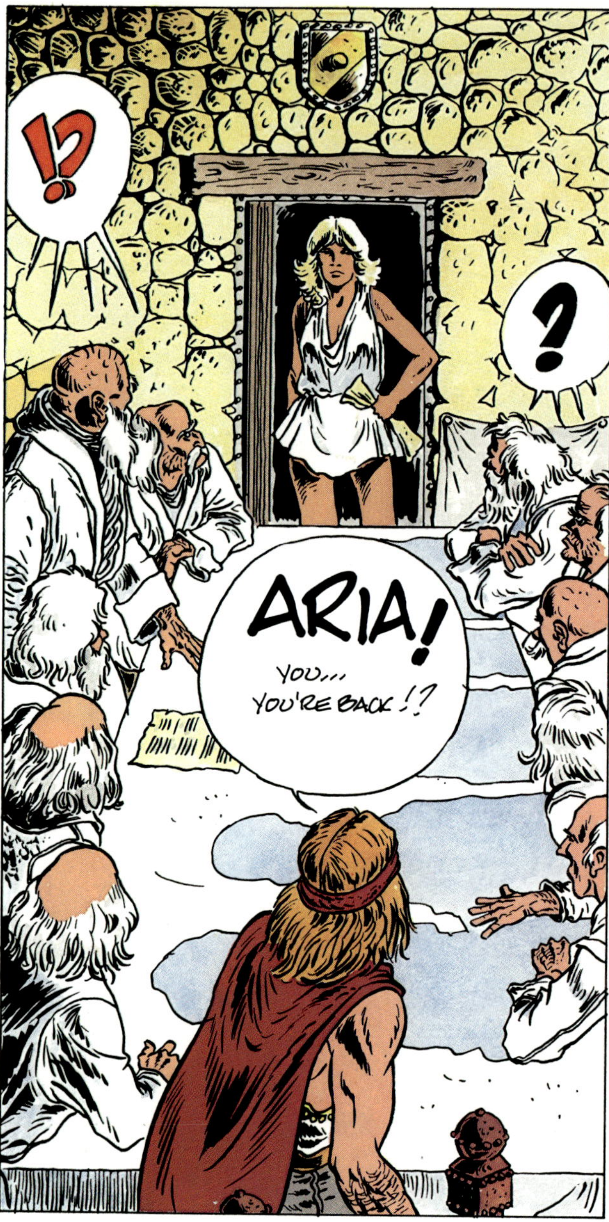
!?
?
ARIA!
YOU... YOU'RE BACK!?

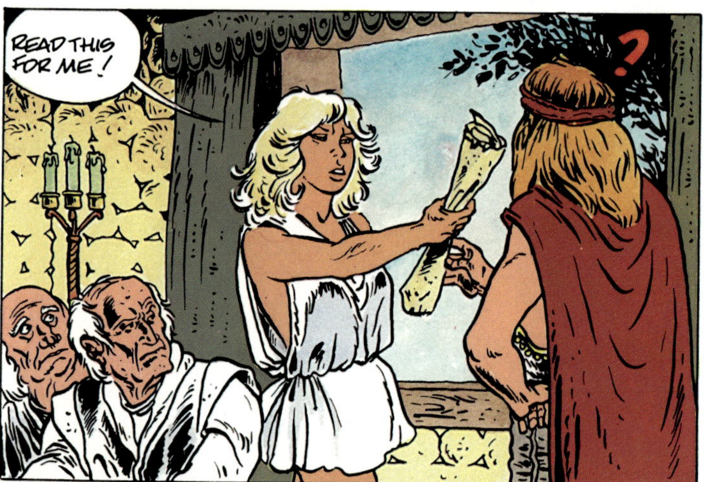
READ THIS FOR ME!
?

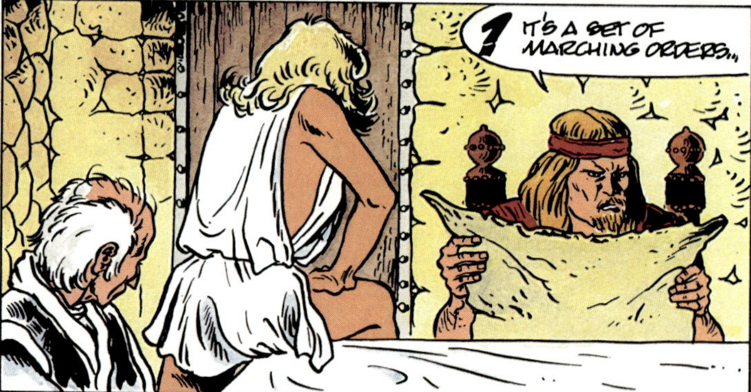
IT'S A SET OF MARCHING ORDERS...

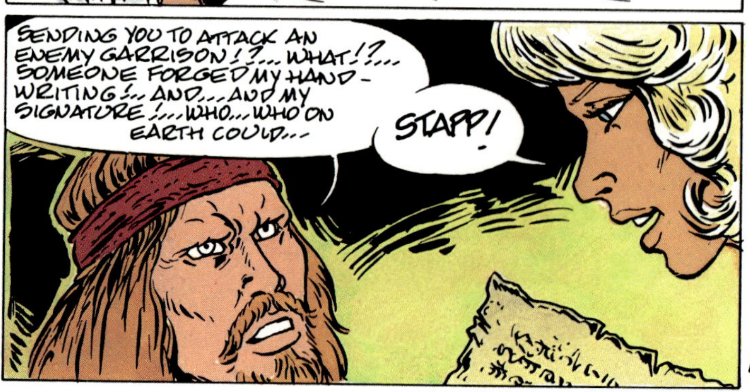
SENDING YOU TO ATTACK AN ENEMY GARRISON!?... WHAT!?... SOMEONE FORGED MY HAND-WRITING!... AND... AND MY SIGNATURE!... WHO... WHO ON EARTH COULD...
STAPP!

42

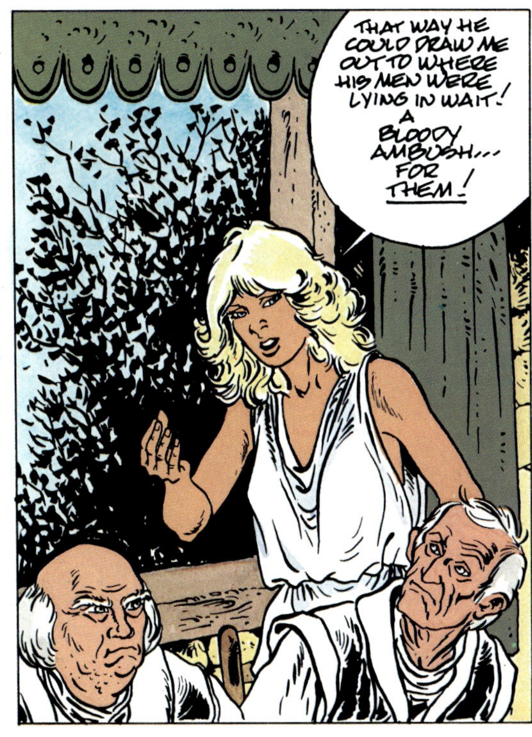
THAT WAY HE COULD DRAW ME OUT TO WHERE HIS MEN WERE LYING IN WAIT!
A BLOODY AMBUSH... FOR THEM!

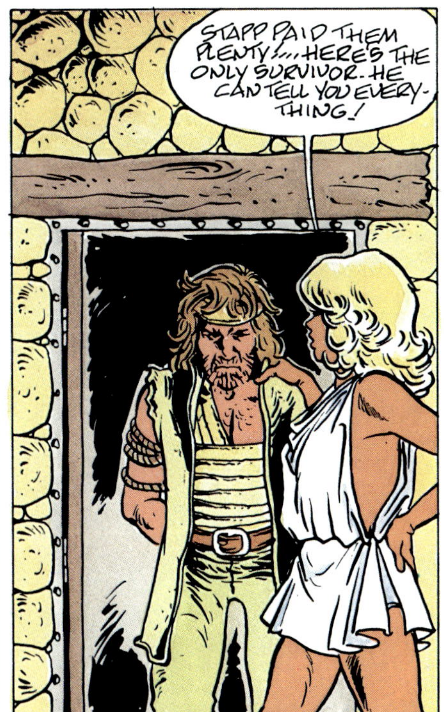
STAPP PAID THEM PLENTY!... HERE'S THE ONLY SURVIVOR. HE CAN TELL YOU EVERYTHING!

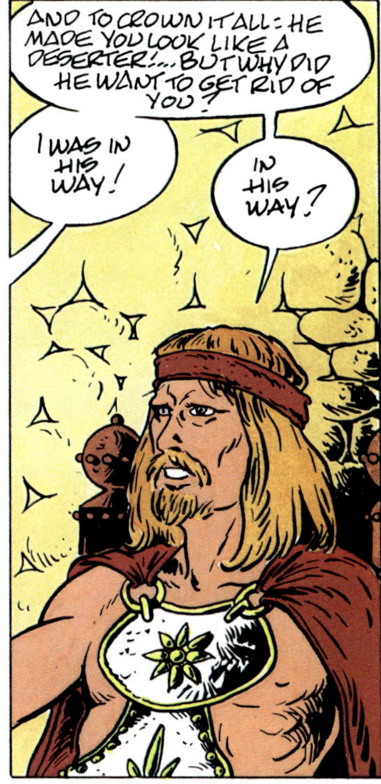
AND TO CROWN IT ALL: HE MADE YOU LOOK LIKE A DESERTER!... BUT WHY DID HE WANT TO GET RID OF YOU?
I WAS IN HIS WAY!
IN HIS WAY?

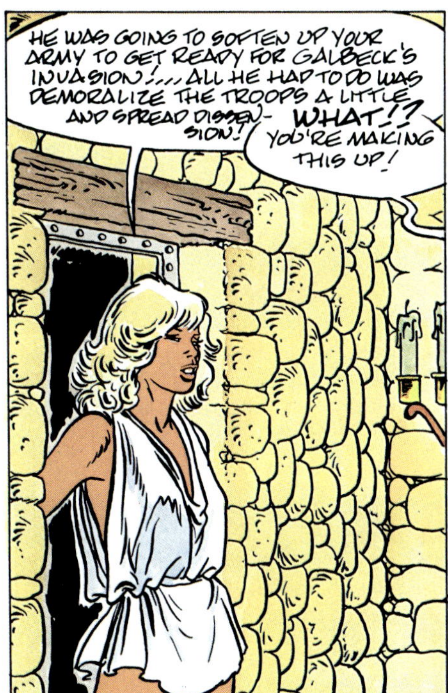
HE WAS GOING TO SOFTEN UP YOUR ARMY TO GET READY FOR GALBECK'S INVASION!... ALL HE HAD TO DO WAS DEMORALIZE THE TROOPS A LITTLE AND SPREAD DISSENSION!
WHAT!? YOU'RE MAKING THIS UP!

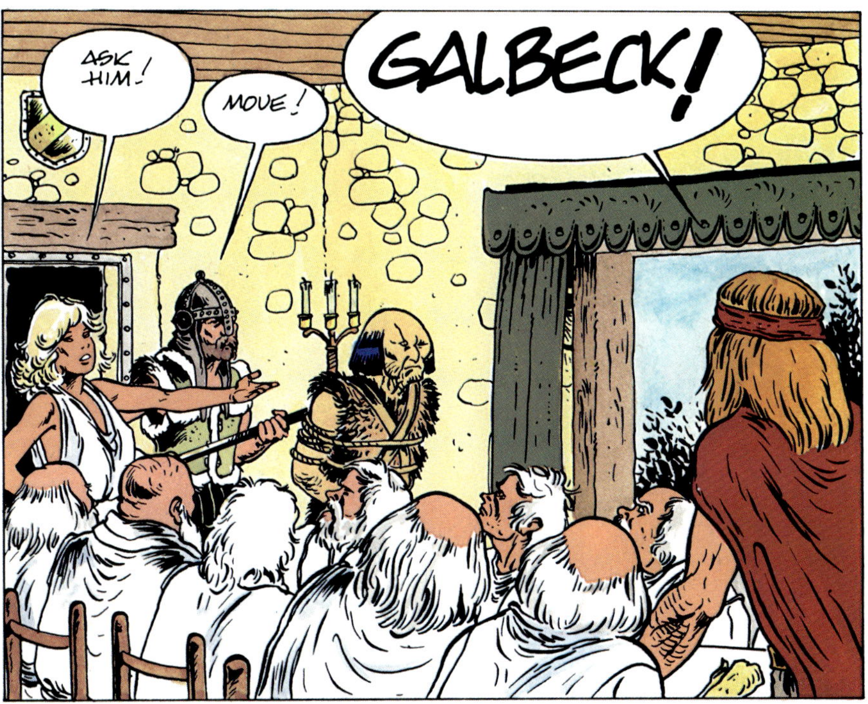
ASK HIM!
MOVE!
GALBECK!

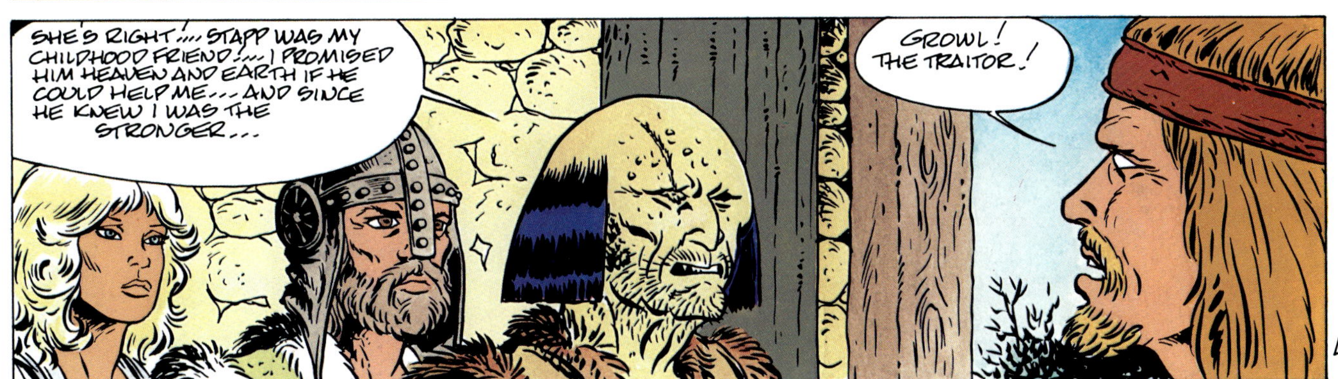
SHE'S RIGHT!... STAPP WAS MY CHILDHOOD FRIEND!... I PROMISED HIM HEAVEN AND EARTH IF HE COULD HELP ME... AND SINCE HE KNEW I WAS THE STRONGER...
GROWL! THE TRAITOR!

43.

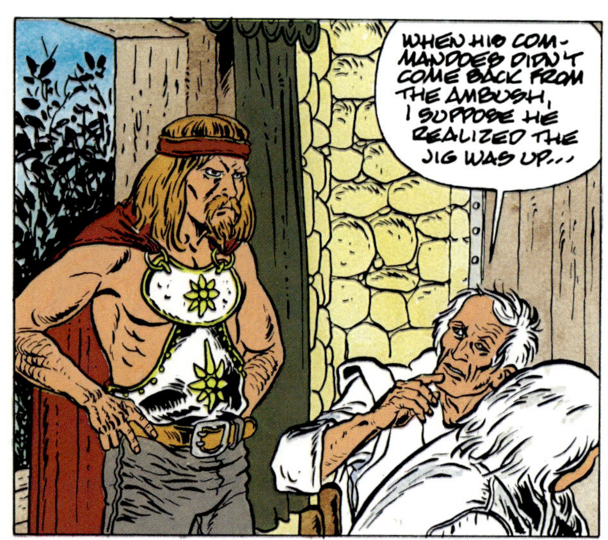
WHEN HIS COM-MANDOES DIDN'T COME BACK FROM THE AMBUSH, I SUPPOSE HE REALIZED THE JIG WAS UP...

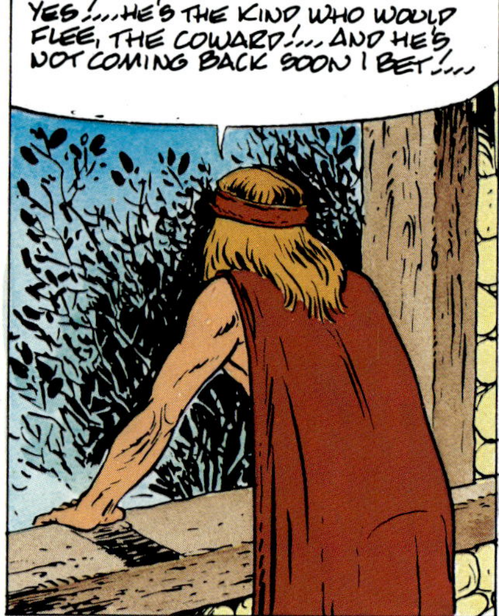
YES!... HE'S THE KIND WHO WOULD FLEE, THE COWARD!... AND HE'S NOT COMING BACK SOON I BET!...

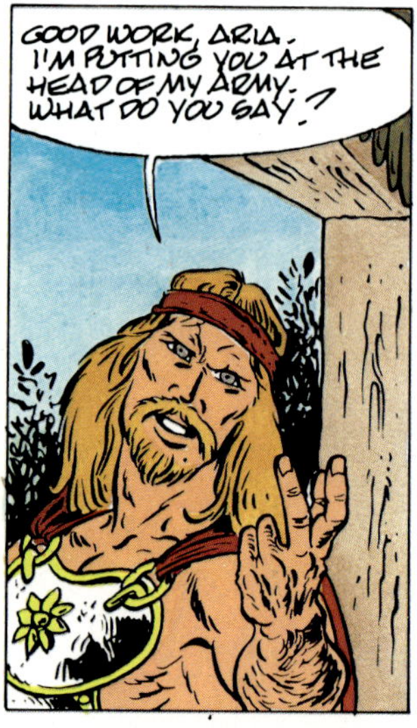
GOOD WORK, ARIA. I'M PUTTING YOU AT THE HEAD OF MY ARMY. WHAT DO YOU SAY?

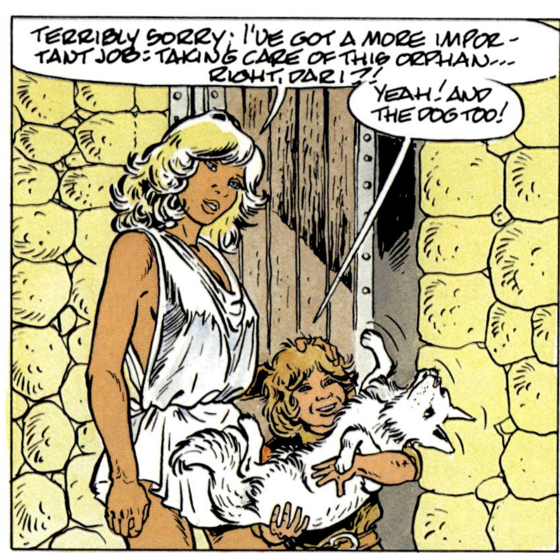
TERRIBLY SORRY; I'VE GOT A MORE IMPOR-TANT JOB: TAKING CARE OF THIS ORPHAN... RIGHT, DARI?!
YEAH! AND THE DOG TOO!

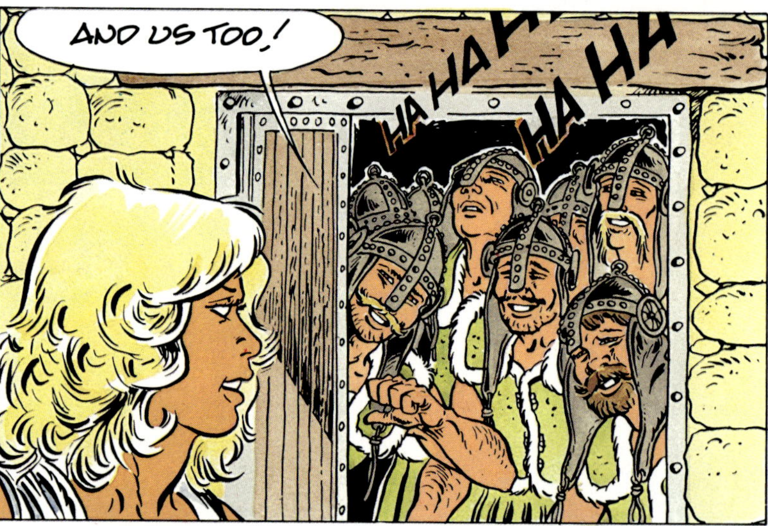
AND US TOO!
HA HA HA
HA HA

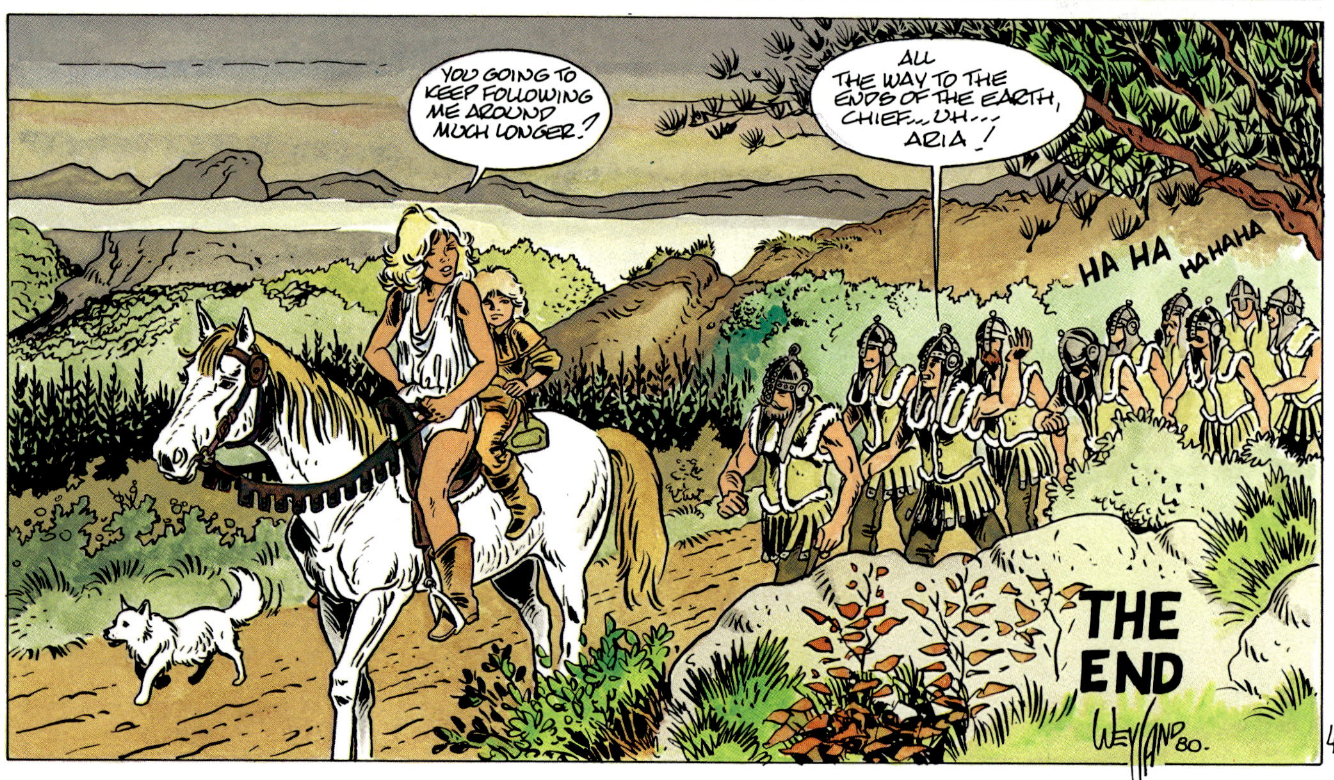
YOU GOING TO KEEP FOLLOWING ME AROUND MUCH LONGER?
ALL THE WAY TO THE ENDS OF THE EARTH, CHIEF... UH... ARIA!
HA HA HAHAHA
THE END
WEYLAND 80.

44.

PRINTED IN BELGIUM BY
proost
INTERNATIONAL BOOK PRODUCTION

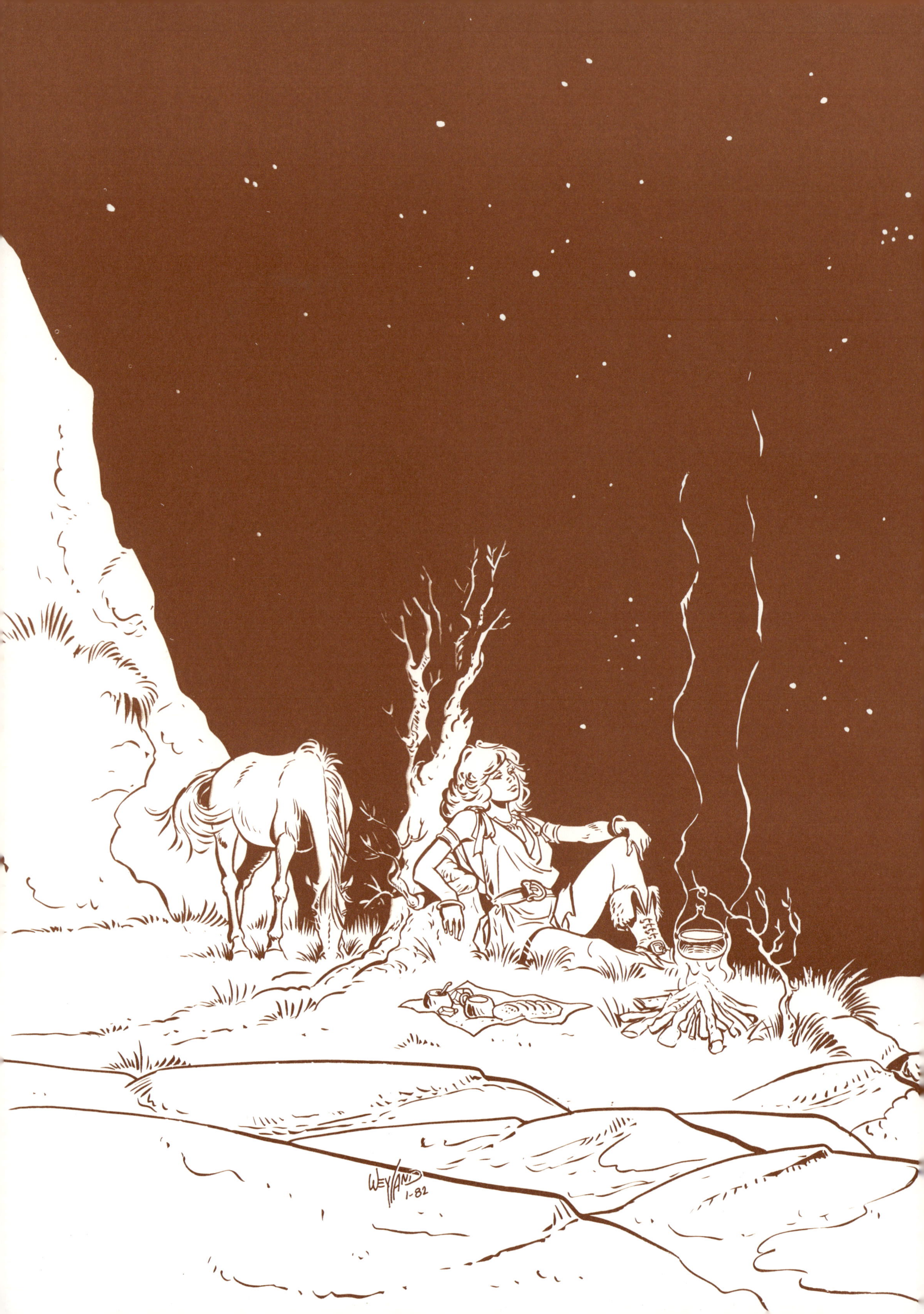